T0301629

Markets on the Margins

Related James Currey titles on South & Southern Africa

South Africa. The Present as History:
From Mrs Ples to Mandela & Marikana
John S. Saul & Patrick Bond

Liberation Movements in Power: Party & State in Southern Africa
Roger Southall

The New Black Middle Class in South Africa
Roger Southall

Mandela's Kinsmen: Nationalist Elites & Apartheid's First Bantustan
Timothy Gibbs

Women, Migration & the Cashew Economy in Southern Mozambique
Jeanne Marie Penvenne

Remaking Mutirikwi:
Landscape, Water & Belonging in Southern Zimbabwe
Joost Fontein

Writing Revolt: An Engagement with African Nationalism, 1957–67
Terence Ranger

Colonialism & Violence in Zimbabwe: A History of Suffering
Heike I. Schmidt

The Road to Soweto: Resistance & the Uprising of 16 June 1976
Julian Brown

The War Within: New Perspectives on the Civil War in Mozambique,
1976-1992*
Eric Morier-Genoud, Michel Cahen & Domingos M. do Rosário (eds)

Township Violence & the End of Apartheid: War on the Reef*
Gary Kynoch

* forthcoming

Markets on the Margins

Mineworkers, job creation
& enterprise development

KATE PHILIP

JC JAMES CURREY

James Currey
is an imprint of Boydell & Brewer Ltd
PO Box 9,
Woodbridge, Suffolk IP12 3DF (GB)
www.jamescurrey.com

and of

Boydell & Brewer Inc.
668 Mt Hope Avenue
Rochester, NY 14620-2731 US
www.boydellandbrewer.com

British Library Cataloguing in Publication Data
A catologue record for this book is available on request from the British Library

ISBN 978-1-84701-176-3 (James Currey hardback)

This publication is printed on acid-free paper

Typeset in 10/12 Melior
by Kate Kirkwood Publishing Services

Printed and bound in Great Britain by
TJ International Ltd, Padstow, Cornwall

Contents

Illustrations

Table

Figures

Photographs
All photos by Kate Philip unless otherwise stated

Preface

Just when I thought the manuscript for this book was done and dusted, a final reviewer came back with the comment that I am never introduced to the reader; that, in particular, an explanation is needed for how a white middle-class woman ended up running the development programme of South Africa's National Union of Mineworkers during the apartheid years. It's not a question I had thought to answer – the focus of the book is on development strategy – it is not a memoir. Yet, once asked, it is hard to argue that race, class and gender are irrelevant.

Where, however, to start? Age eight years seems as good a place as any: in a history class at school. We were studying the Great Trek: the moment when the Boers leave the Cape, a pivotal moment for Afrikaner identity and South African history. They table a list of grievances against the British: many no doubt legitimate. The last on the list, however, registers their protest at the anti-slavery campaign led by Dr John Philip. The same picture of him as hangs in our dining room looked out of the history textbook at me with a quizzical expression that asked: so what side of history are *you* on?

I grew up in a family that knew the answer to that question. By the time I got to high school, my parents had started a small independent publishing company to tilt at windmills – and to contest apartheid ideology, too. David Philip Publishers operated from our home. So after school, I would often find renowned authors on the stoep, unknown poets under the lemon tree, or artists unwrapping the tissue paper from their illustrations in the lounge. They all seemed to stay for drinks. There was no question that ideas mattered – and that yours did too.

Each year my parents would go to the Frankfurt Book Fair, often leaving my sister and me in the care of Tessa Fairburn who was, at the time, an English teacher at Livingstone High School. This was a 'coloured' school – at a time when schools were strictly segregated by race. On a series of Saturdays, Tessa took me there to rehearsals of Joan of Arc, which she was directing. From a fold-up wooden chair in the school hall, I watched, entranced by the teenagers strutting their stuff on the stage. They were older than me, and seemed dazzlingly sophisticated. I had a crush on at least two of the boys – and Joan of Arc, of course. I don't think they even noticed I was there.

Then came the Soweto student uprising of 1976. I was sixteen years old. Cape Town was not untouched, and in anticipation of who knows what, buckets of sand were put outside our classrooms at my whites-only, girls-only school. Then one day, we heard that the students from Livingstone High were marching – over Claremont bridge, across the railway tracks – and in our direction. We could hear them, singing and chanting. I could imagine them – Joan of Arc in front, flanked by the others, fists raised. Then we heard the sirens, the *doef-doef* of shots, the acrid smell of teargas wafting across the playing fields. For the rest of my school-mates, their apparent rout was a cause of celebration and relief. For me, however, the students marching over the bridge were not 'the other'.

Small wonder, then, that when I got to the University of Cape Town I joined the student movement, under the auspices of the National Union of South African Students (NUSAS). NUSAS had a long history of mobilising opposition to apartheid on the mainly white university campuses, politicising a core within each generation, who were urged to use their skills in the interests of change. Many did and, although always a small cohort within the wider movement, white anti-apartheid activists could be found in the trade unions, in civil society, in the media, in the arts, as lawyers and across society, trying to find ways to make a difference in support of mass-based struggles.

The 1980s were a particularly heady period in this regard, with a myriad of forms of organisation mushrooming across the country in opposition to then Prime Minister P.W. Botha's 'reforms' of apartheid. At the end of 1982 I was elected President of NUSAS. It was also during this period that the United Democratic Front was formed, echoing the African National Congress's clear message of non-racialism, reflected in the opening lines of the Freedom Charter, which says: 'South Africa belongs to all who live in it, black and white'.

NUSAS joined the United Democratic Front (UDF), placing us clearly within the fold of the democratic movement. The formalisation of a non-racial student alliance took place then too – a culmination of years of strategic engagement by student leaders who came before me.

So when, in 1984, the Congress of South African Students (COSAS), who organised students in schools, called on workers as their parents to support their struggles with a stay-away from work, NUSAS campaigned in support also. While this form of general strike later became a regular occurrence, this was the first time the mining and industrial heartland of South Africa was brought to a standstill, in what was termed the Transvaal Stay-Away.

There was an immediate clamp-down; many activists were detained. I was one of them. The nature of racial profiling in the media at the time, however, meant my detention certainly received more than its fair share of attention.

After NUSAS I joined the editorial collective of *SASPU National* – a newspaper produced by the South African Student Press Union that had a wide readership in the mass democratic movement, because of the in-depth coverage it provided on grassroots struggles. This in turn meant traversing the country, often to remote areas, to engage with student, youth, civic and trade union activists, to report on what were often otherwise untold stories.

When Matthew Goniwe, Fort Calata, Sparrow Mkhonto and Sicelo Mhlauli ('the Cradock Four') were brutally assassinated in the Eastern Cape in 1985, it was another indication that repression was reaching new heights; a trend reinforced when, on the night of their mass funeral in Cradock, a state of emergency was declared.

Activists scattered to safe houses; raids took place throughout the night. *SASPU National* was however working on a special edition on the Eastern Cape which had taken on new urgency in the light of these events. So, keen to meet deadlines, I made my way to the *SASPU National* offices the next morning anyway. I parked a few blocks away – just in case. As I rounded the corner, I stopped in my tracks. The building, which housed a range of anti-apartheid organisations, was gutted – a burnt out shell. Police swarmed in the parking lot. I turned on my tail and beat a hasty retreat.

Like many others, we all went into hiding; but – albeit erratically – we still managed to bring out the newspaper. With student and youth networks smashed, we relied increasingly on the newly launched Congress of South African Trade Unions (COSATU) for its distribution.

All of which is my way of explaining why, when the job interview in NUM described on page 22 took place, it started with handshakes, and greetings of 'comrade', which was just the way it was in those days.

Acknowledgements

It was a pleasure and a privilege to head the development strategy of the National Union of Mineworkers (NUM) in the period that I did; providing me with a fascinating and formative opportunity in a critical period in South Africa's history. NUM's support to development initiatives for its members long after they had left the industry – as well as for their wider communities – was remarkable; with NUM's vision of a social plan for mining communities as relevant today as when NUM first proposed it.

I thank the leadership of NUM and the MDA Board for entrusting me with this role. In particular, NUM General Secretaries Cyril Ramaphosa, Kgalema Motlanthe and Gwede Mantashe all provided significant guidance and support, as did Presidents James Motlatsi and Senzeni Zokwana and Treasurers Paul Nkuna and Derek Elbrecht. Special thanks also go to Moremang Montsi, Chair of MDA's Board in the final period of my tenure.

I also want to thank the co-op members and of course the staff in MDA and its centres, all of whom contributed to this amazing learning journey. While I have no doubt we might still debate many of the issues reflected in these pages, I hope we can all agree that they are approached with the 'warm spirit' referred to in Chapter One. While some names are mentioned in the pages that follow, many other people also contributed in significant ways. Amongst these, I would like to recognise the key roles played by Mary Cobbett, Zane Dangor and Ace Puso in the turbulent early co-op period and of Elton Jones and Daphney Matjiu in later years. Amongst the often unsung heroes and heroines of finance and administration, I'd like to recognise the support of Sam Mphaka and Fassy Phiri.

There are also many parts of the MDA story in the period covered here that did not make it into these pages – even if some anecdotes are captured in boxes in the text. Marks Masoetsa and the Lesotho Taxi Co-op don't even get a mention; Kolo Diamond Co-op is a line in a table, yet caused quite a stir when its members found a particularly large diamond in Lesotho. For the Basotho ex-miners, this vindicated their long-held view that the diamonds found further down the Orange River – in South Africa – always originated in their mountains. De Beers, however, held a somewhat different view of how these diamonds came to be found upstream. What all the anecdotes reflect is the human factor in the story of any organisation or development process: a dimension to which I have barely been able to do justice.

I would also like to acknowledge the many donors who supported MDA over the period covered here. Given the complexity and volatility of donor funding priorities – as discussed in these pages – NUM's establishment of Mineworkers Investment Trust and its commitment to generating resources to support initiatives such as MDA was far-sighted, with access to core funding through this mechanism providing MDA with a degree of strategic independence that was very valuable – and much appreciated.

Also far-sighted was NUM's inclusion of demands for development funding for affected communities in its retrenchment negotiations. It was through these joint NUM/mining industry funds that many Development Centres were established. DFID Southern Africa also played a crucial role, with funding support to the institutional development of MDA, the Development Centre strategy, the marula programme and the Lesotho programme. Particular thanks go to Sam Sharpe, Richard Boulter and Tony Polatajko for their support at a formative time; also to the Kellogg Foundation, which contributed to the marula and Lesotho programmes.

My gratitude goes to Puseletso Salae for his comradeship throughout, as well as for his insights and commentary on the manuscript; also to Professor Eddie Webster, for his intellectual input and support over many years.

The artwork entitled 'Rural Markets' on the cover is by Andile Msongelwa. When artist Andrew Lindsay was doing murals for the business supply store in Lusikisiki, he noticed beautifully painted signs on many local shops and tracked down the artist – Msongelwa – in a nearby village to involve him in the project. When Msongelwa came to Johannesburg shortly thereafter, Lindsay secured commissions for him; this was one of them. Thanks are due to Lindsay for his remarkable generosity of spirit in working to promote local artists everywhere and for the difference the murals made to every MDA facility.

In terms of the complex logistics of actually producing this book, I'd like to acknowledge the rigour, patience and support from Jaqueline Mitchell and Lynn Taylor in Boydell and Brewer.

My wonderful family already knows how grateful I am for their love and support throughout this process – despite the book's incursions into summer holidays over many years.

Last but certainly not least, I want to use this opportunity to remember the colleagues and comrades in the MDA family who lost their lives over this period. Every one of these untimely deaths was a blow to the heart. This book is dedicated to their memory.

Abbreviations

AAC	Anglo American Corporation
AIDS	Acquired immune deficiency syndrome
Amcoal	Anglo American Coal
AMCU	Association of Mineworkers and Construction Union
ANC	African National Congress
BCP	Basotho Congress Party
BDS	Business development services
BNP	Basotho National Party
BMLC	Basotho Mineworkers Labour Co-operative
CBNRM	Community-based natural resource management
CCDI	Cape Craft and Design Institute
CORDE	Co-operative Research, Development and Education
COSATU	Congress of South African Trade Unions
CRIAA	Centre for Research, Information and Action in Africa
CSFS	Co-operative Self-Finance Scheme
CSIR	Council for Scientific and Industrial Research
CUSA	Council of Unions of South Africa
CWP	Community Work Programme
dti	Department of Trade and Industry
DFID	Department for International Development
DWAF	Department of Water and Forestry
HIV	Human immunodeficiency virus
ILO	International Labour Organization
KWV	Koöperatieve Wijnbouwers Vereniging
LLA	Lesotho Liberation Army
LED	Local Economic Development
Lega	Lega Nazionale delle Cooperative e Mutue (Legacoop)
M4P	Making markets work for the poor
MDA	Mineworkers Development Agency
MDC	Mhala Development Centre
MGNREGA	Mahatma Gandhi National Rural Employment Guarantee Act
MNP	Marula Natural Products
NEC	National Executive Committee
NGO	Non-governmental organisation

NTFP	Non-timber forest product
NUM	National Union of Mineworkers
PAWCO	Phalaborwa Workers Co-operative
R	Rand or ZAR
RFF	Rural Finance Facility
Rutec	Rural Technology Company
SA	South Africa
SAB	South African Breweries
SACP	South African Communist Party
SAWCO	Sarmcol Workers Co-operative
TEBA	The Employment Bureau of Africa
TEMCOP	Transkei Ex-Mineworkers Co-operative Project
UNIDO	United Nations Industrial Development Organization
USA or US	United States of America

1 Introduction

SETTING THE SCENE

In 1987 the National Union of Mineworkers (NUM) called a national mineworkers strike: an epic twenty-one-day showdown between the five-year old NUM and the far more established South African mining industry backed by the might of the apartheid state. One of the many consequences of this strike was that some forty thousand workers lost their jobs. The dependence of South Africa's mining industry on migrant labour meant these workers returned to homes scattered across the sub-region, with the largest numbers returning to the rural Transkei, in South Africa, and the small neighbouring mountain Kingdom of Lesotho.

In the aftermath, and as a response to these events, a job creation unit was established within NUM, but the job losses from the strike proved to be just the start of a period of restructuring in the mining industry during which over three hundred thousand jobs were shed over the next fifteen years. This period also coincided with dramatic changes in South Africa. At the start of the period, the political system of white minority rule known as apartheid was still in place; by the end of it, South Africa's transition to democracy was nearly a decade old. Over the same period, democratic struggles were also unfolding in neighbouring states such as Lesotho, Mozambique and Swaziland – with their fates closely tied to events in South Africa.

While this book relates the story of one particular job creation initiative in a particular southern African and historical context, it nevertheless has wider implications and contemporary relevance for enterprise development strategies that aim to create jobs and reduce poverty in developing contexts. A core part of this challenge involves grappling with the role of markets in development, and whether and under what conditions enterprise development strategies in rural and peri-urban contexts can provide pathways out of poverty: or simply serve to lock people into it instead. These issues remain a current development priority.

The story that unfolds in this book is told from a particular perspective: I joined NUM in 1988, tasked with heading the new job creation unit and creating alternative forms of employment for workers dismissed in the strike. In 1995, when this NUM Unit was transferred into a non-profit company called Mineworkers Development Agency

(MDA), which became the development wing of NUM, I became its Chief Executive Officer and continued in that role until I left the organisation in 2002. This book tracks the journey in enterprise development that unfolded over this period, the detours and dead-ends we stumbled into – and out of – and the causes and consequences of the many strategic shifts that took place as our understanding of the task at hand grew.

The action takes place against a backdrop in which NUM's leaders and members were active agents in the struggles for social and political change rocking the wider society. While NUM's role on the national stage in South Africa is widely recognised, the union's involvement in the rural labour-sending areas from which its members were drawn added an often unseen level of influence in rural politics, not just in South Africa but beyond its borders also.

It was in this context of turbulent times that NUM's development programme grappled with how to empower people in poor communities to create employment for themselves through enterprise development activities, in a context in which entry points into formal employment in the core economy were largely closed to them. This was then – and is still today – an unusual role for a trade union to play; yet NUM invested heavily in this development agenda and in the rural labour-sending areas from where the mining industry drew its labour. NUM's vision was broad, providing support not only to its former members, but to their wider communities also, as a contribution to local economic development and employment creation. For NUM, this was part of its contribution to promoting the concept of a 'social plan' for the mining industry, in which it envisaged the private sector, government and labour all investing in the development of mining communities across southern Africa.

The negative social legacies of the mining industry and the need for such a social plan were cast into new relief as part of the context in which the police massacred thirty-three mineworkers at Marikana in October 2012. This took place against a backdrop of mounting tension, with mine employers undermining collective bargaining arrangements, and rising conflict between NUM and a new rival union, the Association of Mineworkers and Construction Union (AMCU).

These events placed a renewed spotlight on the continued role of mining in post-apartheid South Africa, on its impacts on South African labour markets and on the conditions of structural violence, poverty and inequality in which so many mineworkers and their dependants still live. In many senses, the Marikana massacre generated a sense of déjà vu in relation to the struggles over wages and working conditions on the mines, the challenges of organising workers in the industry, the relationship between industry leaders and the state, the role of the police in that mix, the role of migrancy, of ethnicity and warlordism: all these issues were characteristic of the period covered in this book; they are also all still present in old and new forms, more than twenty years after the advent of democracy in South Africa.

This sense of déjà vu was coupled by a profound sense of dissonance, with no escaping the ironies, in particular in relation to the changed roles of some protagonists, then and now. In the early period covered in this book, Cyril Ramaphosa was one of South Africa's most powerful trade union leaders, who achieved what even experienced unionists did not believe could be done: building a trade union of mineworkers in the highly repressive context of the time. Under his leadership, NUM grew to a membership of over three hundred thousand people and became South Africa's largest trade union, despite the significant hurdles put in its way by the Chamber of Mines and by the apartheid state. Yet, in 2014, when Ramaphosa, then Deputy President of the country and in 2018 elected President of South Africa, took the stand in the Marikana Commission, he did so in his capacity as a shareholder and director in Lonmin: called upon to defend his role in the build-up to the massacre. In the context of an unprotected strike supported by AMCU, violent enforcement of the strike had claimed several lives and was spiralling out of control. Ramaphosa appealed to the Minister of Mineral Resources to intervene in the situation and called for more-effective policing to deal with criminal conduct in the strike.

At the time, despite the rising body count, police had been notable for their absence. When they did enter the fray, their ill-conceived attempt to disarm striking workers and to gain control of the situation ended in the massacre of workers. Certainly, this was one of the lowest points in South Africa's democratic era. Ramaphosa's role in calling for police involvement led some to accuse him of responsibility for the events that followed, but the Farlam Commission into the events at Marikana rejected this interpretation.

While these events focused global public attention back on South Africa's mining industry and its labour relations, the focus in this book is on a far earlier period of NUM's history, on the unusual role NUM played in supporting small enterprise development in the marginal and mainly rural contexts from which mine labour was drawn, and on the wider lessons this experience still holds for enterprise development strategies.

The mining industry and South African history

For those less familiar with South Africa's history, this section of the introduction clarifies the central role of the country's mining industry in shaping labour markets, the interconnectedness between land dispossession and the creation of a working class, the system of apartheid that was built on these foundations, and the critical role of organised labour in the struggle against that system.

In the late nineteenth century, when diamonds and gold were discovered, South Africa was a patchwork of British colonies and small
republics established by breakaway groups of 'Boers' – or farmers –
mainly of Dutch descent, now speaking the uniquely South African
language of Afrikaans. The economies within this patchwork were all
largely agrarian, but the discovery of minerals raised the stakes. The
Anglo-Boer War followed, from 1899 to 1902. Britain won and mining
started in earnest.

This created an unprecedented need for labour; but black South
Africans preferred their existing land-based livelihoods to working
underground in dark and dangerous conditions for a pittance. While
colonial conquest had stripped them of many rights, many still had
access to land, including freehold tenure in some contexts. At the time,
the growth of mining towns was creating new markets for agricultural
produce, and many black farmers were responding well to new opportunities (Callinicos 1980).

So, coercive methods were used. South Africa's infamous 1913 Land
Act was passed, limiting the rights of black people to own or rent land
to that in designated reserves that constituted a mere 7.6 per cent of
all land in South Africa (later increased to about 13 per cent). The Act
was designed to force black South Africans off the land and into the
labour market – in particular, onto the mines. It was coupled with the
introduction of taxes that had to be paid in cash, creating additional
pressure on black people to enter the cash economy. It was also a system
in which the supposed ability of families to continue to engage in
subsistence agriculture in the reserves was used to justify cheap wages
(Wolpe 1972, p. 434).

The strategy relied in part on co-opting traditional leaders in the
reserves, with the mine labour recruitment system requiring approval of
labour contracts from a given tribal area by the relevant local headman.
Those traditional leaders who resisted these roles were removed from
their positions.

These policies caused an influx of black workers to the mines, but black
people were only allowed into urban areas as workers. Mineworkers
were housed in vast single-sex hostels adjacent to the mine shafts; their
families were not allowed to join them. This separated families for
extended periods, depriving children of their fathers and devastating
the social fabric of African communities.

In South Africa therefore, issues of land and labour were integrally
linked, with the laws dispossessing people of land and those regu-
lating migrant labour forming the backbone of the system called
'apartheid', introduced formally in 1948, after the National Party was
elected in South Africa's whites-only parliament. This system, which
translates literally from Afrikaans as 'being apart', was based on an
ideology of separate development that aimed to separate white, black,

coloured[1] and Indian groups in South Africa – and then further divide black South Africans by ethnicity, by devolving their citizenship to the bantustans. This was supposed to justify denying them rights in the rest of South Africa. In the 1970s, four of the bantustans, including the Transkei, became self-governing territories with all the formal symbols and institutions of independent states: including their own border gates, passports, flags – and local despots.

Under apartheid, a complex set of rules governed society. Some took the form of racist incursions into everyday life, such as whites-only beaches, park benches and railway carriages, but other aspects of apartheid created deeper, structural differences in access to rights, opportunities and wealth, with intergenerational effects. These included the establishment of different education systems for each group, with education for black people infamously excluding mathematics from the syllabus on the basis that they would not rise above the level of manual labourers and would not therefore need it; it included job reservation, which reserved more-skilled jobs for white people, including on the mines and it prohibited black people from running many categories of business outside of the bantustans. These dimensions of apartheid left legacies that continue long after the transition to democracy.

Not surprisingly, this system generated resistance. In 1912, the African National Congress (ANC) was formed to assert the rights of black people. By the 1950s, the ANC was leading a wider movement that included all races and in 1955, an inspiring popular manifesto called the Freedom Charter was adopted at a mass event called the Congress of the People.

This opposition generated a repressive response, with many people detained without trial, jailed and intimidated. In 1960, in response to protests against the pass laws limiting the rights of black people in urban areas, protesters were massacred in a place called Sharpeville. This was a turning point, with organisations like the ANC being banned and forced into exile. This in turn led to a decision for the ANC to embark on an armed struggle. Nelson Mandela played a leadership role in this process and, along with others, was caught, tried and sentenced to life imprisonment for treason.

After years of oppression, student uprisings in 1976 marked a turning point. Less high profile but equally significant however, was the rise during the 1970s of trade unionism. In addition, by the 1980s, a wide range of local community organisations, religious groups, youth groups and many more had started to mobilise against apartheid. Internationally, apartheid was also under pressure. Sanctions against South African products played a role in raising the costs of the system; the costs of

---

[1] In South Africa, under apartheid, the term 'coloured' was used to describe people of mixed descent and the descendants of Malay slaves.

repression internally, coupled with South Africa's engagement in wars on its borders were also taking their toll on the economy. The apartheid government started to talk of introducing reforms but when these came, they were a new form of divide and rule, in which whites, coloureds and Indians would all participate in three linked but separate parliaments – with the white parliament holding veto power. For black people, bantustan independence and greater voice in black township councils were envisaged. This catalysed the formation of the United Democratic Front (UDF) which brought together a myriad of opposition groups in support of the demand for full democracy.

For the duration of the 1980s, South Africa was at war with itself, with the apartheid state confronting an ongoing armed struggle as well as intensified popular uprisings. The ANC called for the society to be made 'ungovernable' and to a significant extent, this was achieved. Repression was intense. In this context, the trade unions, under the banner of the Congress of South African Trade Unions (COSATU), played a catalytic role in regularly bringing the economy to a standstill. NUM – only formed in 1982 – became the country's biggest trade union. The scale of disruption to the economy and the costs of maintaining apartheid persuaded the private sector that the system might not be worth defending any longer. By the late 1980s, private-sector and other leaders within the white constituency had started to meet with the ANC outside the country. By 1990, the writing was on the wall and the National Party Government announced that the ANC and other banned organisations would be unbanned and that Nelson Mandela and other political prisoners would be released. A process of constitutional negotiations began, co-chaired by NUM's General Secretary, Cyril Ramaphosa – by then elected as the first Secretary General of the ANC after its unbanning. These negotiations culminated in agreement on a rights-based constitution. South Africa's first democratic elections were held in 1994. The ANC won a landslide victory and Nelson Mandela became the first democratically elected president. The priorities shifted from overthrowing an oppressive state to building a democratic and developmental one, able to overcome the triple challenges of poverty, inequality and unemployment.

In the period covered here, the global context was also one of significant change. When the first NUM co-operatives (hereafter co-ops) were being established, the term globalisation still had limited currency, the Cold War was a going concern and the Berlin Wall was still standing. While the 'young lions' (as activist youth were then called in South Africa) could still be heard roaring locally, the 'roaring 1990s' were yet to come. Thatcherism and Reaganomics were rampant, democratic socialism was the Third Way and Cuban soldiers were still in Angola. By the end of the period covered here, however, the Soviet Union no longer existed, the Cold War's hot wars were no longer being fought in southern Africa, the post-Washington consensus was rediscovering poverty, the Millennium Development Goals had been agreed and 9/11 had just brought a new era of geopolitics into play.

Shifts in enterprise development strategy

Against this rapidly changing backdrop, the story here starts with the unexpected – and unwelcome – transition confronted by those mine-workers dismissed in the 1987 strike: from a trade union struggle to trans-form labour relations on the mines to a different kind of struggle within the same market economy – the struggle to create alternative forms of livelihood through self-employment and enterprise development.

At the time, this was not only a new frontier for NUM as a trade union. Within the wider democratic movement, the focus at the time was on the struggle to secure political rights. The nuances of future economic policy were still the subject of slogans and the broadest of brush strokes; small enterprise development was largely unknown territory. This was compounded by a context in which, under apartheid, the participation of black people in business ownership had been legally restricted to a narrow set of forms of enterprise. Those that were permissible required licences from the discredited Black Local Authorities and were often deemed to reflect patronage relationships with councillors and, hence, a form of collaboration with apartheid. Businesses in black townships were often torched as part of strategies aimed at making these areas 'ungovernable' at the time. Yet because co-ops were understood as a socialist form of enterprise and an alternative to existing employment relations, they were treated as an exception and hence became the first entry point into enterprise development activity supported by organisations that formed part of democratic struggles.

The first section of the book deals in depth with the initial transition mineworkers had to make: the continuities and discontinuities con-fronted, the ways in which ex-miners – and NUM – tried to discover this new logic of enterprise development, at the same time as trying to transform that logic through an alternative form of work organisation in co-ops. It explores the ways in which we did and didn't manage to do so, the sometimes violent struggles over development resources and development direction and how the lessons of this experience informed changes in approach, with lessons from implementation experience informing a series of shifts in strategy.

Each of these phases of strategy had its own distinct drivers and characteristics, but the role of markets in development remained a constant theme. In the initial co-op phase, this entailed the discovery of what was, at the time, an inconvenient truth: the centrality of markets in determining co-op success or failure and the iron logics of profit and loss, even in what were understood to be alternative, socialist forms of enterprise. While thirty producer co-ops were established, the impacts of these were mainly limited to the direct participants; nor were these impacts necessarily always positive. Against the backdrop of a massive crisis of lay-offs in the mining industry, the scale and scope of the programme's reach was simply inadequate.

By 1993 – just before South Africa's first democratic elections – we were attempting to craft a new strategic direction, grappling with what would soon become a wider concern in the post-apartheid context: how to achieve scale and depth of impact in employment creation in marginal areas.

In this second phase, the focus shifted away from co-ops to a service-delivery role, allowing for wider outreach and for such services to be made available to all forms of enterprise activity at a local level, in a context in which the importance of small enterprise development was starting to feature in the first post-apartheid economic policies.

A network of seven development centres was established, providing a range of business and financial services to local enterprises. The strategic focus of these centres was on local production for local consumption: aiming to diversify the production of goods and services serving local markets, with the explicit intention of increasing the circulation of money to create multipliers in the local economy. What this did not take sufficiently into account, however, was how the highly unequal and centralised structure of the South African economy limited the scope for small-scale producers to compete, in a context in which the vast majority of items in the consumption basket of poor people were – and still are – mass-produced in South Africa's core economy.

Recognition of this precipitated a further shift in strategy, in an attempt to move beyond the constraints of local markets to break into higher-value and/or higher-volume markets outside the local economy. In practice, this required participation in value chains and/or access into the formal retail sector. This brought new opportunities – but also meant an end to the kinds of informal transactions enhanced and enabled by local knowledge, networks and trust relationships. Instead, participation in wider markets required more formal processes. This in turn required a step-change in business sophistication and, therefore, in the forms of support provided. Amongst a range of initiatives undertaken by MDA to assist entrepreneurs to break into such wider markets, two are considered here. Firstly, MDA's involvement in the craft sector and secondly, its involvement in the first commercial production of a juice from the indigenous marula berry, as well as in the development of marula oil as a cosmetic product: building a value chain from below that linked four thousand women in forty-two villages into national and global markets.

While our skill and expertise in understanding market conditions and constraints grew with each phase, our starting point was still a critique of the core logic of the market structure – and wider market system – within which we were operating. What were the alternatives to this system? It was against the backdrop of such soul-searching that we were confronted with a paradigm shift in the small enterprise development sector globally, characterised by an approach called 'making markets work for the poor'.

This paradigm emerged against the backdrop of sharp ideological differences and debate internationally. While South Africa was in the final throes of its struggle for democracy, the wider world had entered the post-Cold War period, which soon included the aggressive promotion of free market fundamentalism. While South Africans were trying to craft developmental roles for our new democratic state, the role of the state was being gutted across the rest of the continent. When the concept of 'making markets work for the poor' first came onto the agenda, it certainly seemed to fit within this wider narrative. In response to this new paradigm, some of the hollow laughter to be heard from the left was certainly my own.

Yet while there was much in the 'making markets work' approach to critique, doing so required a much sharper analysis of how markets work, whether there is scope to change how they work at a systemic level – and what that all means for the role of development actors, in order to attempt to answer the question: can markets be made to work for the poor? Or, in the less ambitious formulation that followed, can they even just be made to work *better* for the poor? Or is the process of market participation always inexorably one of making the poor work for markets? If so, was that all that our efforts were achieving?

Just to deepen our existential crisis over our role, in the new South Africa, small enterprise development was increasingly being positioned as the preferred neo-liberal solution for unemployment and poverty. So, despite unemployment levels in South Africa of over 25 per cent and rising, policies for employment creation were becoming increasingly marginalised from core trade and industrial policy, ring-fenced instead to a focus on small enterprise development. As Judith Tendler argued in the Latin American context:

> No longer considered 'serious' economic development, [concerns about employment] are now relegated to the realm of social policy, safety nets, and small-enterprise and informal-sector specific programs – a realm that has become marginal to the central project of economic growth. (Tendler 2002, p. 4)

At the time, this certainly applied to South Africa too. Employment concerns were absent from industrial policy; strategies to address un-employment were routinely focused on small enterprise development with an emphasis on micro-finance as a silver bullet – with a widespread expectation that the poor could self-employ their way out of poverty on the basis of a micro-loan charged out at commercial interest rates. A real win-win situation: banks would profit from ending poverty, while the rest of society could wash their hands of any further responsibility for the poor. This micro-finance 'revolution' was also held up at the time as the best available example of markets being made to work for the poor.

A related discourse from within social policy was also promoting a 'go fish' approach to poverty. Those who used their social grants for enterprise development purposes rather than consumption were implicitly presented as 'the deserving poor,' with everyone else cast as scroungers and freeloaders dependent on handouts. There was an inherent contradiction in this approach however because, in practice, South Africa's social grants are targeted at people who are not expected to be economically active – at children, pensioners and people with chronic disabilities. Yet this acted as no deterrent to a discourse in which the impact of social protection was increasingly measured by the extent to which income support to such target groups was converted into enterprise activity.

A further dimension of the discourse on enterprise development that caused us discomfort was the strident assertion of a new and unfamiliar form of class struggle. Not this time between capital and labour but between the employed and the unemployed (leaving the owners of capital entirely off the hook). In this narrative, despite high levels of working poverty, employed workers had become a labour elite protecting what were deemed to be their privileges (rather than their rights at work) in ways that were presented as the single biggest obstacle to employment creation, with the newly won labour-rights regime creating a regulatory environment that, it was argued, stifled the creation of what would otherwise be masses of jobs in the informal sector.

Mineworkers Development Agency was uniquely placed in these debates. As the development agency of South Africa's largest trade union, we were mandated to work with the unemployed to promote enterprise development in the most marginal economic areas in order to create jobs and fight poverty. While we believed enterprise development had an important contribution to make, this did not translate into support for any of these emerging narratives and polarities. We did not see small enterprise development as an alternative to industrial policy, we saw it as complementary – with industrial policy having crucial implications for small enterprise. We did not measure the value of social protection by the extent to which it led to self-employment, but by the extent to which it reduced poverty. We did not see the unemployed as the victims of an employed labour elite nor set the interests of the informal sector up against those of employed workers in simplistic and opportunistic ways.

Instead, MDA's location at the interface between employed and unemployed workers and between migrant miners and their communities meant that the direct linkages between the forces impacting on workers, the unemployed and the informal sector were inscribed within MDA's day-to-day work as an organisation. While the wider discourse increasingly pitted these categories of the poor against each other, our own experience was that, rather than being locked in conflict, they were far more likely to be found sharing a meal at the same supper table each evening – perhaps with an empty chair for the missing migrant worker – but with significant interdependencies and transfers within households between employed workers, the unemployed, those engaged in enterprise activity and recipients of social grants.

Our roots in NUM as a trade union and in labour market struggles also meant we brought a different prism of analysis into the debate on whether markets can be made to work better for the poor because, ironically, while some of the main proponents of this approach were more than a little hostile to the role of organised labour, the role of trade unions in labour markets provides a rather fascinating example of the proposition that markets can indeed be made to work better for the poor.

Like it or not, workers have found their power in the labour market and have wielded it, whether directly within that market or indirectly through their influence on political institutions, in ways that have changed the terms on which the labour market operates – in some contexts, changing this role from a poverty trap into a pathway out of poverty.

This shift is particularly clear in the South African context. A key part of South Africa's history revolves around the coercion and resistance associated with the creation of a labour market and the exploitative form this took. While much academic work has documented the history of resistance to inclusion in the labour market and in the mining industry in particular, this book starts at the point in history at which the mining industry – and later the economy more widely – starts to eject workers, with the fight now being to keep those jobs.

While the working poor are still a sizeable portion of South Africa's working class, it is nevertheless the case that a labour market that was historically unambiguously exploitative and dehumanising now provides protections and conditions that – in the formal sector – makes it the preferred route out of poverty. Those excluded from the labour market are left with no real alternative but to claw their way into the market economy through other means, with self-employment and enterprise activity often an option of last resort offering minimal returns for the new underclass of South African capitalism.

Markets and society

In labour markets, history has shown that there is scope to contest and change the terms on which this particular market operates – embattled as such shifts may be. Are there analogous ways of shifting power relations in other markets, in ways that change distributional outcomes in favour of the poor?

These questions plunged us into the wider debates of the role of markets in society and the role of society in shaping markets. All these debates have their roots in early political economy, but still remain at the heart of politics and economics today, informing different policy approaches that have real impacts on the distribution of power and resources and on poverty and inequality in societies.

This is explored in the concluding two chapters which focus on linking hard-earned lessons from implementation experience to these wider debates, reflecting on what this means for development strategy. Critical to the discussion are strands of analysis of markets drawn from Karl Polanyi, Douglass North and Ha-Joon Chang, all of whom engage with how to understand markets and their relationship to the state and to society.

According to Karl Polanyi, in *The Great Transformation*, first published in 1944, the concept of markets free of regulation by the state is a fiction, with market development instead relying on the role of the state:

> (T)he road to the free market was opened and kept open by an enormous increase in continuous, centrally organized and controlled interventionism. To make Adam Smith's 'simple and natural liberty' compatible with the needs of a human society was a most complicated affair ... the introduction of free markets, far from doing away with the need for control, regulation, and intervention, enormously increased their range. (Polanyi 2001, p. 140)

Polanyi focuses in particular on the negative effects on society that arise from treating land, labour and money supply as commodities, produced in order to be bought or sold and left to find their price on the market, arguing that these are instead 'fictional commodities':

> Undoubtedly, labor, land, and money markets are essential to a market economy. But no society could stand the effects of such a system of crude fictions even for the shortest stretch of time unless its human and natural substance as well as its business organization was protected against the ravages of this satanic mill. (Polanyi 2001, pp. 71–3)

The heart of Polanyi's argument is that in practice, societies have protected themselves against the ravages of unregulated markets in what he describes as a double movement:

> Social history in the nineteenth century was thus the result of a double movement: the extension of the market organization in respect to genuine

commodities was accompanied by its restriction in respect to fictitious ones. While on the one hand markets spread all over the face of the globe and the amount of goods involved grew to unbelievable dimensions, on the other hand a network of measures and policies was integrated into powerful institutions designed to check the action of the market relative to labor, land, and money ... Society protected itself against the perils inherent in a self-regulating market system – this was the one comprehensive feature in the history of the age. (Polanyi 2001, p. 76)

In the widest sense, the origins of the concept of social protection lie here: as a set of mechanisms through which society protects itself from the negative impacts of markets on society, in particular insofar as land, labour and money are treated as real commodities rather than fictional ones: with social intervention required to protect societies in relation to money supply, to the environment and to the terms on which labour is commoditised. While the dangers of treating labour as a commodity have been evident since the advent of market economies, Polanyi's identification of these risks in relation to the environment and to money supply seem prescient in the current context of climate change and recurring global financial crises, with his concept of the 'double movement' also evident in the struggles taking place within societies in relation to these issues – and, in fact, between these issues – with the impacts of globalisation on labour markets cast into sharp relief by both Brexit and the US election in 2016.

In his work on institutions, Douglass North echoes Polanyi's emphasis on the role of the state in creating the rules of the game within which markets function, with a more in-depth focus on how markets have developed as institutions – understood as the 'rules of the game' in societies. These rules of the game are not limited to laws and regulations, however, but include other formal and informal norms and practices that govern how societies work.

His work identifies markets as the institutions that govern exchange in society and focuses in particular on how the rules of the game in markets have developed to limit uncertainty in the process of exchange. These have facilitated what Adam Smith referred to in 1776 in the *Enquiry into the Nature and Causes of the Wealth of Nations* as 'anonymous exchange': forms of exchange that no longer rely on trust relationships and that take place across distance, with the development of contract law an example of this process. According to North, with a growing division of labour and increased specialisation in society:

societies need effective, impersonal contract enforcement, because personal ties, voluntaristic constraints and ostracism are no longer effective as more complex and impersonal forms of exchange emerge. It is not that these personal and social alternatives are unimportant; they are still significant even in today's interdependent world. But in the absence of effective

impersonal contracting, the gains from 'defection' are great enough to fore-
stall the development of complex exchange. (North 1991, p. 101)

The greater the division of labour and of specialisation, the more
complex the forms of transaction and the more important the issue
of transaction costs. Without contract enforcement mechanisms, the
transaction costs will reflect the associated risk that the other party
will defect on the contract. North argues that, throughout history,
the size of this risk premium has acted to limit the development of
complex exchange and where this is limited so is the possibility of
economic growth, with markets limited to local contexts in which trust
relationships dominate (North 1990a, p. 33).

Somewhat unexpectedly, Adam Smith's early concept of the role of
anonymous exchange in expanding market opportunities and North's
much later analysis linking contract security to the scope for economic
growth in societies proved to be directly relevant to our experience
of enterprise development in marginal contexts. Here a reliance on
simple and direct exchange placed limits on the scope for growth of the
informal sector, while breaking into wider, external markets brought
with it the complexity of anonymous exchange – and the need for the
clearer contractual rules of the game that drove the early development
of markets as institutions.

Chang is critical of the New Institutional Economics that builds
on North's work and the focus on governance reform that follows, as
reflected in the World Bank's 'World Development Report 2002: Building
Institutions for Markets'. This report argues that efficient and inclusive
markets are critical to poverty reduction and growth, and identifies the
need for institutions to enhance market development. Such institutions
need to perform three key functions: they need to reduce information
asymmetries, reduce transaction costs such as dispute resolution and
contract enforcement and they need to enhance competition in markets.
Chang argues that the focus on institutions has provided a new lease of
life for neo-liberal economics, allowing them to argue that the reasons
their economic policies fail is because of institutional weaknesses
rather than the disconnect between orthodox economic economics and
the real world (Chang 2006, p. 1).

Chang also critiques the 'property rights reductionism' that glorifies
private property rights as against any other form of secure rights in
property, and calls into question the assumption in the literature that
the protection of existing property rights is always optimal for economic
growth – because this assumes that the status quo is also always optimal
for growth. He also highlights the extent to which existing rights and
endowments are politically constructed:

> To begin with, the establishment and distribution of property rights and
> other entitlements that define the 'endowments' of market participants,

which neoliberal economists take as given, is a highly political exercise. The most extreme examples are the various episodes of 'original accumulation' in which property rights were redistributed through the most naked forms of politics, involving corruption, theft and even violence, such as the Great Plunder or the Enclosures in the early days of British capitalism, or the shady deals that dominate the privatisation process in many developing and ex-communist countries these days. (Chang 2001, p.12)

For South Africa, in its transition from apartheid to democracy, the role of politics and history in shaping inequality in the present were stark; in the debates over market development approaches to small enterprise development that followed, the tendency to treat existing endowments as given confronted us as a regular theme, despite consistent evidence that such inequality skewed market outcomes in favour of those already well endowed.

In considering the heated debates over the relative roles of the state and markets characteristic of this period, Chang argues that the terms of the debate are rooted in a flawed set of assumptions, because of a failure to give the concept of markets sufficient institutional specificity. As a consequence, even many of the critics of neo-liberalism focus on justifying state intervention in markets. Chang states that this reflects a flawed conception of markets and of what constitutes intervention, arguing that implicit in the debate about how much or how little the state should intervene in markets is an underlying neo-classical assumption: that markets can or ever have developed on their own. In *Kicking away the Ladder* (2002), he illustrates the critical role of the state in market formation in the developed world, illustrating how forms of state intervention generally considered out of bounds for developing countries today formed the backbone of successful development policy in countries that now no longer need the protection such policies afforded.

Chang argues that what defines a market as 'free' and what is seen to constitute 'intervention' are both context-specific and based on an underlying set of assumptions about the rights-obligations framework. He uses the changing terms on which labour markets have developed to illustrate the point. In relation to child labour, for example, he argues that few people in the advanced countries consider the ban on child labour to be a state intervention artificially restricting entry into the labour market, whereas in some developing countries, such intervention is resisted as impacting on economic efficiency. The same applies to the issue of slavery. This is no longer considered an 'intervention' that limits labour market flexibility, yet it was over a hundred years into the development of capitalism and only following significant struggles and a civil war in the United States of America (USA) that the ban on slavery stopped being considered an unjustified intrusion of the state into the market. Many environmental regulations were similarly initially resisted as intrusive – with the struggle certainly continuing on this front, despite the achievements of the 2016 Paris Accord.

The underlying and sometimes implicit thread linking Polanyi, North and Chang is the notion that, far from developing independently of society or outside of society in a separate 'economic' realm, markets (and economies) are social constructs: governed by social rules. This begs the question: if markets are socially constructed, how might they be constructed differently – to achieve different social and distributional outcomes? This is not a question that was explicit in the early phases of the journey covered here and there is no attempt to super-impose this concern into the evolution of strategy retrospectively. Instead, the aim is to reconstruct the dialogue that took place between experience and a changing context and changing discourse, to demonstrate the ways in which all of these led towards an increasing focus on the role of markets and on what the insight that they are socially constructed might mean for effecting change in their impacts on poverty and inequality: with the onus in this regard placed squarely back in the realm of societal choices rather than externalised as immutable economic forces.

In reflecting on this learning process, full note is taken of the comment made by a staff participant in one of MDA's many internal reviews, which reflects the kind of robust interaction that was typical, both in terms of defence and correction:

> There was tension in debating some issues – some comrades were harsh: it seems they were trying to hide their mistakes. We should discuss issues with a warm spirit, we are all learning and anyone who says they never make mistakes is lying. (Author's notes from MDA Strategic Planning meeting, 1995)

This book aims to discuss the complex issues confronted with just such a warm spirit.

2 The 1987 Mineworkers Strike

In Harold Wolpe's classic work *Capitalism and Cheap Labour-Power in South Africa: From Segregation to Apartheid* (1972) he explains how subsistence agriculture in the bantustans contributed to reducing the costs of labour on the mines:

> When the migrant labourer has access to means of subsistence, outside the capitalist sector, as he does in South Africa, then the relationship between wages and the cost of the production and reproduction of labour-power is changed. That is to say, capital is able to pay the worker below the cost of his reproduction. In the first place, since in determining the level of wages necessary for the subsistence of the migrant worker and his family, account is taken of the fact that the family is supported, to some extent, from the product of agricultural production in the Reserves, it becomes possible to fix wages at the level of subsistence of the individual worker. (Wolpe 1972, p. 434)

Over time, however, Wolpe anticipated that pressure on land in the bantustans would place pressure on the contribution that subsistence agriculture could make, that this would increase conflict, not only over wages but over the entire structure of the society, and that such conflict would be met by political measures that would in turn generate a political reaction (Wolpe 1972, p. 444).

The 1987 Mineworkers Strike for a living wage represented a critical moment in such a cycle. By then, the crisis of rural reproduction was acute. Arguably, a tipping point had been reached in bantustans such as the Transkei. Not only was the rural economy unable to fulfil its designated role in underpinning cheap wages, but rural households had become dependent on cash transfers from the mines and the urban economy.

These pressures contributed to NUM's remarkable growth and made the call for a living wage resonate deeply. A mere five years after NUM was formally launched in 1982, it had become South Africa's largest trade union, able to organise the biggest industrial strike in South African history:

> The massive 1987 mineworkers strike, the biggest and costliest wage dispute in the history of South Africa no doubt marks one of the highpoints in the

development of militant progressive worker struggles here. Not only does the strike stand out for the large amount of workers mobilised to fight for a 'living wage' and decent working conditions, 340,000 at its height, but because of the strategic economic and political importance of the mining industry in South Africa. (Markham and Mothibeli 1987, p. 58)

The 1987 Mineworkers Strike changed the mining industry forever. For NUM, it was 'the twenty-one days that rocked the Chamber' (i.e. the Chamber of Mines). Twenty-one days was far longer than the industry or NUM had anticipated the strike would last – and, while it inflicted significant damage on the industry, it nearly destroyed NUM.

It was a brutal, violent strike, in an industry characterised by the institutionalised violence of the migrant-labour system, manifested both by high and recurrent outbreaks of violence within the hostels, and the routine use of force to maintain control.

In one of many interchanges between NUM and the industry over the causalities and responsibility for the recurrent pattern of violence on the mines, NUM placed an advertisement in the *Weekly Mail* in early 1987 to present its view:

> Let it be known once and for all that the source of conflict is rooted in the institutions of oppression and exploitation that exist in the mining industry. The hostel system, migrant labour and induna system were pioneered at the turn of the century by mineworkers' lives. It is from this brutal and draconian system that the AAC (Anglo American Corporation) has benefited. Over time these structures have been refined but kept intact. AAC has identified and acknowledges some of the issues which have caused the tensions. But what has it done? AAC wants industrial relations to be sound and orderly yet it is not prepared to remove the archaic structures which are the source of the conflict. It wants to publicly articulate its liberal views and distance itself from the violence and deaths, when the very cause of the problems emanates from the institutions it has created. (*Weekly Mail* 10 January 1987, quoted in Allen 2003, p. 236)

The hostel (or compound) system is a deeply entrenched institution in South Africa's mining industry – with some hostels continuing to this day. Workers lived adjacent to their place of work in large, single-sex, access-controlled barracks. In the gold mines, the number of residents in a single hostel ranged from three to five thousand, with ten to eighteen men a room (Allen 2003, p. 6). Hostels were under the authority of *indunas* – miners appointed by management to represent workers, often through referrals from tribal authorities in workers' home areas, where chiefs historically also played a role in mine recruitment processes (Callinicos 1980, p. 35). This created a link between traditional authority in rural areas and the mines, with such authority co-opted as an instrument of labour market control. This was compounded by the ethnic segregation of certain job categories in the mines, as well as within the hostels, and embedded the ethnic dimensions of apartheid's divide and rule strategy. This had implications for trade union organisation:

> In industry at large, the interface between workers and employers was at the point of production but in mining it also occurred in the hostels for the hostel managers regulated and controlled the after-work life of the mineworkers and thus extended the area of potential conflict between workers and management. (Allen 2003, p. 210)

Even when trade union organisation started to gain momentum in the wider economy, the mining industry was still seen as impenetrable. However, once NUM was able to recruit an initial core of members within the hostels, the opportunity to organise workers room by room during off-duty hours meant the hostels became a crucial locus of trade union organisation. NUM's mobilising slogan for 1986 was to 'take control of the hostels'. As Allen notes, this was a threat to management but, in particular, it spread alarm amongst the *indunas* (2003, p. 210).

Their power was further eroded when NUM introduced a system of electing shaft stewards at mine level, whose role was to represent workers and take up grievances with management: 'Once management agreed to the shaft system, the induna system rapidly became redundant (at least in its representative functions) and a new regime ruled the compounds, a NUM regime' (Moodie et al. 1994, p. 255).

The displacement of the power of the *indunas* and the challenge to management's unilateral authority was often accompanied by violent conflicts. In the build-up to the 1987 strike, both sides prepared for what was, in practice, more of an industrial war than a strike. Reuters correspondent Christopher Wilson described the scene in the days before the strike began:

> South Africa's strike-bound Western Transvaal gold mines this week looked more like military installations than the major profit centres that form the backbone of the economy. Most ... were sealed off by heavily armed mine security men backed by plainclothes police. Armoured vehicles crammed with steel helmeted soldiers and police patrolled the main roads of the goldfields. (Quoted in Allen 2003, p. 317)

Each mining house had its own security force. The best armed and most notorious was in Goldfields. A confidential report leaked to NUM by a former Goldfields employee revealed that Goldfields had an armoury of six thousand shotguns, anti-riot vehicles and dog units, ran a mine security training camp where security personnel from other mines were trained and had even patented its own rubber bullet (Philip 1989, p. 214).

A key feature of the strike was the way in which control of the hostels was seized. As workers barricaded themselves inside – facilitated by the single-access entry points – management and the security forces laid siege from outside, using mediaeval tactics such as cutting off food supplies and power for cooking, and arresting workers who came to seek medical attention (Allen 2003, p. 335). At Western Deep Levels Mine, miners claimed to have been forced underground at gunpoint.

A dismissed worker who was later a member of NUM's Flagstaff Co-op explained that workers had locked themselves into the hostel when six green Hippos (armoured personnel carriers) from Western Deep Levels security and six white Hippos from another mine arrived:

> those Boers rammed the gate with the Hippos, broke it open and rode into the hostel. They said over the loudspeakers: 'Now we are taking control, no-one is going to control again, you are too late with your controlling'. They told us to go to our rooms and then they just started to attack us with their dangerous weapons, shooting at us, without even giving us five minutes, using teargas, rubber bullets and pistols with proper bullets. When we were in our rooms, they turned off the water and they stopped food from coming in.
>
> At nine o'clock that night, they told us to come out, we are going to work now. They shot teargas into the rooms and chased us out with batons and forced us to stand in line. They then forced us into the lifts at gunpoint and we were faced with no choice but to go underground, all the shifts at once and also the surface workers, forced down underground at gunpoint. (Quoted in Philip 1989, p. 215)

Some workers were barefoot; few were in work gear. Once underground, they began a sit-in protest. On Level 66, workers made weapons out of metal objects, vandalised mine property and threatened the white miners who had been deployed to supervise the work – who ran away and hid underground. When cages finally came to collect workers at the end of the shift, they were met on the surface by security officials, dismissed and escorted to buses to take them home (Allen 2003, pp. 365–6).

By week three, fifty-four thousand workers had been dismissed. In the end, when news reached NUM General Secretary Cyril Ramaphosa that Anglo American Corporation had taken a decision to dismiss its entire workforce, NUM's leadership agreed to accept the most recent offer from the Chamber – despite a strike ballot by workers two days earlier that had rejected these same terms (Allen 2003, p. 385).

The gains won appeared marginal: a 10 per cent increase on the annual leave allowance and an increase in the death benefit from two to three times workers' annual salary. There was no wage increase. The minimum wage on the gold mines at the time was R230 a month and R335 on the coal mines with 85 per cent of black mineworkers earning wages below the poverty line (Markham and Mothibeli 1987, pp. 59–60).

The fate of the dismissed workers became a key issue. Ramaphosa believed the agreement that ended the strike included their unconditional reinstatement. The Chamber denied it. The lack of a common understanding became evident only when the strike had been officially called off – providing a salutary tale about the risks of reaching 'gentlemen's agreements' when you are not dealing with gentlemen.

Despite NUM's attempts to fight this issue, including extensive litigation, reinstatement was selective. About forty thousand workers were not reinstated and were blacklisted from future employment on the mines. This included NUM President James Motlatsi, almost the entire NUM National Executive Committee, many Regional Committee members, education officers and shaft stewards. Organisationally, NUM was decimated.

NUM leaders faced a difficult balancing act in the aftermath of the strike. Despite the limited gains and the significant losses, it was crucial to cast the strike as a victory, which, in his inimical style, Ramaphosa tried to do: 'Defeating the bosses' aim of destroying the NUM is clearly a resounding victory' (Ramaphosa quoted in Allen 2003, p. 389).

Despite the apparently back-footed nature of this victory, Ramaphosa was not wrong. Powerful industry players were indeed intent on destroying NUM; but the cost of doing so was, in the end, more than even the Chamber of Mines was willing to pay – and they stepped back from the brink. As a consequence, the mining industry had no alternative but to deal with NUM as a legitimate presence. This fundamental change was acknowledged by the President of the Chamber of Mines, Naas Steenkamp, at the end of the strike. He said that the mines had learned 'about the effectiveness of the NUM's muscle, organisational capacity and skill' and that the strike was 'the beginning of a new learning phase in the relationship between the union and the Chamber' (quoted in Allen 2003, p. 389). It certainly was. The strike changed the nature of industrial relations in the mining industry. The mines had taken heavy losses in the strike also and mine management did not want to repeat the experience if it could be avoided. There has been no strike on that scale in the industry since.

More than twenty-five years later, against the backdrop of the massacre of striking mineworkers at Marikana, too much appears unaltered. At the same time, the dispute at Marikana cast the issue of mine wages into the public glare once again and at this level at least, some important shifts are notable. In 1987, mineworkers were amongst the worst-paid industrial workers in South Africa, earning on a par with agricultural workers. Today, they are amongst the best paid. No such shift has however taken place in the fortunes of agricultural workers, with a critical difference between these sectors being the level of trade union organisation achieved.

In the aftermath of the 1987 strike NUM had to re-constitute its battered structures at mine level and respond to the crisis of forty thousand core members and activists now outside both the union and the industry. Organisationally, this was a double-edged issue. On the one hand, NUM needed the skills and commitment of this cadre of dismissed union activists, who had built the union and whose organising and conflict management skills were sorely missed in the organisational mayhem that followed the strike. Yet at the same time, this powerful lobby of union leaders was now unexpectedly unemployed and outside the union. There was no precedent to inform the terms of their continued relationship with the union. If things went wrong, their potential to damage NUM was significant; these NUM stalwarts were now a potential threat.

According to the NUM constitution, the President of the union had to be a working miner; but NUM needed its dismissed President to remain in his post over this crucial period and Motlatsi did so until the constitution could be changed at the 1989 Congress. Some former National Executive Committee members were absorbed as staff and some were given ad hoc responsibilities for organising dismissed workers in the key labour-sending areas – mainly Lesotho and the Eastern Cape.

To do so, they needed living allowances, accommodation and transport and, by providing these, NUM was responding to the urgent need to convey the message to dismissed workers across southern Africa that NUM had not forgotten them and was fighting their case, with their return to the industry still envisaged.

In the chaos after the strike, the distinction between imperatives and choices was not always explicit; decisions were made in the heat of the moment that set precedents, created expectations and divisions that resonated well beyond this period. Little was scripted about it, however: this was new terrain and the stakes were high.

So, when the hotel bookings and hired cars were first arranged, these were largely pragmatic decisions informed by organisational impera-tives. The difficult politics of how and at what stage to remove such facilities from now-unemployed former worker-leaders of NUM was not anticipated. And, because only a relatively small cadre of dismissed leaders could be permanently employed by NUM, access to these organisational resources became highly contested.

Small wonder then, that power struggles were intense, as a much weakened NUM tried to conceal the extent of its injuries not only from the apartheid state and mining industry employers, but from its own members too. The arrests and dismissals had left a gaping power vacuum in NUM's structures and leadership at many mines.

Amongst the many challenges, NUM had to urgently find ways to support the forty thousand dismissed workers. This was the constituency – and the set of imperatives – that was passed on to NUM's job creation programme, tasked with establishing co-ops for these workers. I was interviewed for the post of head of this new unit by Motlatsi, Ramaphosa and Vice President Elijah Barayi and I came prepared to answer ques-tions about co-ops. The only question I was asked, however, was: 'What is the relationship between the struggle for national democratic revolution and the struggle for socialism?' Discussion on this topic and interrogation of my answers took well over an hour, but at a certain point, Ramaphosa exchanged glances with the other two and gave a nod. I was appointed.

I still had to earn the acceptance of the ex-miners, however. Soon after my appointment, I accompanied a team including Ramaphosa and Barayi to the Transkei, for a meeting with ex-miners. The Transkei had only recently seen General Bantu Holomisa overthrow Stella Sigcau in a coup in 1987. Trade unions were still banned in the Transkei at the time and this was the first time an NUM leadership delegation had formally visited or addressed a meeting in this so-called independent territory. Ramaphosa argued that the visit could not be considered illegal, as its purpose was not to undertake trade union activities but to support the establishment of co-ops. That logic had not, however, been tested with the Transkei authorities.

We flew in to Umtata airport. Elliot Bhala (former Chair of Randfontein Region, dismissed in the strike and now head of the newly formed Transkei Ex-Miners Co-op – TEMCOP) had arranged for a top-of-the-range Mercedes Benz to fetch the delegation. Ramaphosa refused to travel in it. When we finally left the airport, in a small Toyota, so did a convoy of uninvited (and unmarked) Transkei security police vehicles.

After a lengthy meeting in a community hall in Umtata, the same convoy bumped along rough tracks to a homestead on the outskirts of the town, where a meal was being prepared. A bull was to be slaughtered in honour of the event and we expected to provide an appreciative audience. The bull put up more of a fight than anticipated; more ex-miners had to join the team in the *kraal* (the cattle enclosure) to assist in bringing it down. This is a brutal process under any circumstances, but was made worse in this instance by the evident distress of other cattle watching the slaughter. Finally a young bull broke through the fence and charged the men, but this act of solidarity was to no avail.

With the slaughtered bull giving its final kicks on the ground, we were led to a tented area where food was to be served. Within minutes, men arrived with a platter of liver, offered with great deference to the NUM leadership – and also to me. Ramaphosa leaned over in anticipation of my response and his instruction was clear.

'You have to eat it', he said. 'It's an honour.' So, under the watchful gaze of the assembled company, I did. Charred on the outside, the inside was still warm from life.

Meanwhile, the convoy of Transkei security policemen was still there, sitting on the sidelines in their cars, watching. After eating, Ramaphosa ambled over, greeted them and invited them to eat also. Somewhat sheepishly, they joined the back of the long queue for food that had by now formed.

3 Conflict in the Transkei

In the aftermath of the 1987 Mineworkers Strike, some forty thousand workers were dismissed and sent home. A large cohort of these was from the Transkei bantustan, in what is now the Eastern Cape. Many were from Pondoland on what is known as the Wild Coast, with its steeply rolling hills, indigenous forests and ragged coastline. Despite its natural beauty, this was then and still is one of the poorest places in South Africa, deeply dependent on incomes from migrant labour, and one of the areas hardest hit by job losses in the 1987 strike. Little did we know at the time that this was just the start of a decade-long period in which the mines would haemorrhage more than three hundred thousand jobs.

For the men sent home on the buses, the transition from a trade union battleground to a very different terrain of struggle in labour-sending areas across southern Africa was a significant rupture. The considerable power that arose from collective action on the mines did not translate into any equivalent form of power for ex-miners suddenly dispersed onto the outskirts of the economy, nor did the strategies used on the mines have any traction in facing down the competitive market pressures soon to confront them in the co-ops and other forms of enterprise.

So, while there was a political continuity of purpose, this could not be translated into a continuity of practice. Yet the early patterns of action saw the ex-miners attempting to create just such continuities in both their organisational structures and strategies. Nowhere was this more evident than in the Transkei.

Two of the main protagonists – and antagonists – amongst the ex-mineworkers in the Transkei were Elliot Nomazele Bhala and Sipho Nqwelo. Bhala, who had been the Chair of NUM's notoriously violent Randfontein Estates Mine in Westonaria, took the reins of leadership amongst ex-miners in the Eastern Cape.

Randfontein Estates Mine was notorious for an incident in 1986, during which mineworkers had paid a *sangoma* (traditional healer) for *muti* (traditional medicine) to make them invincible. In particular, the *sangoma* promised it would make police bullets turn to water. When police came to disperse a gathering, mineworkers charged them; when police responded with the use of water canon – not in common use at the time – many interpreted this as vindicating the *sangoma*'s claims, emboldening them further. In the clashes at Randfontein Estates over this period, police shot and killed nine mineworkers, with many injured; mineworkers killed two policemen (Allen, 2003, p. 197; Malan 2015, p. 303).

Nqwelo had been a shaft steward at Vaal Reefs Number Two Shaft and Chair of its Strike Committee. He became Chair of the first co-op to be established, at Qwe Qwe outside Umtata and was later in charge of NUM's Mobile Job Creation Unit, a twenty-ton truck that delivered training to mineworkers on the mines during retrenchment processes. He also led the opposition against Bhala in the struggles that unfolded in the region.

Both of their stories illustrate just how tough and often dangerous these years in NUM were, with a volatile mix of tribalism and anti-tribalism, tradition and a challenge to tradition, violence and anti-violence, the building of democracy and the building of fiefdoms. All these elements were happening simultaneously in the union's early years, with the struggles over the trajectory of the union's development and who would control it particularly acute during the 1987 strike and its aftermath.

The emergence of a large trade union in which democratic practices became significantly institutionalised, which was able to unite workers across the ethnic divides and across all sectors within the mining industry (mainly gold, coal, platinum and diamonds) and to act as a constraint on the violent faction fights that had been a feature of mine life until then, was never a pre-determined outcome. It depended then – and depends still – on the role and calibre of leadership at every level.

A story from James Motlatsi, NUM's President at the time, illustrates this – and also serves to introduce Bhala. As Motlatsi recounts, during the build-up to the strike, he was invited to address a mass meeting chaired by Bhala at Randfontein Estates. About six miners were seated on the platform behind him. He assumed they were local branch or shaft level leaders, gave his speech and was leaving the venue when a miner pulled him aside and said: 'Comrade Motlatsi, why did you ignore the *impimpi*s (spies) on the platform? Why did you not congratulate us on catching them? They are going to die now.'

Motlatsi made his way back to the platform where he berated the leadership and the crowd, explaining that killing these men would be completely unacceptable to the union. He personally escorted the six hapless men to safety.

Bhala was amongst the NUM National Executive Committee members dismissed in the strike, and in early 1988 he announced over the radio that ex-miners should elect District Committees in all twenty-eight districts in the Transkei, in preparation for a meeting to be held in Butterworth, for which he had secured the permission of the magistrate, to establish a Regional Committee for the Transkei Ex-Miners Co-operative (TEMCOP).

At this meeting, a Planning Committee was elected, with three representatives from Eastern and Western Transkei and with Bhala as Chair (interview with Nqwelo, 2003). Sipho Nqwelo had been elected Secretary of the District Committee in Willowvale District and at the Butterworth meeting he was elected onto the Planning Committee.

My first encounter with Nqwelo took place soon after my appointment in NUM, at a workshop held at Wilgerspruit Centre near Johannesburg for representatives from the ex-miners, to develop proposals for the first set of co-ops. While I was making a presentation, a dove flew into the large glass doors of the venue and fell, stunned, to the ground. A man leapt to his feet, grabbed the bird, wrung its neck and then laid it out – feet up and head hanging on its broken neck – on the desk in front of him. In the lunch break he built a small fire, plucked and gutted the bird, and then cooked it and ate it with relish. This was Sipho Nqwelo.

Nqwelo was born in Willowvale in Pondoland, the first-born of six children. His father was a miner. He left school in Standard Six; to get a contract to work on the mines, he had to go to the local offices of The Employment Bureau of Africa (TEBA), the mine labour recruiting agency owned by the Chamber of Mines, where a friend of his father's was able to secure him employment. He was sent to Vaal Reefs Mine, where he worked from 11 November 1978 until 1987, at Number Two Shaft where he stayed in a hostel room with sixteen men. His first job was to load rock into the locomotive underground. Then he became a *picanin* to a white miner:

> There was this thing of a *picanin* in the mine, you carry this bag – the *skaf* tin [lunch tin] for this person [the white miner], his food and water, iced water and you go with him, carrying this thing ... You have to take his overall out and wash it after knocking off... but it was just a better job than the one of loading (rock), because you were just moving with this guy and it was hot ... I was then transferred to the engineering department where I worked, assisting there, because even if you went on a course of boiler maker, you couldn't do it during that time, it was reserved for whites, so you would still be an assistant there, so I worked at the boilermaker department. At least it was becoming better, that was the situation. (Interview with Sipho Nqwelo, 2003)

Nqwelo joined an English class after hours at the mine, where he was recruited to NUM and became a union organiser in Number Two Shaft – a role with significant risks. This was a time when ethnically based strategies of divide and rule permeated mine life and faction fights were common. According to Nqwelo, the key to faction fights was the power of rumour. Following a build-up of such rumours between Pondo and Sotho workers at Number Two Shaft in 1986, a fight broke out one night. Nqwelo and another union leader tried to intervene:

Photo 1 *Sipho Nqwelo (in the NUM jacket on the left) prepares to address a mass meeting of mineworkers being retrenched at Durban Deep Mine; 2000.*

> We decided to go inside. I said, no, we want to know, why are they fighting, because they didn't tell us. We are their leaders, so if they decide to kill us, they must kill us. So we went through this mob, we passed the Basothos, they didn't do anything; we went straight towards the end of the hostel, where the Pondos were. They were divided; the Xhosas were sitting on another block, all of them, well armed, they said, we don't want to be involved, we don't know this fight between the Basothos and Pondos. Then we went to the Pondos, already eight people were dead, a lot were injured ... So I decided to go to the resting station and I called the ambulances on my own. I was just making my way up and down going towards West Vaal Hospital with these ambulances, going to help those who were still injured, we didn't care about those who were already dead, we were just jumping over them. (Interview with Nqwelo, 2003)

Despite attempts by management to disarm workers the next day, the fighting continued, until finally, according to Nqwelo, the workers from Pondoland were defeated and opted to leave.

Nqwelo was from Pondoland himself. He offered to leave the mine with the other Pondo workers, but workers from other ethnic groups persuaded him to stay. He uses this to illustrate the challenges NUM confronted in building a solidarity that transcended tribal divisions – despite how deeply these divisions were institutionalised in mine life.

Nqwelo also uses the experience of a proposed national strike in 1984 that was called off at the last minute to illustrate the volatility – and personal risk – confronting union organisers at the time. In the build-up to this strike, shaft stewards from the mine had gone to Johannesburg as part of NUM's national negotiating team. At the eleventh hour, based on agreements negotiated, NUM decided to call off the strike. The shaft stewards returned to the mine just before the strike was supposed to start. It was a Sunday evening. Nqwelo was Chair of the Strike Committee but had not attended the negotiations – he had stayed behind to organise. He describes the report-back given by Oliver Sokhanyile (Soks) to the workers:

> It was already at night past six to seven and you must remember people were drunk already, knowing that they are not going to work, they are going on strike; there was that spirit; so people filled the arena. When we arrived there they [the union representatives] started now addressing the crowd: 'Okay, these are the issues that have been agreed upon – but there was no agreement on the wage increase.' So even some of the shop stewards started now mixing around the workers to say: 'No, these people have been bought'; and there was chaos, they wanted to kill Soks. Even the songs now changed, they were singing about Soks ... the song said: 'Soks is selling us to the Boers, let's kill him'. So, wearing the strike committee T-shirt, I jumped over the platform to cool the crowd, calling 'Amandla! Amandla!' and they calmed down. I said 'look guys' – I didn't even want to consult Soks and others because I could see this situation is getting out of control – I said: 'Look, let's agree we are not going down (the mine), even the day shift, tomorrow, we are not going to work. Let's meet tomorrow and have a meeting so that we can all understand this agreement.' And they were happy, they started now going out of this arena singing and marching all over the hostel. (Interview with Nqwelo, 2003)

So, despite the national agreement reached between NUM and the Chamber of Mines, the exigencies of the moment meant NUM at Vaal Reefs went on strike anyway. 'Exigencies of the moment' were to dictate a similar pattern in the co-ops – and would require similar levels of local leadership to determine the outcomes.

The extent of the challenges that lay ahead in the co-ops were, however, still unknown. NUM and the ex-mineworkers were keen to initiate the first co-ops as soon as possible; to do so, NUM would use resources left from international strike solidarity funds, which were sufficient to set up two co-ops in Lesotho and two in the Eastern Cape. One of these was planned for Qwe Qwe village just outside Umtata; the other in the Eastern Cape was to start on a site just outside the small town of Flagstaff.

Shortly after I joined NUM, I was tasked with undertaking quick feasibility studies for both of these, to be ready in time for Ramaphosa's next visit to the Transkei. These showed that the anticipated scale of local markets meant each co-op could viably support only twenty members. Unfortunately, however, the first opportunity I had to brief Ramaphosa about the outcomes of these feasibility studies was over breakfast in the Transkei Hotel in Umtata.

Ramaphosa was aghast – forty thousand ex-miners were expecting jobs in the co-ops – and the first two would accommodate only forty people? By the end of breakfast, based on some calculations on the back of his cigarette box and against the backdrop of the sounds of workers singing and *toyi-toying*[1] in the hall next door, the *realpolitik* of the situation dictated that there would instead be sixty members in each co-op, drawn evenly from all twenty-eight districts in the Eastern Cape, with the balance drawn from the Regional Committee and they would share the jobs, on a rotational shift basis.

Against a benchmark of forty thousand, this didn't close the gap much and caused enormous harm to the viability of the co-ops, but it was done. The imperatives that informed this decision seemed legitimate and compelling at the time and given the tightrope being walked by NUM in the Transkei, who's to say Ramaphosa's judgement was wrong? In practice, it was not wrong for NUM as an organisation: it was one amongst many strategic responses that contained and averted a level of potential crisis that could have changed the course of NUM's history.

However, it was certainly wrong for the co-ops as business entities. It was a cardinal error that too many co-ops set up to create employment in South Africa have repeated since: taking on more people than the co-op can support, because the need for jobs is so dire. The dramatic oversupply of labour in these co-ops compounded many other problems that later arose. Earnings that would have been low anyway were now much lower. The target wages in the co-op in the initial feasibility study for twenty people had been set at R350 (about US$140 at the time) a month, which was just above existing minimum wage levels in the industry at the time. Now each of these wages had to be shared between three people. In addition, at a single stroke, the complexity of management was significantly compounded.

The next key battle was over the control of co-op finances. Bhala opposed the idea that co-ops would control their own funds; instead, he wanted the Regional Committee overseeing the co-op development process to control them and argued that the profits of these co-ops should be distributed by this committee to all ex-mineworkers in the twenty-eight District Committees:

> He wanted monies to come to the region and then you will agree with him that this budget must be sent to the co-op – but not direct to the co-op, he was against that, because now you are killing his influence because for him having control over money is everything; then we kneel in front of him. (Interview with Nqwelo, 2003)

This issue was to be decided at a crucial workshop held with the Transkei regional structures in Lusikisiki. The workshop took place in a community hall and was run jointly by myself and Kgalema Motlanthe,

[1]   A *toyi-toyi* is a form of protest dance in South Africa.

then head of the NUM Education Department (and much later, President of South Africa from 25 September 2008 to 9 May 2009, after the removal of Thabo Mbeki and before the appointment of Jacob Zuma).

The meeting was tense, not helped by the arrival of the Transkei police, who informed us that we were under suspicion of organising a trade union in the Transkei and that we were to accompany them to the police station. It was not entirely clear whether this meant we were under arrest, but with Motlanthe and I in front, flanked by two police officers, the entire workshop was then escorted to the police station, walking down the centre of Lusikisiki's main street, stopping traffic and attracting crowds of curious onlookers.

The station commander was a corpulent man, seated behind his desk in an office adorned with homilies and idioms such as 'Do not put off until tomorrow what you can do today', printed on fading pastel-coloured cards. Somehow, we were able to convince him that our purpose was legitimate; no doubt Motlanthe's quiet aura of authority and gravitas saved the day.

We all marched back to the community hall – to continue our own tense stand-off. When Bhala realised NUM was immoveable and that control of the finances would vest with the members of the co-op, he stormed out – grabbing the keys to the hired car we'd been using off the table in front of me and taking them with him. It was a bumpy ride back to Umtata in the *bakkie* (van) of Regional Secretary Sonwabo Msezeli, but at least the battle for the NUM co-ops to control their own finances had been won.

The next big battle was at the 1989 NUM Congress, where a large delegation of ex-miners led by Bhala was present, demanding representation and voting rights. A huge struggle ensued. Despite Bhala haranguing the delegates in a deep Xhosa than not even the NUM translators could translate, the ex-miners could not muster the voting support required to change the constitution, in which membership rights are terminated six months after a member exits from the industry: for whatever reason. In the two years since the strike, National Executive Committee and Regional Committee members had been elected in place of those dismissed; they had little interest in seeing the re-instatement of previous leaders. Bhala's power in NUM was on the wane; but it was not over yet.

This was not the only battle at the 1989 Congress, however. The Congress took place against a backdrop of heightened tension in the country. It is said that the darkest hour is before the dawn and in 1989, it was simply unimaginable that in just a year, the ANC would be unbanned and political leaders would start to be freed. Ramaphosa summed up the mood in his speech:

> The scenario reflects cracks within the ruling class, where no coherent orientation exists on the way forward and where the potential for disintegra-

tion exists. But we must not confuse the cracks and divisions within the ruling class as a sign of the imminent collapse of the apartheid system. (Ramaphosa, quoted in Allen 2003, p. 473)

The slogan for the Congress was 'Defend and Consolidate the NUM': a reflection of the tough times the union faced after the strike. Ramaphosa described relations with the mining bosses as being at 'an all-time low'. While Bhala's attempt to secure continued voting rights for those workers forced to leave the industry was unsuccessful, it was also a reminder that in almost every NUM region, new leadership was in place in the aftermath of the strike and this created its own set of dynamics – which included the risk of leadership challenges in the national elections with which the Congress would conclude.

Gwede Mantashe, then a formidable worker leader from Matla Colliery in the Witbank Region (and later General Secretary of NUM before becoming Secretary General of the ANC) was NUM's national organiser – a powerful position of influence in the build-up to the elections. The outcome of these would provide the grand finale of days of deliberation, accompanied by a great deal of singing and *toyi-toying* – all of which was to be followed by a celebratory dinner for the hundreds of delegates.

For the first time (and I believe the last one, too) NUM had decided to self-cater this dinner, starting with the slaughtering of an ox – in recognition of the added cultural resonance this would have with mineworkers. In what was either a short-sighted tactical manoeuvre to remove Mantashe from the scene of the election action in the final hours – or simply an oversight – he had been made responsible for slaughtering the ox. It should have come as no surprise that Mantashe's priorities lay with election lobbying, in which he remained deeply immersed right up until the end. The result was that when worker delegates finally left the Congress venue after a tense and protracted election process, 'dinner' was still walking around in an enclosure outside.

As a consequence, Mantashe had to slaughter the ox in front of a critical audience comprising all of NUM's Congress delegates. That he managed this with little difficulty certainly did his stature in NUM no harm. The rest of the staff had been similarly gripped by the election process. The cabbages for coleslaw were still in their large mesh bags; those of us on chopping duty had a long night ahead. It was many hours before dinner was served. Luckily, there was plenty to drink.

Thwarted at the Congress, Bhala tried another approach and, a few weeks later, I was informed by an exasperated Ramaphosa that Motlatsi was on a plane to Lusaka – at the ANC's request – to fetch Bhala and his secretary in the region, Sonwabo Msezeli. Although the winds of change were already blowing, with a flurry of visits between different groupings in South Africa and the ANC in Lusaka, it was still a banned organisation, operating in exile from there. Bhala and Msezeli had found their way there and tried to play ethnic politics. They informed

Photo 2 *No visit to the Transkei was complete without a detour to Nomazele Bhala's homestead to see his sheep. On one such occasion, Deputy Secretary General Marcel Golding asked Bhala whether they were sheep or goats. For mineworkers present it was unclear which was more plausible: that this was an intentional insult – or that Golding really couldn't tell the difference. Bhala is in the centre; NUM President James Motlatsi and Treasurer Paul Nkuna are on the left; 1989.*

the ANC that NUM was a Sotho-dominated organisation and a threat to the ANC (the sub-text being that the ANC was a Xhosa organisation) and that inter alia 'James Motlatsi and Kate Philip should be destroyed'.

The ANC heard them out and then contacted Ramaphosa to ask what they should do with these renegade NUM members. It was agreed Motlatsi would go to Lusaka to fetch them. A few days later, Bhala and Msezeli were found looking rather sheepish and dishevelled in the office of Ramaphosa's secretary, waiting for the union to provide them with taxi money to go home to the Transkei – which NUM did.

They returned to Umtata, but tensions within the Eastern Cape structures ran high and Bhala started to face a challenge from below. When other committee members removed a union *bakkie* from him on the basis that he was failing to keep to agreed procedures for its use, Bhala laid charges of theft against them at the local police station – and accused them of being ANC members also, for good measure.

Bhala's next move was to mobilise the District Committees to demand payment from NUM for the work they had done in organising ex-miners after the strike, acting as the communication channels for the legal cases of the dismissed workers. The District Committees had, in fact, done a significant amount of liaison between NUM and the dismissed workers and this demand appeared reasonable and united the region. A delegation representing all the districts – which included Nqwelo – arrived unannounced at NUM Head Office to demand payment, which NUM – most ill-advisedly – agreed to make.

An amount of R52,000 (about US$20,000 at the time) was transferred to the Transkei account, as a once-off honorarium for distribution to members of the twenty-eight District Committees. While there may have been a case for some form of payment for the work performed, the method by which it was negotiated significantly empowered Bhala and validated these tactics. The unannounced arrival of combi-loads of ex-miners demanding money from NUM became common. But ironically, this victory for Bhala had unintended consequences that were his downfall in the end; because although NUM paid the money into the Transkei regional account, it never reached the ex-miners. They became increasingly suspicious, as Bhala made promises, slaughtered oxen – but never paid. Workers accused him of 'chowing' the money. He then faced not only an enquiry by NUM's NEC, but the wrath of ex-miners also – which no doubt catalysed his next move.

Bhala arrived at NUM Head Office with a combi-load of armed men and took Ramaphosa and Motlatsi hostage, demanding more money. Ramaphosa managed to alert Nqwelo:

> We were phoned in the Eastern Cape that Bhala is here [in Johannesburg] and that they were in trouble. We said to Cyril, no, don't refuse him ... you know, there is danger in life ... What you do, tell him that you are busy preparing the cheques and they are going to get them tomorrow. And then we organised ourselves, we were twelve. We went and took the *bakkie* in the evening at about six o'clock. We were well armed, with guns and swords. We came here to Johannesburg and we were well organised, even including people from the eastern side, from Pondoland. (Interview with Nqwelo, 16 April 2003)

Even in times of crisis, when the urgent task was to rescue the General Secretary and the President of NUM, Nqwelo recognised the strategic importance of ensuring that the delegation sent to deal with Bhala was ethnically even-handed – hence the emphasis on including people from Pondoland:

> So we arrived in the morning, I think it was five o'clock ... we went up to where the national leadership was. We found Bhala there, I think he was with Ramaphosa ... The national leadership didn't sleep. So we started beating him there – I remember Motlatsi was the one now who was appealing to us not to kill Bhala.
>
> We went to search those combis, taking whatever, confiscating whatever, there were some weapons there ... But we made a blunder and now we started going to this bottle store, buying some beers and Bhala escaped. Somebody saw him running to the lift and we have to wait for another lift now to get Bhala. When we reached downstairs, Bhala was already gone. He never came back – that was the last. (Interview with Nqwelo, 16 April 2003)

It may have been the last of Bhala in the NUM co-ops but not in the Eastern Cape – or in the mining industry or national politics. Sometime later, he was involved in a taxi war in Flagstaff and – as the story goes – the youth in Flagstaff attacked him and cut off his leg. When he was taken to the Holy Cross Hospital near Flagstaff, his reputation was such that the nurses were too afraid to treat him: he had to be taken to Umtata Hospital. Whatever the truth – and the anecdotes vary on the detail – half of one of his legs was indeed amputated.

Despite all of this, he made it onto the ANC list in the Eastern Cape as a candidate to become a member of parliament in the first parliamentary elections, but was too low down to make it. In 2003, he had formed a new organisation and was representing ex-miners in a bid for increased compensation. More recently, he was leading protests at the Union Buildings in Pretoria, in a context in which Motlanthe had become President of South Africa.

With Bhala removed from the immediate context of the battles in NUM, however, the focus in the Transkei co-ops could finally shift to co-op issues.

4 Power Struggles in Lesotho

South Africa's mining industry drew workers from labour-sending areas across southern Africa, but the small mountain Kingdom of Lesotho had become particularly dependent on such migrancy, with the large cohort of Basotho mineworkers playing an active role in the development of the National Union of Mineworkers (NUM). They were hard hit by the dismissals following the 1987 strike and, while the post-strike struggles described in the previous chapter were playing out in the Transkei, an analogous process was unfolding in Lesotho.

Lesotho was not always dependent on migrancy. Instead, when gold was first discovered in South Africa, Lesotho became known as the granary of the goldfields, increasing its agricultural output in response to the associated rise in demand. This changed when South Africa imposed new borders in 1912, pushing Lesotho further up the mountains and transferring vast swathes of productive agricultural land from Lesotho into South Africa's Orange Free State.

With Lesotho largely forced out of South Africa's agricultural markets, its people became increasingly integrated into the labour market instead. The 1986 census found that nearly half the working male population of Lesotho worked on South Africa's mines; in 1988, mining remittances contributed to 62 per cent of Lesotho's gross national product, dropping to just 18 per cent over the next ten years (Hassan 2002, p. 3).

Lesotho also has its own complex political history, securing independence from Britain in 1966 to become the Kingdom of Lesotho. Two main parties competed for power. However, when, in 1970, the Basotho Congress Party (BCP) won the elections on a progressive and anti-monarchist ticket, the ruling Basotho National Party (BNP) annulled the election and declared a state of emergency. The BNP ruled for the next sixteen years, banning the opposition and forcing its leaders into exile or into the mountains, from where they fought a low-key guerrilla war (Gay and Hall 2000, p. 7).

This did not stop massive international aid flowing into Lesotho. A case study of a World Bank funded development project in Lesotho in the period 1975–84 is provided in James Ferguson's classic ethnographic study, *The Anti-Politics Machine*. Ferguson describes the aid-funded development apparatus as 'an anti-politics machine, depoliticising everything it touches, everywhere whisking political realities out of sight, all the while performing, almost unnoticed, its own pre-eminently political operation of expanding state power' (Ferguson 1990, p. xv).

For Ferguson, this depoliticisation of development is illustrated by the way development texts, such as the World Bank's Country Strategy Paper, studiously avoid mention of the causal linkages between Lesotho's underdevelopment and the colonial wars that saw it dispossessed of significant arable land; or the link between its economic options and the political choices made about its relationship with apartheid South Africa – and with the ANC. Lesotho is also consistently projected as a subsistence and backward rural economy only now waking up to and integrating into agricultural markets, yet, as indicated above, this is entirely ahistorical.

Ferguson further argues that in the highly political context of the 1970s and 1980s and under a form of authoritarian rule backed by South Africa, the use of international aid money to run development projects played an insidious role, treating development problems as technocratic challenges and the extension of the role of the state through the delivery of government services at village level as a bureaucratic exercise devoid of political meaning.

In his conclusion, Ferguson made a plea for a different kind of development – a development from below. He says:

> the 'development' problematic tends to exclude from the field of view all forces for change that are not based on the paternal guiding hand of the state; it can hardly imagine change coming in any other way. But, from outside that problematic, it seems clear that the most important transformations, the transformations that really matter, are not simply 'introduced' by benevolent technocrats, but fought for and made through a complex process that involves not only states and their agents, but all those with something at stake, all the diverse categories of people who craft their everyday tactics of coping with, adapting to, and, in their various ways, resisting the established social order. (Ferguson 1990, p. 281)

He noted the massive change coming in the region and pointed, amongst others, to 'mineworkers joining the large and rapidly growing National Union of Mineworkers' as potential agents of such change.

The events covered in this book are in many ways a reply to Ferguson's plea, with Basotho ex-miners as agents of development and agents of change, engaged in just such struggles as he describes and in a context in which the links between the politics of Lesotho and of South Africa could not be more explicit – and travel in both directions. In fact, in this story, politics is the starting point. In the period in which Ferguson's World Bank project was doing its depoliticising damnedest, many BCP members had fled Lesotho – and many had fled to the mines in South Africa. Puseletso Salae was one such exile.

The reason why we actually supported NUM, we saw it as another vehicle that will assist us to fight the BNP in Lesotho. It is true that they were talking about, you know, issues of dismissals at work and injuries, but when we were sitting somewhere in the corridors, we could see that no, this is exactly the organisation that we wanted to take us back to Lesotho, because many of us – including myself – could not go back to Lesotho. You remember, when I was deported the first time in 1986 (from South Africa to Lesotho), it was my first time to go to Lesotho after ten years. I left Lesotho as a young boy to come here to the mines, but I could not go back because my family were BCP members. (Interview with Puseletso Salae, 18 July 2003)

During these years, however, the conservative and monarchist BNP had undergone a political volte face:

The Basotho National Party, while it was ruling Lesotho, it was supported by South Africans, but early in 1979 when Leabua Jonathon went to Red China and the Eastern Bloc and so forth – when he came back after meeting the ANC – strongly now he came up and declared himself, that I don't want to support these wild Boers anymore. I still remember that paper called *The Rand Daily Mail*, I read it – where he was saying 'I have changed my mind, I am no more supporting the South African government. The Cubans and the Russians are here to stay in my country permanently in order to make South Africa behave.' The Soviet Embassy was there in Lesotho. So South Africa was panicking to say, no, this guy has changed – now the ANC will move into Lesotho. Now it was, you know, a threat to the government of South Africa, so they actually now moved back to the BCP because they were aware that the BCP was having some problems in guerrilla training outside there ... Then the BCP could now move freely to Lesotho to destroy the BNP government. (Interview with Salae, 2003)

The BCP underwent a similar change in this period – although in the opposite direction. With the tacit support of the South Africans, the BCP's Lesotho Liberation Army (LLA) operated from bases in Qwa Qwa (a South African bantustan that bordered Lesotho) allowing the BCP 'free movement' into Lesotho.

The BNP's conversion did not extend to holding democratic elections, however and shortly after a form of quasi-election was held in 1985, in which only BNP candidates stood, a military coup was led by a faction in the army led by Major General Lekhanya. This was recent history at the time of the 1987 strike and Lesotho remained under military rule until the BCP won a landslide victory in 1993.

The Basotho miners who were part of NUM had not, therefore, necessarily learned all their politics in NUM. Many key NUM leaders from Lesotho were effectively political refugees from Lesotho. They brought with them political experience and a political agenda that not only aligned with NUM's goals, but also influenced the character of NUM and the direction it took: including a critique of traditional authority and the role of the chiefs. While Motlatsi is the most high profile example of this, Salae's story encompasses these struggles in Lesotho, the formation of NUM – and the history of the Mineworkers Development Agency in Lesotho also.

Salae was an organiser for NUM from its earliest days, as a union within the Council of Unions of South Africa (CUSA) and before its formal launch. Below, Allen describes Ramaphosa's first days as an organiser in CUSA – and in the process, introduces Salae also:

> Piroshaw Camay [then General Secretary of CUSA] gave Ramaphosa his new organising assignment on a Saturday morning and he immediately went to have his first glimpse of a mine shaft and a mine hostel in the Johannesburg area ... When he began the practical work of organising he was given one assistant, Puseletso Salae, a dismissed mineworker from Lesotho who was an active member of the Basutoland Congress Party. (Allen 2005, p. 88)

Salae had been working for The Employment Bureau of Africa (TEBA) as a fingerprint expert, before being transferred to Vaal Reefs Number Six Shaft, where he worked for about three years before being transferred to Johannesburg, where he was expected to train the white staff who would become his supervisors. He joined CUSA and started trying to organise workers in TEBA. He was dismissed – and returned to Vaal Reefs to organise for NUM. He is credited with 'virtually single-handedly' organising the entire Vaal Reefs complex with its ten shafts (Moodie et al. 1994, p. 252). Vaal Reefs Mine was located in Klerksdorp in what was then the Western Transvaal. It was South Africa's largest mine at the time, with forty thousand employees, and signing up a significant majority of this workforce was a crucial milestone in NUM's growth. During this period, Salae was twice deported to Lesotho. The following is what happened the first time:

> You remember, during apartheid, you are not supposed to have lunch in these Wimpy Bars. So I organised some few comrades, mineworkers and I said: 'Guys, all of you: put on your white shirts, ties and your jackets and make sure that you are as clean as anything; comb your hair and do everything and let's go to Klerksdorp, to a restaurant, to a Wimpy Bar.'
>
> We got there and many of the whites were so shocked; some of them even moved out of the restaurant immediately. We had all brought newspapers, you know, so we can sit in the restaurant reading newspapers. We said to the comrades: 'Even if you can't read, have that newspaper there as if you know how to'.
>
> And we had a lot of money, you know, cash in our hands, so that now we can pay and buy food like everybody. So we occupied the benches and many of the whites were so angry they moved out. The owner was prepared to offer us a service, but the wife of the owner was not happy, so they started clashing. 'No, tell these guys to move or I have to call the police and blah blah.' So the gentleman said, 'But no they are here to eat, why don't you just serve them and then they will go, instead of pushing them out?' So the wife took all the cutleries and everything and moved them away from our

Photo 3 *Puseletso Salae with a member of the stonecutters' co-op in Lesotho; 2002.*

table and throwed them out, you know and immediately the police were also called and I was deported to Lesotho; they didn't even hand me over to the police, they just dropped me in Lesotho and they came back. So I had to find my way back again to South Africa. (Interview with Salae, 2003)

The second time Salae was deported was during the preparations for a strike to celebrate May Day in 1986 and only two days after he had been released from one of many stints in detention. He was taken to the Klerksdorp police station, where he was told 'we know all about you'. Since his first deportation, Salae had returned on a Bophuthatswana passport. Bophuthatswana was one of the bantustans that had been granted a nominal form of independence from South Africa. Somehow, Salae managed to get a Bophuthatswana passport – exploiting a loophole in the system that he and no doubt others were quick to identify. Salae tells the story:

'We know all about you', they said. 'You are originally from Lesotho, from Leribe, so today is the end of Part One, my brother and you will never see Part Two. Bring your passport.' They took my passport, they cancelled it and cancelled it, they put a stamp on it.

They said, 'You have to go back to your country. You are messing us up here; there is peace here in the Western Transvaal, now you are bringing this Soweto *toyi toyi* and riots in here and you guys from Lesotho must go and organise these things in your country'...

Then they handed me over to the Lesotho police, with a long list that I have been making bombs, I am a terrorist and blah, blah. So the Lesotho guys said, 'No! Then how can you hand over this terrorist guy to us openly here, we should get some back-up support, we need South African and Lesotho soldiers as well so that we are sure that we are also secure, only then can we take this man'...

Then in Lesotho, honestly the police didn't say anything, they just searched me and then said: 'But we don't see anything wrong with you ... you are a human being like other people'. (Interview with Salae, 2003)

Salae was free to go and began working for the Migrant Labour Project of the Christian Council of Lesotho, acting as a link between NUM and mineworkers in Lesotho until he was drawn into the Basotho Mineworkers Labour Co-op (BMLC) – the entity set up by NUM for its ex-members after the strike. The Lesotho Council of Churches actively supported the 1987 strike, calling on workers not to become scab labour. Salae was in charge of reception committees set up by the church to meet and provide soup and support to dismissed workers arriving at Lesotho border posts.

From the time of his second deportation, there was a photograph of Salae on display at the South African border post with Maseru, identifying him as a 'wanted terrorist'. Instead, its effect was to provide at least one familiar face to say a silent *khotsong* (a greeting of peace) to wish Basotho mineworkers well each time they crossed the South African border. Salae became Secretary of the BMLC and was later appointed as the Lesotho Co-ordinator for the Mineworkers Development Agency (MDA), which, as at 2018, he still is.

By the same logic applied in the Transkei (that setting up co-ops was not the same as organising a union) NUM sent a delegation to initiate co-ops in Lesotho, made up of four former NEC and Regional Committee members. They set up base at the Lakeside Hotel but dissatisfaction with their performance mounted as they appeared to be living in luxury in the hotel without serving workers.

Before NUM could act, however, events took an unexpected turn, with the four announcing the formation of a new organisation called Miners and Dependants Welfare Association, funded by USAID as an alternative to NUM's initiatives. NUM's first inkling of this arose because Salae attended a barbecue at the American Embassy, in his capacity as a staff member – at that time – of the Lesotho Transformation Centre. He was mistaken for one of the Lakeside group by a US Embassy official (for whom all ex-mineworkers clearly looked the same) who engaged him in discussion about these plans. This official also confirmed the time of a meeting to be held at the Lakeside Hotel, at which the associated donor contracts were to be signed. Salae 'just happened' to be at the hotel at that time and made a point of greeting the four former NEC members as they sat with US officials. While NUM was initially sceptical of Salae's report-backs in this regard, which seemed bizarre even in that era of Cold War paranoia, a rival organisation headed by these four former

NUM leaders was indeed funded by USAID (interview with Salae, 2003).

Luckily, the Lakeside group had performed their mandated tasks sufficiently badly for workers to be unimpressed by this development and there were few defections, but it certainly raised the stakes for NUM in Lesotho and the pressure on the co-op strategy.

In another dimension of the Cold War context, around this time, in 1988, I was called into Ramaphosa's office and told that the Pope's visit to Lesotho provided the perfect cover for a meeting with a delegation from the Soviet Union. So, while the Pope-mobile wended its way slowly to the purpose-built stadium in Maseru, Billy Cobbett (then with PlanAct) and I met a Soviet delegation at a discrete venue in Maseru. Although the purpose of the meeting was never specified, I expected intelligent conversation – new insights into the link between the national democratic revolution and the struggle for socialism, perhaps. Instead, it was like being trapped in a bad anti-Soviet propaganda movie in which a great deal of vodka was consumed. I soon had reason to be very glad that Cobbett was there as a nominal chaperone.

Unlike the Transkei, Lesotho had a Co-operative Law, a Co-operative Ministry, a Co-operative Commissioner and a level of application of the rule of law that made formal registration of NUM's co-ops necessary. Lesotho's co-op institutions were modelled on the approach to co-ops taken in many African countries post colonialism: a way of doffing the cap towards socialism and towards a kind of surrogate social ownership, under the auspices of one ring-fenced department of government, which was also often the only locus of continued rhetoric about socialism, disconnected from the rest of government policy.

Co-ops were 'owned' by their members, but the terms of this ownership were circumscribed by the powers of the Co-op Commissioner. Ownership of co-op assets vested partly in the Ministry of Co-ops: if a co-op collapsed, its assets were taken over by the Ministry and the Ministry had a range of powers to intervene in the internal decision making of co-ops also – in the name of protecting the members.

Workers in Lesotho registered the BMLC under Lesotho law. While NUM was not a legal entity in Lesotho and its activities in Lesotho came under intense scrutiny, the BMLC now provided a legal vehicle through which the ex-miners were able to operate.

The first elected Chair was Moses Mokhehle. Although an NUM member, he had not been prominent in NUM, but he claimed to be the son of Dr Ntsu Mokhehle, the head of the exiled BCP – a filial status that was at best unclear. Politics found its way into the centre of the NUM Co-op Programme:

> That is exactly where the whole thing started because [Moses Mokhehle] happened to be claiming to be the son of Ntsu Mokhehle and yet he was not. Threatening 'Comrades, comrades if you don't do this, I will have to bring

the LLA.' The LLA is the Lesotho Liberation Army that was in exile – that was formed by the BCP. So that caused problems again, because the very same people, Jack and including myself – we were still members of the BCP but we were actually disillusioned, we didn't even want to get back to the party any more because of internal politics and the relationship with South Africa and so forth ... So we were no more interested and this caused again a conflict between us. And the guy kept on saying, 'I'll have to inform my father, if you don't do this' and other threats, anyway. But unfortunately that took a very serious direction. (Interview with Salae, 2003)

By this time, both the NUM Co-op Unit and the BMLC committee were unhappy with a serious lack of accountability over financial issues. Things came to a head over a desk purchased by Mokhehle (with no mandate) that was made from a rare imported wood and was so large it couldn't even fit into the BMLC offices. Salae persuaded the Swedish Embassy to buy it from them. Removing Mokhehle from his post, however, required a formal process overseen by the Commissioner of Co-operatives in Lesotho; but because he was believed to be the son of Mokhehle, officials were unwilling to enable this process.

Salae describes how they then went to the family home of Dr Mokhehle and found that Moses Mokhehle was not recognised as his son. Yet the Commissioner continued to refuse to allow the BMLC to call a special Annual General Meeting to attempt to remove him. With formal channels closed to them by the Commissioner, fair means turned to foul.

Mokhehle was known to greatly enjoy his signing powers as President, without necessarily paying much attention to the contents of the documents put before him. He was taken a pile of cheques and papers to sign, including a document supposedly verifying that he was no longer the President of the BMLC and a resolution from the BMLC executive to this effect. He signed them. On the basis of these documents, the BMLC removed him as a signatory at the bank and – confronted with the 'evidence' – the Commissioner of Co-ops finally agreed to allow the BMLC to proceed with a special AGM.

Mokhehle had been tricked and he in turn turned to dirtier tactics. The BMLC offices, located in a building at the main circle in Maseru, near the cathedral, were attacked by Mokhehle and a group of ex-miners armed with knives and sticks. The committee was routed, some were injured and the offices were ransacked. It was the first of many such attacks in the following weeks.

When the AGM finally took place, we required the protection of the Lesotho police and army, with soldiers cordoning off the venue, because of concern of a violent attack. In elections presided over by the Co-op Commissioner, a new leadership was elected. Mokhehle was removed: for the time being, anyway.

The establishment of the BMLC, with its links to NUM and the ANC, also attracted the interest and support of progressive intellectuals in Lesotho. Salae explains below how this strengthened the Lesotho programme:

> We got support from the intellectuals in Lesotho, progressive forces, but intellectual guys who were very much behind the ANC who actually see these co-operatives as a backup, a tool that they would also use to support the structures of the progressive organisations in Lesotho … So intellectual support was there – which was not actually happening if you get to Eastern Cape, if you get to Swaziland, that was not happening, guys were on their own.
>
> So that is the right thing, because on our own we are fighting from eight o'clock until four o'clock, nothing is done in the office, fighting, fighting, fighting. But in the presence of an external person from the university, who says guys, let's sit down, today what is happening. Now we need to meet the EU [European Union], right, make an appointment; and write what we are going to do, to present to the EU … those were the guys who could analyse even the cash flows and help us to understand … They did a lot, honestly. Then came fear again from other forces, from the government, let's say, because they could see that the BMLC was very close to the university. (Interview with Salae, 2003)

Their concerns were not entirely unfounded. Together with this network of university-based intellectuals and professionals, they were able to stop Mandela from visiting Lesotho in 1990: because they did not want him to confer legitimacy on the military regime. Through his links to Ramaphosa, Salae, who happened to be in Johannesburg at the time, was able to table concerns over the proposed trip into a meeting of the ANC Working Committee:

> So they [the ANC Working Committee] said, okay stay outside, we want to discuss this and find out exactly what is happening and they took about an hour. At 5.30, Joe Slovo came out of the meeting to report that, 'No, no, Mandela is no more going to Lesotho' and we were so happy that you know, we have stopped Mandela. A small team has managed to do that. Then I rushed back driving that red *bakkie* to Lesotho drrrrrrrr … the border gates were closing at 10 pm at that time. I drove very fast to make sure that I report back to say: 'Guys, you have succeeded, Mandela is no more coming'. Imagine, in that time when Lesotho was busy talking about Mandela coming to Lesotho, they had bought many blankets, you know, slaughtered so many cattle and sheep. (Interview with Salae, 2003)

The influence of the ex-miners at the highest levels of South African politics did not go unnoticed within Lesotho politics:

> That thing made the government distance itself from the BMLC, saying now these organisations are politics not co-operatives. I remember we were told by the [Co-op] Commissioner, he called us and said are you guys running a co-operative or a trade union? Then we said: 'No, no, we are running a co-operative'. He said: 'No, Salae you are lying, look at all these photos' –

he was confronting the old man *Ntate* [term of respect for an older man] Jack Mpapea, at the co-op and he said, 'What are these: Mandela, Mandela, Ramaphosa, ANC what what. This is Lesotho, but you don't have a picture of the Prime Minister of Lesotho here?'

And then *Ntate* Jack answered in a very clever way, he said: 'No, no, no, all these are friends, if you want to be a friend of the BMLC, you can be a friend as well, we won't say no. This Mandela is a friend of ours, you know'. Even the Minister of Co-operatives, who was the secretary of the BCP – he told James Motlatsi when he was in Lesotho: 'Guys I am watching these co-operatives, these are not co-operatives'. (Interview with Salae, 2003)

Ferguson would no doubt enjoy the irony. 'Depoliticised development' meant development was not politics and so, in an environment in which political activity was not allowed, 'development' was nevertheless legitimate terrain for the ex miners to occupy – and as long as what they were doing could be justified as development, it could not be condemned as politics, despite the explicitly political dimension of the BMLC's role.

In Lesotho, development as an integral part of a wider political agenda remained integral to the way NUM and MDA's programme unfolded and it was against this backdrop that the process of co-op development finally began in earnest.

5 Co-ops Capture the Imagination

When NUM started its co-op programme, the idea of co-ops as an alternative to traditional forms of ownership and to the organisation of work was starting to capture the imagination within the democratic movement in South Africa. Within the Congress of South African Trade Unions (COSATU), interest in co-ops was given impetus during the 1980s by the establishment of the Sarmcol Workers Co-operative (SAWCO) in Howick, near Pietermaritzburg. SAWCO was initiated by the National Union of Metalworkers of South Africa (NUMSA) and was intended to provide income support and solidarity to workers who had been dismissed in a bruising battle with metal-industry employer Sarmcol.

Co-ops were not new on the South African landscape. A network of credit unions existed, along with scattered community-based initiatives. Most visible, however, were the large agricultural marketing and supply co-ops set up by white farmers. These were constituted as racially exclusive entities and represented a powerful conservative farming lobby in South African politics, through which significant subsidies and support to farmers were channelled.

The emergent co-op movement was at pains to differentiate itself from this tainted tradition, looking to the rest of the world for more democratic and socialist examples on which to build. Close to home, the emergence of co-op movements in Zimbabwe and in other countries across the region provided inspiration, as they grappled with post-liberation challenges, providing a window into future possibilities for South Africa that, in the 1980s, still seemed very remote.

Globally, the co-op tradition includes a diverse and dynamic range of forms of co-op. The main categories include user co-ops, such as consumer co-ops, credit unions, child-care and utility co-ops, where the members are users of the services of the co-op; producer co-ops, where the members are self-employed producers such as farmers, fishermen or taxi drivers, who come together to create economies of scale in relation to inputs, processing activities and/or marketing; social or community co-ops, often multi-stakeholder in form, bringing members together around a social goal; and worker co-ops, whose main purpose is job creation and are owned and controlled by workers in the enterprise (Roelants et al. 2014, p. 17; Zamagni 2012, p. 22).

Within this wide range of forms of social and economic co-operation, it was primarily worker co-ops that caught the popular imagination in the trade union movement in South Africa at the time, in turn influencing the wider discourse. A feature of these is that the members are also workers in the enterprise, dependent on the co-op for their livelihoods. This is not the case in other forms of co-op. In a consumer co-op, for example, the benefit of membership is based on access to affordable groceries or other household needs. Insofar as they get any additional financial benefit or return from their participation, this is typically based on the co-op's annual performance, with their share of any surplus generated linked to how much they bought at the co-op over the year. Such members are not dependent for their livelihood on the co-op, even if their participation brings economic benefits. By contrast, in a worker co-op, members are employed in the co-op and it is usually their main source of livelihood. This certainly raises the stakes for such members.

A further distinction relates to employment relationships in co-ops. In most forms of co-op, the relationship between the co-op and its employees is little different, in contractual terms, from employment relations in a conventional business. Worker co-ops are owned and controlled by the workers who work within them and, as a consequence, this model offers a more radical alternative to conventional firms than other forms of co-op necessarily do.

This attempt by worker co-ops to redraw the relationships between owners and producers significantly increases the complexity of the endeavour, however and while other forms of co-op have thrived in many parts of the world, proving resilient even in the face of the recent global economic crisis, the establishment of viable worker co-ops has posed a more significant challenge – with worker co-ops historically the least successful form of co-op, despite 'the disproportionate amount of attention' accorded to them in the theoretical literature (Zamagni 2012, p. 22).

Yet despite the difficulties, there are remarkable success stories. The most famous of these include the worker co-ops within Mondragon Co-operative Corporation in Spain as well as within the *Lega Nazionale delle Cooperative e Mutue* (the Lega) in Italy, where co-ops have been sufficiently influential to be defined as 'the third sector' of the economy, with over 8 million members. By 2011, the Lega had over 13,505 member co-ops, employing 480,435 people (Jensen et al. 2015, p. 45).

In both cases, while worker co-ops are an important part of the story, they are dwarfed by the scale of participation in other forms of co-op, with consumer co-ops having the largest membership – and employing the most people.

In South Africa in the 1980s, however, it was the notion of worker co-ops as a strategy for job creation and as a radical alternative to the traditional firm that most resonated.

Co-ops: A radical alternative?

In the enthusiasm for co-ops as a radical alternative to capitalist firms, what was often missed was that within Marxist and socialist traditions there was quite some scepticism about the extent to which worker co-ops really did offer such an alternative. The critical limitation of co-ops from a Marxist perspective was characterised by Bettelheim as follows: 'the contradiction between capital and labour, abolished at the level of the unit of production, is maintained on a social scale' (quoted in Cornforth 1983, p. 12).

So, while structures of ownership and the organisation of production within the co-op might differentiate them from traditional firms, this has no wider systemic effect on the structure or logic of the market economy. Despite such internal changes, capitalist relations of production still define the parameters within which co-ops operate, with the role of the market directly affecting a co-op's chances of economic survival: forcing co-ops to play by the rules of the capitalist game.

Also sceptical of the scope for co-ops to offer a radical alternative were Fabian socialists Beatrice and Sydney Webb, whose 'Special Supplement on Co-operative Production and Profit Sharing' was published in 1914 in *The New Statesman*. After extensive study of 'associations of producers' in France, Belgium, Britain, Italy and Germany, the Webbs concluded with little optimism for co-ops as a form of enterprise – transitioning from idealism to disillusion in the course of their research.

Their controversial conclusions have been central to debate on the economic and political limits and potential of worker co-ops ever since (see Cornforth 1995; Major 1996; Storey et al. 2014; Langmead 2016).

There are two main strands in the Webbs' argument. Firstly, they argue that 'self-governing workshops' or worker co-ops have a tendency to fail; they reflect on 'the melancholy uniformity' of their collapse:

> They are extremely unstable, springing up with comparative ease, but dying with equal rapidity. They are born, in fact, at the rate of about one a week, but the death-rate about equals the birth rate ... They often arise immediately after strikes. They attract usually workmen of exceptional zeal, energy and self-denial, who display the utmost industry and self-denial in building up their enterprise. (Webb and Webb 1914, p. 6)

After examining a wide range of factors, the Webbs attribute the lack of competitiveness of such self-governing workshops to three main factors: inadequate work discipline, insufficient knowledge of the market and a reluctance to adapt existing processes or adopt new technologies:

With regard to workshop discipline, experience seems to indicate, with human nature being as it is at present, it does not do for those who have in the workshop to obey the manager to be, as committee men, the direct employers of the manager. (Webb and Webb 1914, p. 21)

More controversially, the second part of their conclusion was that where co-ops do manage to overcome the challenges that threaten their viability as businesses, such co-ops tend to leave key elements of the co-op form behind, abandoning democratic practices and reverting to more conventional forms of enterprise. Economic success, they suggest, precipitates political failure:

Moreover, those societies which have had any marked financial success, or have grown to any size, prove, for the most part, to have departed considerably from the form of the Self Governing Workshop – to such an extent, indeed, that it is not far off the truth to say that the chance of success seems to increase the further that form is left behind! (Webb and Webb 1914, p. 20)

The Webbs termed this phenomenon 'degeneration', associated with the characteristics, summarised as follows:

1 A breakdown of internal democracy in the co-op; manifest as a shift from more direct forms of democratic control in production, to more indirect forms of democracy, including, for example, the appointment of external management rather than the election of management internally.
2 The dilution of worker-ownership, or of the principle of 'indivisibility of co-op capital'. either through the partial sell-off of shares in the business or the full conversion of the enterprise to a conventional form of share ownership.
3 The introduction of wage labour – workers in the enterprise who are not members and who do not have any automatic right to become members by virtue of working in the enterprise.

Certainly, worker co-ops often fail, but the reasons why they do so are largely shared with all forms of start-up enterprise. Do the features that differentiate co-ops from other forms of enterprise help or hinder their ability to adapt to such challenges, however? Outcomes vary, but in the recent financial crisis, there is evidence that in certain contexts at least, co-ops actually proved more resilient than conventional forms of enterprise (Roelants et al. 2014, p. 15). Clearly, context and the support framework matter.

More hotly contested, however, is the Webb's theory that successful co-ops tend to degenerate into conventional forms of business: because if this is the case, then the significant effort in getting them to succeed risks becoming an exercise in futility.

Certainly, not all worker co-ops degenerate; but it happens often enough for the debate to have remained live: with co-ops in both Mondragon and the Italian Lega accused of such degeneration (Oakeshott 1990, p. 8; Storey et al 2014, p. 3; Heras-Saizarbitoriaa and Basterretxea 2016).

Within the significant literature around this issue, two main explanatory factors are provided. The first focuses on degeneration as a political phenomenon, manifest by the breakdown of democracy and ascribed largely to voluntarist factors. A lack of commitment or form of betrayal of co-op principles by members is often implied, with the remedies focused on political education and regeneration and institutionalisation of democratic and participatory processes. The second explanation focuses on how the exigencies of competing within capitalist markets create external pressures, often focused on the need to raise external capital.

Preventing degeneration in co-ops

When I first confronted these debates, over twenty-five years ago, I dismissed the Webbs' arguments as excessively pessimistic (Philip 1988). While the risks of failure and the difficulties of competing in the market were certainly taken seriously, conditions in South Africa at the time seemed to provide a supportive context that could enable co-ops to thrive. In particular, the location of co-ops within a wider mass democratic movement held the promise of solidarity markets able to cushion co-ops from the sharpest edges of competition; the threat of bureaucratisation and dilution of co-op principles associated with degeneration also seemed to have little relevance to the heady context in which co-ops were emerging in southern Africa at the time. As a structural constraint on degeneration, I also argued for the development of models of wider social ownership of co-ops such as those in place within Britain's Industrial Common Ownership Movement (ICOM) and copied closer to home by the Organisation of Collective Co-operatives in Zimbabwe (OCCZIM). These models aimed to prevent dilution of the principle that co-op capital is 'indivisible' by vesting ownership of the assets of member co-ops in the co-op federation – limiting the capital that members could withdraw to their original contribution plus nominal interest.

Not long thereafter, I was invited to head NUM's co-op programme: providing an opportunity to put theory into practice – with some unanticipated outcomes.

6 The NUM Co-op Programme

Against the backdrop of the power struggles in the Eastern Cape and Lesotho described in earlier chapters, four new NUM co-ops finally went into production during 1989. In South Africa, these were in the Transkei, in Qwe Qwe (outside Umtata) and in Flagstaff; in Lesotho, they were in the small towns of Quthing and Leribe. These co-ops represented a rather steep learning curve for NUM, in which most of the kinds of problems experienced in the early 1900s in the 'associations of producers' described by the Webbs and discussed in the previous chapter were manifest in stark forms – along with quite a few they could never have anticipated.

With the first four co-ops just up and running, the pressure to roll out more was already intense, with NUM embarking on a co-op expansion strategy focused on establishing agricultural production co-ops in every district of the Transkei and Lesotho. This expansion phase was supported by funding from the European Union through a local entity called Kagiso Trust. This allowed the NUM Co-op Unit to rapidly enhance its staff capacity with a mix of ex-miners, professional financial managers and specialist agricultural capacity.

In this period, the Co-op Unit was exposed to the more established co-op movements in Zimbabwe and Botswana, where experience and thinking on the issues was far ahead. We drew from this experience by recruiting James Sarakusebwa from the Co-operative Self-Finance Scheme in Zimbabwe.[1] Over this period, in 1990, the ANC and the South African Communist Party (SACP) were unbanned; a range of staff members with specialist skills were drawn from amongst these returning exiles.

NUM's Co-op Forum – comprised of representatives from each co-op – became a platform for significant inter-co-op learning and exchange. With meetings translated routinely into three languages at least (isiXhosa, seSotho, sometimes English and sometimes seSwati) these meetings tended to extend through the night. The debates were intense, with co-op members' passion for participation unflagging through to dawn.

---

[1] James was a key strategic role-player in the programme and would have been an invaluable informant for this book, but he died in 1998 after a battle with cancer.

Photo 4 *Members at the Qwe Qwe Block Production Co-op, Transkei; 1990.*

This was all taking place against the backdrop of history in the making, as political leaders started to be released from prison and as the constitutional negotiations began, along with negotiation between the ANC, the Congress of South African Trade Unions (COSATU), the SACP and other democratic formations over the content of the Reconstruction and Development Programme envisaged for the post-apartheid period.

In NUM, these developments were highly influential – and NUM was influential within them. In the Eastern Cape, the terrain shifted from one in which security police regularly raided the co-op house in Umtata, to one in which, for example, I received a phone call to say that General Bantu Holomisa (then in charge of the Transkei bantustan, following his military coup against Stella Sigcau) had come to the office to buy an NUM T-shirt. The co-op staff were not sure whether to sell

Table 1 NUM Co-ops in 1993

Co-operatives	Type of Production	Members (variable over time)
TRANSKEI		
Qwe Qwe Co-op (Umtata)	Block and brick production	10
Noluthando Co-op (Tsomo)	Agriculture	20
Masikhule Xonya (Engcobo)	Agriculture	20
Mangoloaneng East Co-op (Mount Fletcher)	Agriculture	18
Zoko Co-op (Tabankulu)	Agriculture	6
Tsolo Mineworkers Co-op	Agriculture	20
Mtakatye Co-op (Ngqeleni)	Agriculture	20
LESOTHO		
Quthing Mineworkers Co-op	Blocks and bricks, and agriculture	16
Leribe Mineworkers Co-op	Blocks and bricks, and ploughing	28
Peka Mineworkers Co-op	Blocks and bricks	10
Butha Buthe Mineworkers Co-op	Agriculture and poultry	25
Mohau Co-op (Butha Buthe)	Candles	5
Boitjaro Co-op (Butha Buthe)	Knitting and Sewing	10
Lilepe Co-op (Thaba Bosiu)	Agriculture	20
Berea Mineworkers Co-op	Agriculture	16
Kolo Diamond Co-op (Mafeteng)	Diamonds	8
Roma Mineworkers Co-op	Poultry	10
Maseru Mineworkers Co-op	Poultry	10
Mohotlong (pre-production phase)	Baking and poultry	20
SWAZILAND		
Sidvokodvo Farm	Agriculture and poultry	15
Nqwenya Co-op	Poultry brooding	8
Kukhanya Kulanga Co-op (Lubombo)	Poultry and vegetable cultivation	10
PHALABORWA		
Phalaborwa T-shirt Printing Co-op	T-shirt printing	16
Pawco Hawker Network	Hawkers of t-shirts	8
CONSTRUCTION CO-OP TRAINING PROGRAMME		
Qhubekani Construction Co-op (Piet Retief)	Construction	10
Construction Co-op (Steelpoort)	Construction	16
Witbank Trainee Groups	Construction	64

him one, give him one, or refuse to do either. As far as I recall – after much debate – we agreed to sell him a T-shirt.

Within this wider context, certain themes were constant. The first and overarching challenge for the co-ops was to achieve economic viability – measured as the ability to provide a consistent, sustainable income for members. While the goal was to pay at the level of a living wage, the more immediate target was to match equivalent earnings on the mines at the time.

Feasibility studies: Qwe Qwe and Flagstaff

In the first two Transkei co-ops, the feasibility studies undertaken were seen by ex-mineworkers as an irksome delay and a box to be ticked, given that they had already decided to produce cement bricks and blocks. It is not unusual for co-op members to decide to produce a particular product or service with which they are familiar without interrogating its viability: but this potentially sets the co-op up for failure before it has even begun.

Sheer luck and location meant the Qwe Qwe Co-op was essentially a viable business, given Umtata's sprawling peri-urban growth; but the Flagstaff Co-op on the outskirts of a very small rural town probably never was. Either way, the breakfast agreement with Cyril Ramaphosa that tripled the number of workers in the co-ops dealt an early blow to the viability of both of them. While the context of this decision was specific, it is an error often repeated in co-op development in South Africa. In the name of job creation, the enterprise is burdened by an oversupply of labour from the start, which can sabotage its potential viability. The impacts were described in an article I wrote for *Workteam* (the regional co-op magazine produced in Botswana) at the time:

> Co-ops have a hard time when they start. Often, there are months when there is little or no money for wages. If you have more workers in your co-op than the co-op can support, then that little money has to be divided in half again. And half of nothing is not enough to live on.
>
> Having more people in the co-op than it can support cripples the co-op in a number of ways. Co-ops have to keep their prices at market levels and still cover their costs. Even community solidarity won't get the customers to pay more for their blocks! If the co-op has more workers than it needs for production, then it will be hard to keep prices low and still pay wages – unless the wages are so low they are just for survival.
>
> But we have seen that a co-op that only pays survival wages will face the following problems:
>
> > Co-op members end up exploiting themselves just to get a survival wage. They end up working for long hours for the same starvation wages paid by the bantustan factories which we are fighting. As a trade union, we didn't support co-ops with this future in mind for our members.

> When members are only just surviving, it is hard to build up reserve
> funds, or spend the money on maintenance of machinery. It is hard to
> decide to 'feed' a tractor when you haven't fed yourself.
>   As a result, the co-op fails to become self-sufficient. Every time a
> machine breaks down, the co-op has to have another injection of funds,
> or else collapse.
>   [...]
> Most importantly, bare survival is not a long-term solution for workers.
> Workers want to improve the quality of their lives and if the co-op doesn't
> allow that, workers will start to look elsewhere.
>   In practice, it is usually the more skilled members of the co-op who can
> find other jobs. And if they leave, the co-op struggles to develop leadership
> with management skills. Without those skills, it is doomed to dependency.
> (Philip 1991)

Most of the NUM co-ops saw numbers dwindle rapidly as the problems
outlined above became manifest. But the oversupply of labour was
not the only problem in the set-up process. In Flagstaff, the feasibility
study had other flaws. In doing it, we had needed to establish a reliable
source of river sand in sufficient quantities to make cement blocks at
the scale envisaged. Several trips were made to verify the availability
of such sand, but in each instance, the NUM delegation conducting the
feasibility study was diverted into endless seemingly arcane protocol
meetings with chiefs, tribal authorities and local magistrates. In the
face of our protestations, Elliot Bhala and the Flagstaff Co-op members
insisted that we should not worry, 'sand was near'. I made the cardinal
error of accepting this at face value, blinded by my own urban bias that
river sand was the kind of thing that could reasonably be expected to be
'near' in rural Transkei.

Soon after the co-op started, I received a phone call from Regional
Co-ordinator Sonwabo Msezeli, who broke the news: 'Comrade Kate,
we have a problem.' Long pause, deep sigh. 'Sand is far.' There was in
fact no useable river sand within an economic distance from the co-op.

Clearly, this was not a development I was in a hurry to report to
Ramaphosa. Instead, I went to Flagstaff, determined not to show my
face in the Head Office again until the problem was solved. Teams of
ex-miners were dispatched in every direction to find a source of useable
river sand. Visits to countless river-banks yielded only mud and clay,
but finally, Msezeli reported back good news. In a village that was near
enough, there was a river with plentiful river sand. But there was a
problem. To get to this river, we had to pass through a large area of
illegal *dagga* (marijuana) fields policed by local youth. This needed
the permission of the chief. Msezeli was dispatched to do his best and
as usual in matters requiring engagement with traditional authorities,
he was successful. It was agreed that NUM representatives would be
allowed into the area under escort to see the sand. We set off on a route

that could less and less be described as a road – although it was still well within the capabilities of our hired car (which, in NUM's hands, were very versatile vehicles).

Although the fields looked like ordinary *mielie* (maize) fields, the route was flanked by young men. Some stood and watched, arms folded across their chests; others stood and watched with AK47 rifles slung across their shoulders. Some – but not all – of these rifles were carved from wood. In the end, even the hired car could go no further and we set out on foot across a field of *mielies* inter-cropped with *dagga*. And then there it was: a bend in a slow wide river and a great, huge, ancient mound of tons and tons of river sand.

To the bemusement of our watchful guards, I leapt about on the sand, throwing handfuls into the air. I may even have done a cartwheel or two. Not only did the co-op now have a fighting chance of survival – I could also finally go home. I never even had to tell Ramaphosa how close to disaster we had come.

There was, however, no passable route to this sand. This problem was solved through negotiation with the local community, which lead to a community event called an *ilima* being held. This is a traditional form of collective work that usually takes place when a member of the community needs labour beyond what is available within their own household, for a specific effort of asset creation or productive activity. It is a traditional form of economic co-operation. Members of the community participate and in return, a sheep is slaughtered and large quantities of home-brewed beer are consumed.

A road to the sand was then built through the *mielie/dagga* fields, with this sand used by the Flagstaff Ex-miners Co-op for the rest of the life of the project. It is doubtful whether the access to this resource, or the road built to it, would have been achievable if it was not NUM and the ex-mineworkers who were asking for it. In a context in which there is barely a rural village in southern Africa that has not sent men to the mines, NUM's access into the most remote rural areas – and to traditional authorities there – was always remarkable. NUM's power on the mines and in the political processes unfolding at national level had strong spill-over effects in rural areas also. According to Sipho Nqwelo, for example, there was a direct correlation between the return of the ex-miners and the rise of youth organisations and other local formations in the Transkei over this period.

Yet, while this story illustrates the kind of community support and access to local power the NUM co-ops could draw on, it remains an example of a flawed feasibility study. In this instance, the error was mainly mine, but such errors are not unusual in co-op set-up processes. Years later, in reviewing another programme, I found that a peanut butter co-op with state-of-the-art equipment in Limpopo was importing peanuts from Bangladesh because it could not find sufficient local supply –

Photo 5 *NUM General Secretary Cyril Ramaphosa (seated left) and President James Motlatsi (right) at the Flagstaff Co-op, Transkei, discussing the problems faced in the co-op; 1990.*

Photo 6 *NUM General Secretary Cyril Ramaphosa is carried through the streets of Flagstaff by co-op members after meeting with them; 1990.*

because it was all already contracted to existing players. All too often, co-ops have been started on the basis of desk-based feasibility studies that show profits on paper, but in contexts in which the members lack business experience – and their technical advisors lack local knowledge. This is a combination that can sabotage a co-op before it even starts.

Feasibility processes attempting to identify markets are often particularly flawed. Typically, demand is measured by how much of a given product is already being bought within the local economy. 'Yes, demand is high' is the marketing equivalent of 'yes, sand is near'. Yet often, the assumptions on which this is based prove to be erroneous. What is usually being measured is the level of demand already being met – and for which supply is already in place. In the context of the South African economy, many basic needs are mass-produced in the core economy and reach even the most marginal areas. To secure market share, a co-op would have to displace existing suppliers – when these often have well-established brands, produce at mass scale and have large advertising budgets. Time and again, consumers have higher levels of brand loyalty than feasibility studies anticipate. Measuring unmet demand is a much harder task – and is often an entirely speculative affair.

The discovery of management

> The understanding of running the business was a big problem because they could not understand when are we making profit, or how do we make profit, or how should we make profit, or how do we, you know, increase production, or maybe do the best quality of the bricks or blocks so that we compete as well … We could not understand all these dynamics of the market – that we have to compete. Actually we didn't understand business. (Interview with Puseletso Salae, 18 July 2003)

The issue of management – in all its forms – was a consistent headache. The realities of racial authoritarianism in the South African workplace meant the management function was experienced and seen by labour almost solely as an authority function – that could simply be replaced in the co-op by a democratic process. The skills involved in effective management and the catalytic and integrative roles that management plays in the creation of value in an enterprise were not recognised. This is a flaw that Marx's labour theory of value does not help to remedy. This problem was compounded by workers' experience in the mining industry, where the wider functions of management are even more than usually opaque to workers – and where labour relations are more than usually authoritarian and hierarchical.

So, for example, early after the Flagstaff Co-op started, Msezeli reported that the person elected as chair of the co-op had arrived for work the next day in a carefully ironed white suit 'expecting a clean place to be made for him'. The meanings of management had to be renegotiated and existing mental models of the roles – and entitlements – associated with the management function reconstructed.

The need to build alternative forms of management – or 'democratic management' – in the co-op added a further layer of complexity to the purely technical challenges of the management function, which can be broken down into a cursory and no doubt incomplete list as shown below:

- Start with enough working capital in hand to initiate a cycle of production.
- Order inputs in advance of need so that they are available on site at the right time, quantity, quality and price.
- Allocate the labour, skills and equipment in the co-op optimally to ensure the product is produced to the right quality and quantity and within the required timeframes.
- Secure sufficient sales or orders to break even at least.
- Ensure the product is available and/or is delivered when the customer expects.
- Secure payment from the customer; if deposits are secured in advance, make sure this money is not spent on other things and is still available to produce the relevant order.
- Budget for the maintenance and replacement of equipment and ensure this is done in ways that do not interrupt production.
- Record all financial transactions, in order to account for and analyse co-op finances, plan and assess the needs of the next cycle and then assess whether and how much co-op members can get paid – unfortunately often a contingent decision.
- Start the cycle again.

These are not actually a serial set of tasks; they have to be performed simultaneously across several overlapping cycles of production. Constraints on the capacity of the early co-ops to do this were considerable; some never managed. Others, however, became highly skilled at it, but it took patience and time. Malineo Nkhasi, Mineworkers Development Agency horticulturalist for Lesotho, describes below her experience building production planning skills at Butha Buthe Agricultural Co-op:

> I trained them to develop their own production plan ... I will just come and check them and advise them: 'No, if it is planted on the first week of October it will do better than if it is planted first week of November'. I will just polish their production plan
>   [...]
> But it has been difficult for me especially to work with retrenched mineworkers who are mostly illiterate. They take time to understand things. I remember in Buthe Buthe I used to have a hard time with those co-op

members ... They will just say, 'We don't want to be ruled like we were ruled in the mine'.
[...]
I used to agree with them that we will buy a certain amount of kilograms for spinach, carrots, beetroot. Six packets of fertilisers and at least one load of kraal manure. When I came back, nothing had happened. I just sat down with the Chair and said, '*Ntate* why didn't you do what we agreed last time when we had a meeting?' He just said, 'This soil doesn't need fertiliser, it's rich enough, we can just plant anything now, it's okay, you will see when it comes out that the soil is rich'. (Interview with Malineo Nkhasi, 10 December 2003)

The challenge of marketing

If the co-op cannot sell what it makes, the value of members' labour cannot be realised and they will earn nothing. For workers from formal employment, it took time to accept that a return on their labour could only be realised if the product was sold – and that selling the product was as much part of the work of the co-op as producing it.

In addition, experience showed that the assumption that co-ops could rely on consumer solidarity to provide preferential market access in their own communities or constituencies proved to be flawed. Early lessons in the limits of this concept of a protected solidarity market came from the experience of the Phalaborwa T-shirt Printing Co-op – Phalaborwa Workers Co-operative (PAWCO).

PAWCO was set up by sixty workers who had been dismissed from Foskor Mine, in Phalaborwa, for going on strike to demand May Day as a public holiday in 1986. PAWCO's inception predated the wider programme.

PAWCO targeted the solidarity market in NUM and COSATU, assuming that the trade union affiliates of the federation would support the co-op, in a context in which T-shirts printed with logos and slogans for campaigns, congresses and rallies were a dynamic part of union culture. There was just one small problem. NUMSA, the metal workers union, had already set up the Sarmcol Workers Co-operative (SAWCO); this was their strategy too and there wasn't really room for both co-ops in the protected market that COSATU provided – a market that became even more crowded when the South African Clothing and Textile Workers Union set up its own co-op, Zenzeleni – initially producing T-shirts, but later printing them too (Adato 1996, p. 279).

PAWCO also discovered that COSATU unions, including NUM, would only give them preferential market access if they could compete on price and quality – and PAWCO lost major contracts even for NUM events when it could not do so. As a knock-on consequence, any expectation that PAWCO would pay more for Zenzeleni T-shirts meant that PAWCO's own margins would be squeezed. Despite attempts at brokering co-operation between the three co-ops, the reality was de facto competition – and no love lost between them, either. Even within the solidarity market of the trade union movement, the co-ops could not escape the price-setting mechanism of the wider market.

All three co-ops were also at the mercy of another feature of this market: a tendency for trade unions, civic organisations and youth groups to misjudge the quantities for specific events – and to fail to pay for T-shirts ordered (Adato 1996, pp. 279–80). PAWCO developed an innovative response to this which contributed to it outlasting the other two co-ops – surviving long enough to present MDA with a clock as a gift to mark their own tenth anniversary.

PAWCO's strategy was to convert most co-op members into self-employed hawkers, who were deployed to the mines to act as agents of the T-shirt co-op. This created a sales network at the same time as reducing numbers in the co-op from sixty to six.

The co-op gave the hawkers credit terms and rather than the hawkers delivering the T-shirts to the organisations that had ordered them, they sold T-shirts directly at community or union events. In this way, PAWCO optimised the strengths of the solidarity market, overcoming the problem of non-payment as well as the problem of an oversupply of labour in the co-op – all at once. Best of all, the hawkers earned significantly more than they had done as co-op members.

In Lesotho, despite competing with surplus agricultural production dumped by South African farmers, the co-ops did make headway competing in local markets. Nkhasi reports below on the development of marketing skills in the Lesotho agriculture co-ops:

> The first crop that Thaba Bosiu or any of the mineworkers had was tomatoes. They had a very good crop of tomatoes ... It is true that they didn't have the best variety for the market but the way they managed or maintained that crop, it was amazing. It grew up to 1.2 metres, it was tall and it had a very big fruit which was clean, no cracks. But unfortunately, the problem was the variety for the market – it was just good for food consumption but not for storage. It wasn't good for supermarkets. (Interview with Nkhasi, 10 December 2003)

Undaunted by an oversupply of tomatoes they could not sell, the co-op first dried some of them and then had the idea of fermenting them to make tomato beer. With this, the NUM co-ops could claim their first foray into new product development. According to Nkhasi, 'it used to taste very nice and it was nutritious'. They sold it all. With better varieties, they were however able to secure more-formal markets:

> We managed to win a market at Maseru Sun Cabanas and at Shoprite – by that time it was OK Supermarket. We won the market, we were providing them twice a week, on Wednesday and on Friday, we provide tomatoes to Shoprite

Photo 7 *At the Lilepe Co-op, Thaba Bosiu, Lesotho. The author is in the centre; NUM President James Motlatsi is second to the right of her; this is the bumper tomato crop that was turned into tomato beer; 1992 (photo by Puseletso Salae).*

and to Maseru Sun, at 7 o'clock sharp – and we were able to maintain that. (Interview with Nkhasi, 2003)

Lilepe Co-op at Thaba Bosiu had the advantage of relative proximity to Maseru, but other factors differentiated their performance:

Co-op members from Thaba Bosiu were slightly different to those people from other co-ops, they were committed. They won't wait for the office or Salae to come and assist them, they will just go out and seek and search, even in the schools, can we provide you with vegetables? (Interview with Nkhasi, 2003)

By 1994, the NUM Co-op Unit in Lesotho claimed that the Lesotho co-ops were the single biggest Basotho suppliers into the Lesotho market. Nkhasi defends this claim:

It was true. In 1994 we had a massive production in all the co-ops. By that time they understood quite well the importance of following the production plan, using the best varieties and irrigation, and maintenance was perfect. We had a very good crop of potatoes in Buthe Buthe, we supplied supermarkets and restaurants there, even in Maseru, and the grade was first grade, large enough for chips ... For Thaba Bosiu it was so exciting. They supplied Upper Qeme (the Maseru vegetable market), they supplied street vendors with vegetables, they also supplied Shoprite, which is the biggest supermarket, and Fairways with vegetables. We were well known in Lesotho from 1992 to 1996, not only in Maseru ... It was very excellent and the lifestyle of the co-op members changed, they were eating now, they had their lunch packs, they had their wages at the end of the month and they had surplus which they can take home at the end of the day and eat with their families. (Interview with Nkhasi, 2003)

Both PAWCO and the Lesotho co-ops looked set to buck the trend of co-op failure, with the Lesotho co-ops not only becoming firmly entrenched in local markets but out-manoeuvring at least some of the competition from commercial farmers across the border.

Financial management challenges

Financial literacy levels in the co-ops were low. The first challenge was to develop a basic understanding of co-op finances and of the levels of production and sales required to generate enough income to pay regular allowances (as wages were called) at an agreed rate and as a fixed cost – and still break even at least. Yet in reality, whether wages were paid at all was contingent on the business performance of the co-op from month to month.

In this context, the most difficult concept to convey was cash flow and the notion that the money in the bank at the end of the month may not be available for distribution between members. First, because such money may not all belong to the co-op (if it had taken deposits or advance payments); second, because establishing how much can be used to pay allowances to members has to take into account other co-op debts as well as the costs of keeping the business going.

Many co-ops faced months when something went wrong. It was not unusual to come to the end of the month and find that the co-op had been unable to meet the targets in its production plan and faced a shortfall. Sipho Nqwelo explained what would happen in the general meeting when this was the case:

> We don't get money; that is all you have to explain. Because what usually happens at the end of the month, we will have this general meeting, with reports – the first person to report, the sales manager, gives us the sales report; and then workers are starting to calculate, even though there are no papers, they want to know the money that came in.
>
> And then we will go now to the money spent; then we look at the money in the bank that is left. The bookkeeper would talk about all the expenses and the treasurer now will go according to the bank statement ... the withdrawals, what was drawn on such a date, how much for what. Then at the end we have to check what do we share. Now it was when we will encounter problems ... you will see that your operating budget for the month (excluding wages) is about R6,000; and in our account maybe we have got R7,000. Now there will be demands that, no – let's cut a little bit on cement and let's take R3,000 for allowances ... leaving only R4,000 for operations; and this accumulates itself, next month going down, down and your salary goes down, down – that was the problem. (Interview with Sipho Nqwelo, 16 April 2003)

When targets are not met, a co-op is often faced with a choice of either cutting into members' allowances, or cutting into its working capital for the production cycle ahead – which would have the effect of reducing wages in that cycle. A situation where the bank account is empty is hard, but that particular decision is at least easy. There's no money to share. A situation in which the co-op has money in the bank, but has to make a choice between either financing production in the next cycle or paying small allowances at the cost of reduced output (and an inevitable decline in the allowances payable in the next cycle) is far harder. It is hard because it requires a trade-off between the current survival needs of the members of the co-op (which can be real and pressing) and an investment in the enterprise as an entity and the hypothetical returns to members that such investment could mean in the future. The critical issue in general meetings was often effectively over whether the co-op would survive and if so, at what cost to members:

> Sometimes if there is a problem, maybe there is a disease, Newcastle disease for chickens, then there is nothing, there is no money ... or just enough to buy inputs. Then they say: 'Okay fine we want money, nothing else, we are supposed to get money, this is Christmas, we were supposed to get money, let's get money.' They said that to the committee.
>   [...]
> The problem is that the co-operative is run democratically, you have to sit down all of you, you have got only seven people who are the committee members, who say, no, please, let's go and buy inputs; then the rest of the people, about twenty, they pick up their hands and say: 'Fine, we want that money now. The co-operative is run democratically'. (Interview with Lilepe Co-op Chair Jack Mpapea, 10 December 2003)

There were few co-ops in which the members simply plundered the working capital, although it did happen. Timothy Mzoboshe, Education officer in the Eastern Cape, recounts what happened on one of the many occasions on which NUM provided a bail-out to the Flagstaff Co-op:

> Comrade Kate came in order to rescue us in the situation where Flagstaff was collapsing. She came with an R8,000 cheque [about US$3,000] and she tried to make some budgeting plans, production plans and so on. And then we agreed to that, that we should follow those plans. And later on ... She was just 15 kilometres away from us and we started demanding that R8,000, that we should share the money. (Interview with Mzoboshe, quoted in Adato 1996, p. 126)

The money was shared. Adato recounts the events that then unfolded:

> [A]bout eight members decided to invest their share in raw materials in order to produce blocks, while the majority took their portion in cash. This solution caused further conflict, with those who had taken their money threatening to attack the members who had invested their portion. This was part of a series of events which eventually lead to the implosion of the co-op. (Adato 1996, p. 127)

More common than this scenario was that co-op members sacrificed returns to themselves again and again, to feed the working capital needs of the co-op, trying desperately to keep it alive, with whatever resources were available, including their unpaid or underpaid labour, only to see it sink deeper and deeper into a downward spiral with declining returns to their effort and input. Despite often herculean achievements in one sphere, they would all too often find the enterprise falling short in another: producing their targets only to find a glut in the market; ensuring all the necessary inputs were in place only to have the equipment break down; securing advance sales of an entire batch of chickens only to lose them all to Newcastle disease: leading them back, time and again, to a general meeting in which their own immediate material needs would be offset against the survival of the enterprise.

Discontinuity of management

A feature of the co-ops, particularly in the early days, was the tendency to regularly replace elected co-ordinators, in a process referred to as 'reshuffling', that posed a serious constraint on the depth of management capacities that were being built:

> What was happening is that if you are a manager and you are seen maybe to always have a cigarette, there will be some caucus: 'No, they are eating our money, why is he having this?' And then another one is campaigning to come to this position, among us, so he is organising other people that no, we must chase him out of this position
> [...]
> You must remember we were involved with money now. It wasn't like the days of the struggle. When we were elected shaft stewards during those times, it was not easy – nobody liked to be a shaft steward because it is either three things: you are fired by the mine manager, or you are arrested, or you are killed. So nobody wanted to be elected – if you are elected, you know that you are in trouble.
> If you check the union now, because the country is free, there are fights for leadership these days. What is happening now, there are more opportunities if you are elected to be a leader.
> So it was like that in the co-ops, we started fighting for these positions and then they will put this person to be in your position after chasing you out. This person will mess up and mess up and they will realise later and chase him.
> I remember at one time I was chased out and ... the co-op was in chaos, there was no money. I had to start the co-op from fresh and I had to ask for money from Transido [a parastatal development finance institution]. (Interview with Nqwelo, 16 April 2003)

The co-op brought Nqwelo back as Chair, in a context in which it had effectively collapsed. As a matter of pride and even though the collapse

had not happened on his watch, Nqwelo was not prepared to report
it to NUM, nor to request further working capital. Instead, he secured
a commercial loan from Transido against a business plan – the first
time any of the co-ops had done so. The co-op was back in production
and Nqwelo recalls this grudging compliment paid by one of the co-op
members after his return:

> So, Tegeta commented while we were just sitting – he said: 'No, you know
> sometimes a jackal is better, because when he eats the meat of a sheep, he
> will eat only the inside things, the livers and others and leave the rest; but
> just take a wolf, he will eat the whole thing.' What he was trying to say, you
> know, is that it is better to go for somebody better who will just take *some*
> of the money, he won't take it all. And people were laughing – but we were
> in pain, because we didn't have anything, we were not getting even what
> we used to get in the co-op. So, you start afresh. But people forget quickly.
> (Interview with Nqwelo, 2003)

This churning of elected co-op management was cause for serious
concern. Notes of a Co-op Unit meeting, below, provide a snapshot of
the way support staff engaged with this issue:

> There is really a problem of trust in the co-ops. When the management
> structures give reports, the members don't believe them. (Sonwabo Msezeli,
> Transkei Regional Co-ordinator)

> To trust someone is not a petty issue. Trust is a problem at all levels of society.
> But in the co-ops, people are hungry and we have to take into account their
> level of education. For example, at Flagstaff, we have to take time to explain
> if we're dealing with finances. (Timothy Mzoboshe, Co-op Education Office,
> Transkei)

> [S]ometimes the members are right. Sometimes co-ordinators are not doing
> what they should, and act like bosses. Production targets are planned, but
> when it comes to implementation, they set themselves light jobs. Sometimes
> all the members of the committee will be sitting debating nothing while
> the [other] members are working, and, in meetings, they don't give clear
> reports, especially about money. For example, at Butha Buthe, the Chair is
> just roaming about, saying he is taking money to the bank. (Mapota Molefi,
> General Secretary, Basotho Mineworkers Labour Co-operative)

> The co-op members always suspect misuse of finances – but that is because
> there is nothing going to their pockets. It takes some convincing that the
> money is safe, when they are not 'safe' themselves, socially or economically.
> This question of trust is connected to their living standards. (Tux Mtolo,
> Transkei Agriculturalist)

> In order to make the transition to trust, we need to understand and address
> the skills base of trust – the literacy levels of the members and the skills of
> the co-coordinators – so that they are able to do what is expected of them. If
> they are underperforming, it erodes trust. Maybe we need to move from trust
> as an interpersonal issue to 'institutionalised suspicion' – we need to build

better structural mechanisms of accountability. Perhaps the co-ops could institutionalise an internal auditing system. (Prosper Nyirimarunga, Rural Finance Facility)

But it is not only about trust. In some co-ops, there is just resistance to authority in any form. So much so that co-ordinators are scared of giving instructions. (Sonwabo Msezeli, Transkei Co-ordinator)

Sometimes that is because of the way co-coordinators give instructions. By giving respect, you receive respect. (Timothy Mzoboshe, Co-op Education Office, Transkei)

(All from Author's notes of staff meeting c. 1993)

As this discussion illustrates, mastering the functions of management was inextricably linked to the wider issue of democratic management as a way of making decisions, of delegating authority within the co-op and the meanings and practices associated with this.

Getting Motlatsi's goat

In Swaziland, ex-miners had set up the Swaziland National Ex-Miners Co-operative Society (SNEMCOS). Trade unions were banned in Swaziland, but Ramaphosa applied the same logic as in the Transkei and Lesotho: NUM was there to support co-ops – not to set up a trade union; why should there be any problem? As everywhere, the ex-miners were well connected with local traditional authorities; land was secured and planning began.

It was however not possible to hold meetings in Swaziland without government permission and so NUM sought permission to hold a five-day inception workshop for the co-op members. Permission was granted on condition that government representatives could attend the meeting and that the venue for the meeting would be determined by the government of Swaziland. This was agreed.

When we arrived, we discovered that the venue deemed appropriate was actually inside the prison in Mbabane. The NUM team and the thirty co-op members all had to check into the prison for the period of the workshop – accompanied by ten government 'minders' who attended all sessions and dominated discussion. We were served our meals by prisoners in the kind of black-and-white striped prison uniforms normally reserved for cartoon characters.

Once the Sidvokodvo Co-op began, the members achieved significant levels of production and there was a real possibility of their farm being a viable enterprise. Yet it was wracked by internal conflicts. All kinds of allegations and counter-allegations were reaching NUM Head Office and it was agreed that NUM President James Motlatsi should visit the co-op to get to the bottom of what was going on.

The NUM delegation arrived; everyone was convened in a circle under a huge marula tree and the meeting was about to start when the Chair of the co-op, Robert Hlatshwayo, announced that there had been a terrible oversight – it was absolutely necessary to slaughter a goat to mark the auspicious occasion and to show proper respect for the NUM President. He would not take no for an answer; he and I should quickly go and get a goat, so that due protocol could be observed. Getting a goat, he insisted, was no problem at all: there were many goats and they were (of course) near.

So off he and I went, in the hired car, to find a goat. It didn't take long before our route on bad back roads had confused me sufficiently that there was no option of turning around and finding my way back without his directions. We went from homestead to homestead in search of a goat. There appeared to be no shortage of goats – in fact it took my best efforts not to run any over. Yet at each homestead, Hlatshwayo would come back from his negotiations to purchase a goat with a shrug of the shoulders and hands out-turned. We returned to the co-op about three hours later – with no goat. An exasperated Motlatsi had a flight to catch and other challenges to deal with in NUM. Little time was left to delve into the problems at the co-op – and it

Photo 8 *Production Co-ordinator Wellington Nghlengethwa addresses members of the Sidvokodvo Co-op, Swaziland, with Co-op Chair Robert Hlatshwayo on the far left; 1993.*

would have been divisive for him to have attempted to do so in the absence of the Chair. The meeting managed only to get through formalities without ever tackling the real issues at hand.

Hlatshwayo – still expressing contrition at his failure to honour Motlatsi with a goat – waved us all on our way.

7 Challenges of Democratic Ownership & Control

A big part of the attraction of the co-op model was the co-op principle that the co-op is democratically controlled by its members. The attraction of this notion was heightened by the lack of democracy at a political level in the wider societies in which the NUM co-ops were operating: with the co-ops appearing to prefigure desired political and economic futures.

Operationalising such democratic control was, however, a real challenge. So while the difficulties achieving economic viability discussed in the previous chapter might apply to any start-up enterprise, these problems were compounded by the need to institutionalise democratic processes of decision making. Elements of the contestation around these issues are reflected in an interview with Leribe Co-op Chair Molefi Molefi in 1993. Molefi was asked how he understood the meaning of production democracy:

> There are many wrong ideas about this one. If some of the interpretations of democracy in production are going to become the order of the day, then our co-ops are going to fail. If members think that because the co-op belongs to them, each one can do as he likes, then that is not co-operation. You can't organise production on those lines.
>
> When we come together as a co-op, we are coming together with a clear purpose: to produce as a means to our livelihood. That is our goal; that is why we are there. And we are agreeing to co-operate together in order to reach this goal. The demands of production in a co-op have to be given priority over anything that a person thinks he has the right to do. If there is no production, there is no livelihood and there is no co-op.
>
> A co-op is a business and a business has its own demands. There are tasks that have to be done, or else you are just playing. Let's say someone is supposed to be mixing cement and he neglects it and says no, I rather think I'll go to town with some excuse and come back in five hours – that is not co-operative behaviour. It is not democratic behaviour. It is selfish. That person is undermining the whole co-op, because production is disrupted.
>
> When it comes to making decisions about our direction and our production targets and goals, that is when we come together and we take democratic decisions. We can criticise each other, we can assess, we can look at different ways of doing things. Everyone has a say. But once we have reached agreement, then our mandate is to get on with the job and implement

those decisions in the most efficient way possible. (Interview with Molefi Molefi, 1993)

The NUM co-ops were not alone in grappling with how best to institutionalise systems and processes that honoured the principle of democratic control on terms that enabled effective and efficient co-operation in production. The challenge was often presented as a behavioural one. So, for example, Botswana-based *Workteam* magazine ran an illustrated series which identified 'Bad Habits' in the co-op, drawn from the De Morais Theory of Organisation, which was influential in the regional co-op movement at the time. This included 'the Risk Taker', who proposes buying a tractor without doing the costings; 'the Centralist', who takes decisions without consulting and monopolises skills; and 'the Anarchist' who doesn't abide by the agreed workplans in the co-op (*Workteam* 1988, p. 31).

NUM's Co-op Unit added two of its own bad habits, more specific to the NUM experience. One was 'the factory floor fighter', who knows how to fight the bosses, but is not used to taking responsibility for production – and uses tactics from the factory floor in the co-op context, when such tactics hold no equivalent power. The Flagstaff Co-op illustrated the consequences of this when workers went on strike demanding wages when the co-op had no money to pay these. The question they confronted, however, was to whom such demands should be addressed? The members *toyi-toyed* around the town before presenting their demands to a local government office.

The other 'bad habit' added by NUM was 'the Chief':

> The 'Chief' confuses democratic structures with hierarchical ones. Once he has been elected to any position, he thinks it is his for life. Once he has been elected, he thinks that means he can never be wrong and cannot be criticised. He forgets that he is elected to represent the members, not himself. He forgets that the members can take his position away the same way they gave it to him. (NUM Co-op Unit training materials, n.d.)

The challenges clearly went far beyond bad behaviour, however, and to the heart of understandings and meanings of democracy:

> Because of the kind of society South Africa is, we tend to confuse authority with authoritarianism. Democratically electing people to positions of authority is still democracy, as is democratically assessing the performance of managers. (Berold, 1991, p. 31)

Against the backdrop of heightened struggles for political democracy across the region, democracy was often understood as an end in itself. The extent to which democracy as a process can deliver variable outcomes was not well understood. The evidence began to mount, however, that achieving the desired results required informed decisions and that these could not rely on the *process* of decision making alone. A range of decisions in a co-op also needed to be informed by experience or technical expertise – from when to service the tractor to what kinds of crops to plant in different soil conditions.

In its attempts to find pragmatic solutions to the problems around decision making in the co-ops, the NUM Co-op Unit attempted to differentiate between 'practical' and 'policy' decisions.

Policy decisions included overarching co-op policies, such as the constitution and disciplinary code and also production plans. The expectation was that they would provide a policy framework agreed by the whole co-op, within which managers could then make the 'practical' day-to-day decisions necessary to ensure implementation of such decisions. So, if the co-op had approved a production plan that included planting a half-hectare of cabbages, the production co-ordinator should not have to come back for a separate decision or mandate to buy cabbage seedlings.

Yet institutionalising this approach to decision making proved to be difficult and contested. In a context in which lack of skills and education had been used for so long as a reason to exclude people from democratic rights in the wider society, co-op members held tenaciously onto what was understood as a core principle in a co-op: that the members make the decisions: all the decisions.

In practice, therefore, the managerial authority to go ahead and pur-chase the necessary cabbage seedlings was rarely delegated – these decisions required yet another full membership meeting. This problem was highlighted by Adato, in her research analysing the way democratic management was understood in the NUM co-ops (Adato 1996). This issue of an inability to delegate authority was recognised as the heart of the problem.

The managerial authority of managers in the co-op derives from the members. If members are not willing to delegate authority to managers, then the managers have no authority to manage. A particularly vexed area in this regard was in relation to the allocation of labour – and the inability of managers to hold workers accountable for agreed actions, as illustrated in this example from Lilepe Co-op:

> There was one time when we came to town to look for the market for carrots; that was towards Christmas and then someone said, 'Okay, bring ten tons of carrots'. That was good, everyone agreed. Then the members took all the carrots and put maybe a heap of them instead of taking those carrots to town as agreed. They said, 'No, this is a hell of a job, why doesn't that customer come and fetch these carrots? No, we'll leave them here'. And they rotted. It was tough [laughter]. (Interview with Lilepe Co-op Chair Jack Mpapea, 10 December 2003)

In those co-ops where levels of authority *were* delegated and where some level of stability of management was achieved, this tended to

Photo 9 *Flagstaff Co-op members debate issues in a co-op meeting; 1990.*

be because the co-op leadership was able to draw its authority from *outside* the co-op: from their status within local structures of traditional leadership, from the leadership role they had previously played in NUM, from their ability to draw on the external authority of the Basotho Mineworkers Labour Co-op (BMLC) or NUM, or from a combination of all of these. Yet none of these factors necessarily combined with good managerial skills.

In search of solutions

In this context, the NUM Co-op Unit sought advice and assistance from CORDE in Botswana and CSFS in Zimbabwe to run a series of workshops with representatives of all of NUM's co-ops to assist in finding solutions to the array of problems being confronted, as expressed in a fax I sent to Carl Brecker (CSFS) and Gavin Andersson (CORDE):

> Let's start at the end. Basically, where we want to get to (really, practically) is: viable, self-managed co-ops; which don't lose their skilled members all the time; which are able to plan for themselves, hope for the future, improve the quality of life of their members; pay regular wages; contribute to their local economy, be independent, empower all their members, even in small, basic ways.
>
> At present, the members are disempowered by the experience, the co-ops

have drained the reserves of the members not the other way around; their viability is in question, intensive agriculture is not sustainable; they are green islands in their villages and the cabbages have water but the villagers do not.

On the other hand; there is a little seed there; there is commitment; many of the members are proud of their co-ops; and rightly so. (Correspondence from the author, 1993)

Workshops were held in Umtata and Maseru, in mid-1993. The following excerpts from the workshop reports prepared by CORDE and CSFS illustrate how the issue of democracy in the co-ops was tackled:

In a co-op, democracy has two systems:
a) For *members as co-op owners* who make the policy, decide the rules, constitution etc. Owners elect officials whose task it is to assure the co-op is running according to its policies and constitution between members meetings. Elections are usually once a year.
b) A parallel or interlocking system of democracy for *members as co-op workers* involved in production. Production is the heart of co-op life. It is under the supervision of a Production Co-ordinator who is appointed by the committee. The Production Co-ordinator is responsible to the committee between members meetings. The Production Coordinator is also accountable to the *members as owners* in members meetings. Between these meetings the *members as workers* are *bound by the rules* (they made as owners) to accept the supervision of the Production Co-ordinator. The Production Co-ordinator oversees the entire production process but involves the team leaders who involve *members as workers*. Because *production* is the life of the co-op and determines success or failure, it allows maximum involvement of *members as workers* but under very strict conditions which protect the production process from stoppages for meetings, from absenteeism or from poor productivity. (CORDE/CSFS 1993, p.13; original emphasis)

In sum, the workshop proposed that members suspend their rights as owners when they are involved in production and accept their status as workers in production, under the authority of a production manager – until the next general meeting, when the production co-ordinator reports to them in their capacity as owners again.

This approach was trying to overcome the core institutional contradiction in the co-op form identified by the Webbs – that a scenario in which members directly elect a manager, who is accountable to them in their capacity as owners, but also manages them in their capacity as workers in production and to whom, in this capacity, they are accountable, is simply rife with real and potential conflict and contradiction.

Attempts to manage these contradictions were evident in the wider southern African co-op discourse at the time, in debates about 'destructive democracy', 'wrong democracy' and 'democracy that will destroy us':

The most important fact to bear in mind is that the technical and the financial spheres of the co-op are separate from the political side. The technical side is not affected at all when elections are conducted each year. ...Co-ops which have not separated political and business organisation do strange things. Members may elect a new bookkeeper/treasurer every year. This causes chaos in the co-op and will cause the co-op to fail. Democracy does not mean choosing people to do jobs they cannot do. False democracy of this kind destroys our hard won achievements. It should be destroyed and burnt to ashes. (All Are One Co-op, Zimbabwe, 1989, p.11)

This 'false democracy' is, in fact, direct democracy in production. These various formulations are all about ring-fencing production decisions away from direct democratic control by 'members as workers'. They are *de facto* about limiting democracy in production, removing it from workers and relocating it at the level of ownership – as reflected in the explanations from CORDE/CSFS:

The Production Co-ordinator should be appointed by the Committee. Because if members are the ones to elect the Production Co-ordinator, then he or she will have big problems doing the job. For example, if the Production Co-ordinator wants members to work hard, or to water in a certain place, he or she must beg and be afraid that 'if I ask the members to do this, next time I will be voted out of this job'. The Production Co-ordinator becomes a prisoner, who cannot do the job. Most of the old and experienced co-ops who earlier tried to elect Production Co-ordinators learned that it is better to appoint one instead. (CORDE/CSFS 1993)

The terrible truth seems to be that direct democracy in production has to be mediated, transformed and institutionalised into a form of indirect democracy if the co-op is to survive and thrive. Complex as it seems, variations on this formula have worked in many developed-country producer co-ops, including in Mondragon and Italy's Lega, where, although a range of mechanisms for member *participation* in production decisions exist, member *control* is ring-fenced to the Annual General Meeting. Managers are appointed by and report to an elected board, and have the delegated authority to make management decisions: including the allocation and supervision of labour.

In Italy's Lega, this separation of production decisions from demo-cratic processes is well established. When I described our problems of democratic management to the Head of Lega Bologna in Italy in 1993 and sought his advice, all he could do was shake his head, aghast and repeat: 'But that can't work; it just can't work. Workers electing their managers? That just can't work' – as if the very idea of direct democracy in production was so foreign to the Italian co-op movement that he had difficulty understanding how a co-op movement could get itself into such dire straits.

By contrast, the same discussion in a South African context is likely to elicit the following response: 'Workers in a co-op *not* electing their managers? That can't work, it just can't work....'

The democracy in production aspired to in the NUM co-ops then and still hegemonic in the discussion of co-ops in South Africa now entails a much more direct democracy than this. In a context in which NUM co-op members were not even willing to delegate practical management decisions, there was little prospect they would agree to ring-fence their democratic rights in the ways envisaged; and, on the whole, they did not.

Ownership and authority

To compound matters, there was more than a little confusion over who really owned the NUM co-ops. For Salae, NUM owned the co-ops:

> The understanding was that the co-operatives were owned by NUM. Not by the members. That one was clear that these are the co-operatives formed by NUM and they are actually owned by NUM, not us. It was a debate, again; some would say: 'No no ... we own the co-operatives – we own the constitution; but the assets belong to NUM.' (Interview with Salae, 18 July 2003)

As far as Sipho Nqwelo was concerned, the members owned the co-ops:

> The members, it was clear, they knew that this is their co-op but this co-op is given to them by NUM and so they have the right to demand whatever from NUM. That was the position ... The assets are theirs, they were given to them. (Interview with Nqwelo, 16 April 2003)

Mapota Molefi confirms the level of confusion that existed and the competing claims to ownership:

> Ja, that issue of ownership brought a lot of confusion, you know ... Some of the members would simply tell you, this property here, all the property here belongs to the union, we are just workers here; but there were those who would argue and say: 'No, it's ours, we have been contributing towards the union, this is our money, so it's paying us back, you can't just simply tell us that it belongs to the union.' (Interview with Molefi, 10 December 2003)

Clearly ownership issues were very far from clear. Given the levels of conflict over access and control over co-op resources in the early stages of the programme, NUM saw little alternative but to use its wider authority to keep a tight formal hold on ownership of the embattled assets, with co-op members expected to account to NUM for their productive use. This was seen as no more contradictory than the 'social ownership' function performed by co-op movements around the world, with NUM in a caretaker role while such a movement was built. Yet as the quotes above illustrate, there was no shortage of contradictions in practice – and NUM was criticised for this 'big brother' role by CSFS and CORDE, which saw the social ownership function as needing to derive from below rather than being asserted from above.

The Amcoal visit to Lesotho

The Anglo American Coal (Amcoal)/NUM Fund played an important role in supporting innovation in MDA: funding several co-ops and later, the Mhala Development Centre and the Lesotho Development Centre. Key to this was an Amcoal manager we will call Denis Jones – as irascible a mine manager as you were likely to find – and yet to his credit, this Fund was more supportive of MDA's initiatives than any other.

At one point, it was arranged that a delegation from Amcoal would visit several NUM projects in Lesotho. For reasons I cannot now imagine, it was agreed that I would drive from Johannesburg with Jones and one of his colleagues. As we left – shortly after dawn – Jones, who was driving, pulled out a six pack of beers and cracked open his first one. Another followed fairly shortly thereafter. Every time he opened a beer, he would cheerily offer me one too. Desperate times called for desperate measures and I decided that my only chance of arriving alive in Lesotho was if I could at least limit his intake by denting his supplies, which I then set about doing. It was to no avail, however; I'd hardly made an impression on a single beer when Jones pulled over at a bottle store and bought another six pack.

Finally, despite the odds, we arrived at Lilepe Co-op at Thaba Bosiu on the outskirts of Maseru. Next on our itinerary was a visit to a co-operative of widows of miners killed in mine accidents, which the Amcoal/NUM Fund had supported, near Butha Buthe, in the north of Lesotho. As we were leaving, however, Jones' vehicle got severely stuck in the mud. It took a great deal of effort by about twenty ex-miners (accompanied by a lot of swearing by Jones, sitting inside) to extract the vehicle, after which he announced that there was no longer time to visit the co-op of widows as he needed to get back to Johannesburg.

There was no way of contacting the widows to let them know the delegation was no longer coming. This was before mobile phones. We knew they would have spent a lot of time and effort preparing food and that in its own way, while the visit acknowledged their loss and showed respect, a no-show did quite the opposite.

'But the co-op is near,' I insisted. 'And it's on your way to Johannesburg'.

So Jones agreed. I joined Salae in his red Nissan *bakkie* (van) and we set off on bad and bumpy back roads to Butha Buthe, leaving the Amcoal vehicle with no alternative but to follow our dust – for a drive of some two hours – during most of which Jones kept his hand on the hooter, trying to signal us to stop. By the time we arrived at the co-op, he was incandescent with rage. But in the face of a large group of women who had all lost their husbands in mine accidents, smiling and singing, he knew there was no alternative but to accept the hospitality offered with good grace, after

Photo 10 *Kate Philip celebrating the gift of a dress at the Butha Buthe Sewing Co-op – one of three co-ops of widows of mineworkers set up in Lesotho; 1992. (photo by Zane Dangor)*

which we led him and his team back to the tarred main road, from where it was easy to find their way back to Johannesburg. As it happened, the tarred road really was near; it had run parallel to our route all along.

To complicate matters further, as leadership within the co-ops and their associated structures grappled with highly diverse challenges, they simply derived their authority from wherever they could get it at the time – above or below – to try to intervene in the best interests of the co-ops as they saw it. Salae explains:

> Of course I was using NUM all the time – it was my weapon: 'Guys, if you don't do this I will have to tell the President of the NUM, as simple as that. Okay, if you don't accept this, let me now phone Cyril Ramaphosa and tell him and Motlatsi and the NEC that you are refusing' – I was using that as a threat ... For instance if people were misusing the equipment, the property of the co-ops, the assets – that one I would immediately say 'I will call NUM'. Again if they were also not reporting – not accounting to their committee – some of the things like money – I would simply say: 'But we went to a course for five days but now you are unable to account, you don't report, blah blah, this matter has to be taken to the NEC of NUM.' (Interview with Salae, 2003)

When NUM did finally, formally, transfer this 'social ownership' function to the BMLC – as a legitimate and co-op-controlled entity – this was ambiguously received. In the context of NUM's programme, ownership was always further complicated by the complex ways in which it related to the identity of the co-op members and of their relationship to NUM. As long as the co-ops 'belonged' to NUM, then so did they; so while the Lesotho co-ops were quick to assert the independence of the BMLC, this somehow went hand in hand with the notion that such independence reflected a betrayal by NUM: a signal that they were no longer part of NUM – and that they were being abandoned.

Success, degeneration and new challenges in the Lesotho co-ops

By 1994, many of the Lesotho co-ops were doing well. In their different ways, they had institutionalised ways of managing their co-ops that worked. Butha Buthe Agricultural Co-op had reserves of over R40,000 (about US$15,000) in its bank account: a huge sum at the time. Lilepe Co-op similarly. Problems at Leribe and Quthing were being mediated entirely by the BMLC. This included taking control of unutilised equipment at Leribe and redistributing it to other co-ops and having the legitimacy to do so, with no involvement of NUM or MDA (interview with Mapota Molefi).

Like the co-ops, the BMLC had consolidated and matured and a range of norms and procedures had become institutionalised as 'the way things are done'. The BMLC drew its authority largely from below.

In parallel processes, NUM, meanwhile, had reviewed the outcomes of the co-op programme overall and had concluded that the strategy was simply not delivering. The scale of jobs created and the quality of those jobs was far from what had been envisaged. The NUM Projects Unit was tasked with developing a revised strategy that would achieve greater levels of scale and better incomes for participants. It was in this context that the decision was made to set up MDA as a non-profit company, as the development wing of NUM, with its Board of Directors appointed by NUM. As part of wider shifts in strategy, MDA had started to establish what were called 'development centres'. The Lesotho Development Centre was one of the first to be launched, to provide support services for enterprise development in Lesotho. While NUM decided not to initiate or fund any new co-ops, it committed itself to continuing to support the existing ones. The BMLC was represented on the Lesotho Development Centre Board and Mapota Molefi was appointed as Centre Manager. Five Cabinet Ministers from Lesotho attended the launch, which seemed like a good sign. The situation seemed stable – a most dangerous assumption.

Shortly thereafter, I received a call at home from MDA's administrator in Lesotho, Keneiloe Tlaitlai. She said: '*Ntate* Salae and *Ntate* Jack have been arrested for the murder of Moses Mokhehle'.

Moses Mokhehle had not featured in the NUM co-ops since the Lesotho army had been called out to protect the BMLC AGM at which he was ousted as Chair in 1988 – seven years earlier. Why and how had he returned into the picture?

While the immediate answer was that he had lodged an appeal against his removal with the Registrar of Co-operatives, the answer lies in the politics of Lesotho. In addition to the connections between the co-ops, NUM and the ANC, within Lesotho an alliance of ex-miners, students and academics at the National University of Lesotho had formed a political party called the Popular Front for Democracy, with Salae as secretary. They had contested the elections in 1993. They were a tiny party taking on the two bulls already in the *kraal*: the Basotho Congress Party and the Basotho National Party. They won only one seat. But in this context, the growing stability and economic success of the co-ops, coupled with the launch of the Development Centre, were probably not welcome in all political quarters in Lesotho. By now it was entirely clear that this kind of development was no 'anti-politics machine'.

On 6 June 1995 the Registrar of Co-operatives made a ruling against the BMLC in their absence 'In the Quasi-Judicial Court of the Registrar of Co-operatives', and in favour of Moses Mokhehle. It reinstated him as President of the BMLC, retrospective to 1988 – a full seven years earlier – and further ordered

> that all the property belonging to the presidential office usurped from the applicant as the de facto and de jure president of the Basotho Mineworkers Labour Co-op Ltd as from the incident on 25 November 1988 and all the property hitherto procured for the purpose, should be restored to his office. (Papers attached to Court Order, 11 July 1995, in the case of Applicant Moses Moeketsi Mokhehle)

The order was confirmed by a magistrate, who further ordered that this should be put into effect 'if necessary by use of police'. The BMLC's bank accounts – including the bank accounts of every co-op – were frozen, pending this handover of assets.

The BMLC, supported by NUM, successfully secured an urgent court interdict in Lesotho's High Court to stop the process, but to no avail: a new order authorising Mokhehle to assume control of the BMLC office was issued by the Registrar of Co-ops regardless.

Shortly thereafter, Mokhehle and a group of his supporters arrived at the BMLC office, armed and excited, intent on taking control of the office and the BMLC assets. Unknown to them, however, the BMLC was holding an emergency executive meeting, attended by representatives of all the BMLC co-ops, in the meeting room adjacent to the BMLC reception area.

In this meeting, the co-op members were confronting the implications of their situation. All their hard work and sacrifice, their sweat equity and in particular their hard-earned cash reserves, were frozen under the authority of the Minister. They were unable to buy inputs, let alone pay wages. The co-ops were at a standstill, their future in the balance, with the assets to be placed under the authority of Mokhehle – associated with the most turbulent, violent and corrupt phase of the BMLC's history: a turbulence that had been tamed through the institutionalisation of norms, procedures and processes within the BMLC. But the maintenance of this institutional stability relied on a framework of governance and of the rule of law and, with the rule of law having failed them, the future for the co-ops looked bleak indeed.

In the context of this discussion, the BMLC members at the meeting heard the administrator scream, as Mokhehle and his armed and blanketed supporters stormed the office. The co-op members burst out of the meeting room and in the fight that followed, Mokhehle was killed. He was shot; his head was also smashed in with a sandstone block from the stonecutters co-op that had been on display in the reception area. Salae and Mpapea were arrested and charged with his murder.

Amongst many things, this incident is a stark illustration of the problems that can arise as a result of forms of 'quasi-social ownership' vested in Co-op ministries. In Lesotho, the Registrar of Co-ops has significant authority to call an AGM (or not), to approve the appointment of office bearers in a co-op and to attach and redeploy the assets of a co-op. It is a model to which many other African countries subscribe.

Where such powers are subject to political capture, or where the rule of law has limited reach or an ambiguous hold, ownership-oversight is high risk. As a co-op becomes stable or successful, it is at increased risk of being targeted for some form of 'asset harvesting'. This is compounded in contexts in which notions of co-op ownership are also further complicated by poorly specified notions of a wider community ownership of their assets.

In the aftermath of these events, it was small wonder that the BMLC co-ops started to explore converting to limited company structures. Far from acting as a structural constraint on degeneration, this particular form of 'social ownership' directly incentivised the opposite.

In practical terms, with Mokhehle dead, the orders could no longer achieve their purpose. In due course, as a result of legal challenges, the accounts were unfrozen. The murder case was postponed for several years, until finally a plea of self-defence was accepted and the charges were dropped.

The co-ops returned to business and, while there have been no further events to match this level of drama, a number of developments are of interest for the concluding analysis.

The co-op members at Lilepe Co-op at Thaba Bosiu – Lesotho's most successful co-op – wrote a letter to the MDA office in Maseru, requesting that it take over the signing powers on the co-op's accounts and appoint a manager to the co-op. According to Philemon Ralenkoane, Technical Support Officer for Poultry Projects, this was prompted partly by the co-op witnessing the establishment by MDA of two poultry supply centres at Maputsoe and Mafeteng, which provided a supply service to local communities. These were managed as business entities by MDA, which appointed managers and employed staff, who earned regular wages. These poultry supply centres benefited growing networks of self-employed poultry entrepreneurs, who were earning significantly more than the co-op members from selling live birds in their communities:

> Thaba Bosiu wanted to have a manager, even if it is a manager from outside, who will be able to manage the project and everything and they are answerable to him, so that he can pay them at the end of the month....
> They said, 'Let's suspend this thing of a co-op, let's run this as a business ... We notice that Mafeteng is doing well and Maputsoe is doing well, therefore we want to do exactly like Maputsoe and Mafeteng for a period of twelve months'. (Interview with Ralenkoane, 10 December 2003)

After some debate, the office agreed, and appointed Mpapea to manage the co-op – as he had been doing for several years. He was paid more than the members in the co-op, but he was paid out of the co-op's own income. The benefits of this arrangement did not involve any form of subsidy to the co-op, nor any change in its actual management. The only difference was that democracy was removed from the equation. When the agreed time period came to an end, the co-op asked MDA to continue the arrangement, but MDA did not want to become the custodian of the co-ops once again and did not see why the co-op could not just appoint him themselves: but the co-op did not want that authority returned to them.

In April 2004 the BMLC held an AGM. This was more than a decade after NUM's strategies had moved away from a focus on co-op support.

The following co-ops were still functioning and were present: Butha Buthe, Berea, Pheka, Lilepe, the stonecutting co-op, Quthing and Kolo Diamond Co-op.

The stone cutting co-op had twenty-one members; the combined membership of the rest of the co-ops was about thirty people. All of them, except for the stone cutting co-op (which works on a piece-rate system) employed workers as casual labour – often more workers than there were members in the co-op. At Lilepe Co-op, the members were by now earning regular wages of R550 a month; their target was R600 (about US$230 at the time).

When asked why the co-ops were now employing workers rather than taking them in as members, the answer was to point to events at Leribe Co-op. One of the first NUM co-ops set up after the strike, Leribe Co-op had become one of the most stable, mature and successful of the Lesotho co-ops: until it had accepted new members.

These new members, newly retrenched from NUM, dragged the co-op back into struggles and debates over ways of working that destabilised the institutionalised forms of consent and – years after such practices had ended in other co-ops – they plundered the working capital of the co-op to pay themselves out of deposits made by customers. According to Molefi, the co-op collapsed because the new members were not willing to abide by the processes and practices established by long-serving members: these rules and procedures had been made internally by members – but new members were able to overturn them. Instead, he argued, the co-ops needed a framework of rules that could not be violated in this way:

> By rules, we mean rules that are, say, drawn from legal documents, they must be organised. They must bear the stamp from the legal office, you know, all those things: 'If this is a co-op, the co-op should be run in this way'. The co-op must be guided by all those rules ... So, they just destroyed that co-op. (Interview with Mapota Molefi, 10 December 2003)

For Molefi, policies and rules made by co-op members did not protect the co-op. To be beyond the reach of potentially destructive democratic processes, the rules needed to be external – to be 'stamped in a legal office' and hence not open for renegotiation by new members in the co-op.

The employment of workers who are not members of the co-op is a key feature of 'degeneration'. As the Leribe experience illustrates, there are real risks to the co-op from incorporating new members – particularly when these may outnumber the existing membership. In Italy, in many worker co-ops, workers have to work in the co-op for at least five years before they can be considered for membership – and, even then, it is entirely at the discretion of the existing members.

Rather than representing backsliding on co-op principles or degenera-tion, approaches such as these may just represent the wisdom of cumulative experience in co-ops, aimed at protecting their survival. Certainly, this was the lesson drawn by the surviving Lesotho co-ops – none of which planned to take in any new members – although they did not hesitate to employ workers when the co-op needed more labour.

8 Rethinking Degeneration in Co-op Theory

The NUM co-op development experience took place in a specific historical context and was not without flaws or contradictions – many of which the previous chapters have laid bare. At one level, this limits the extent to which lessons from this experience can be generalised. Yet a number of the approaches taken were reproduced, particularly in the state-led co-op development strategies that followed in the post-apartheid period.

In particular, co-ops were promoted as a strategy for job creation in poor and economically marginal areas of the country, with the job creation imperative driving 'number of jobs created' as the lead indicator of success (and the main criterion for funding). This in turn led to a pattern in which co-ops were established with an oversupply of labour relative to their productive base or to the absorptive capacity of their target markets, with decisions on what to produce often based on familiarity with a given product as a consumer rather than on prior experience of production or on any meaningful assessment of business viability. Membership was often based on externally driven selection processes rather than on self-selection or on the skills or experience required in the enterprise. The combined effect of these conditions set such co-ops up for failure, exacerbating all other challenges to viability, with 'the melancholy uniformity' of co-op collapse witnessed by Beatrice and Sydney Webb in the early 1900s evident – despite the significant effort and commitment often invested by members.

The reasons why worker co-ops might fail – particularly in the kinds of circumstances described – are not a great mystery. Surviving in competitive markets is challenging for any enterprise: all the more so when the process also involves reconfiguring internal relations of ownership and control – without much support or guidance.

Far less clear, however, is why worker co-ops that manage to surmount these considerable obstacles and to succeed should be at any risk of degenerating: with such degeneration posing a different kind of threat to the idea of co-ops as an alternative form of economic organisation.

Despite significant odds, the story of the NUM co-ops is not just a story of co-op failure; there were co-ops in NUM's programme that did manage to succeed – not against the kind of benchmarks anticipated at the start, but simply in that they achieved a level of economic sustainability, surviving at least five years as self-sufficient economic entities, able to provide very modest but predictable incomes for their members. As discussed in the previous chapter, issues of degeneration started to arise within this group, in unanticipated ways.

In my 1988 analysis of the degeneration debate, I had been sceptical of the notion of degeneration as an inexorable tendency; it also certainly seemed to be a risk of more concern for the developed world where successful co-ops were competing in the global economy at a level of sophistication and scale that seemed all too distant from the survivalist concerns we were confronting. Yet in practice, even in the economically marginal context of the NUM co-ops, complex sets of incentives and disincentives specific to the co-op form started to manifest themselves, with co-ops responding with adaptations that fell within the three main categories of degeneration flagged in these debates, making it necessary to consider the Webbs' proposition that something 'in the very form' of worker co-ops makes them unstable as economic entities and 'ill-adapted to survive' (Webb and Webb 1914, p. 21).

While degeneration is a pejorative term, were such adaptations always a sign of 'backsliding' on co-op principles? Certainly, there are instances in which enterprises lose their co-operative character. It seems counter-intuitive, however, that it should be the most successful co-ops that appear most susceptible to this effect. Is it plausible, instead, that a consistent pattern of adaptations undertaken by successful co-ops around the world is less about them abandoning co-op principles than it is about a common set of experiences leading to common conclusions about what institutional changes in the classic model might best ensure co-op sustainability?

These arguments are explored in relation to the three main areas of degeneration identified by the Webbs: in relation to democracy in production, to ownership structures, and to the employment of non-members in the co-op.

Recalibrating democracy in production

In relation to democracy in production, the NUM co-op experience – and experience across the sub-region – reinforces the Webb's early point:

> With regard to workshop discipline, experience seems to indicate, with human nature being as it is at present, it does not do for those who have in the workshop to obey the manager to be, as committee men, the direct employers of the manager. (Webb and Webb 1914, p. 21)

Few things are as contentious in co-ops as the question of how democracy in production is interpreted and institutionalised. At one end of the spectrum are collectives in which there is no hierarchy and all decisions are made collectively. To work, this requires a high level of common purpose, a common skills base and a limited division of labour. A critical element of the productivity unlocked by the industrial revolution was, however, the introduction of a division of labour and with it, the need for a managerial function responsible inter alia for connecting the different elements within the production process.

In some co-ops, where the need for a managerial function is recognised, managers are directly elected. The tensions and contradictions this can bring were observed by the Webbs and illustrated in the NUM co-ops; they were also the focus of intensive debate in the region at the time – with some manifestations of such direct democracy characterised as 'democracy that will destroy us'. In the NUM co-ops, while the need for a managerial function was recognised, this was seldom accompanied by any meaningful delegation of managerial authority to allocate co-op resources or labour, even against an agreed production plan. In effect, the concept of democracy in production was interpreted as direct democracy, with the enterprise operating as a collective, with no hierarchy and full, equal participation in all operational and financial decisions. Tensions over roles, responsibilities and expectations in this regard were rife, often sabotaging the viability of a co-op, with this in turn escalating the divisions and plunging such co-ops into an economic death spiral.

By contrast with these approaches, many co-ops, particularly in Europe, have institutionalised more-mediated and indirect expressions of democracy in production, that separate the rights of members as owners and the day-to-day decision making in production. While structures for *participation* in the latter might exist to varying degrees, managerial authority and control is derived via appointment by the annually elected Board, not in any unmediated or direct way from below. This approach now seems obvious and immutable to them – even as it is decried as 'degeneration' by others.

Within this model, a further spectrum exists, with co-ops that actively enable ongoing participation in ways that keep co-operative principles live – as well as examples of bureaucratised approaches associated with a decline in co-op values within the enterprise. While this more-mediated model has its critics, it is a model that is common in Italy's Lega and elsewhere in Europe – where worker co-ops have achieved the highest relative levels of scale and longevity compared to other parts of the world – and showed greater levels of resilience than many conventional companies in the aftermath of the 2008 crisis (Roelants et al. 2014, p. 14).

The indivisibility of co-op capital

The next critical issue in the degeneration debate relates to ownership structures. It is central to co-op theory that the members own the co-op: but some of the ways in which this seemingly straightforward principle has been interpreted can actually remove the materiality of ownership – and the benefits of ownership – from co-op members, in the name of defending co-op principles, with trade-offs to be balanced between benefits in the present and in the future.

This relates in particular to the co-op principle that co-op capital is indivisible, with co-op members having only a limited claim to interest earned on the capital they have contributed. This principle has serious impacts on incentives; so much so that in 1995, after extensive debate, the International Co-operative Alliance (ICA) Principles were changed for the first time since 1966 to address exactly this issue, replacing the relatively straightforward clause on the indivisibility of co-op capital with the following:

> Members contribute equitably to, and democratically control the capital of their co-operative. At least part of that capital is usually the common property of the co-operative. Members usually receive limited compensation, if any, on capital subscribed as a condition of membership. Members allocate surpluses for any or all of the following purposes: developing their co-operative, possibly by setting up reserves, part of which at least would be indivisible; benefiting members in proportion to their transactions with the co-operative; and supporting other activities approved by the membership. (ICA 1995)

This is a far more agnostic principle than the one it replaced, allowing significant latitude in interpretation – reflecting significant ambiguities within the global co-op movement on these issues, with debate still continuing and a wide diversity of approaches accepted in practice (ICA 2017). Yet despite these shifts in the global discourse, the principle that all capital in the co-op is indivisible continued to be asserted in South Africa long after this change. 'The legal definition and principles of a co-operative are very straight-forward about ownership: assets of a co-operative are "jointly owned". The assets are indivisible and not linked to member share contributions' (Satgar 2007).

The fundamental problem with the concept that all co-op capital is indivisible is that it can be unfair on co-op members, particularly once the co-op starts to grow. It means that even where co-op members have invested years of unpaid or low-paid labour in the co-op, and have reinvested surpluses that they created, had a claim over, but chose to reinvest in the expansion of the co-op instead, they have no claim against the capital value so created. If they leave the co-op, they leave with only the value of their initial capital investment, perhaps plus interest. This creates a direct tension between the redistribution of annual surpluses to members and the investment of such surpluses in the co-op: a tension that is not conducive to building up vital reserves.

In this sense, any reinvestment of surpluses means the beneficial rights of ownership are removed from them by the notion of 'indivisibility'; rights over any surplus value they reinvest into the co-op are effectively ceded, becoming as inaccessible as in a capitalist firm. In the early days of the life of a co-op, this could be embraced as part of the common endeavour of building a collective asset; over time, it can start to rankle, leading even committed co-operators to start looking at how to adapt the model: to find a more appropriate balance between the long-term interests of the co-op as an entity and the well-being and financial security of those on whom its future depends. In the developed world, where robust social protection systems exist, for example in relation to pension provisions for co-op members when they retire, the impacts of this are cushioned. But in the developing world, where such protections are far more limited, a desire by members to benefit from their investment in the co-op is not necessarily in tension with their commitment to co-op principles. These issues are made more complex in contexts such as South Africa, in which many co-ops are initially funded with grants, often with no capital contribution by members at all. Such funding often comes with conditionalities that seek to use the indivisibility principle to maintain the social character of the capital transferred, by creating proxy forms of social ownership, sometimes in the form of an ill-defined notion of 'community ownership'. Yet even where such a donation means individual members indeed have no legitimate claim to this start-up capital, it does not change the problem that arises over time, when surpluses generated by the direct sacrifices of co-op members create choices between investment in capital growth – such as through the purchase of new machinery – or the distribution of such surpluses to members.

The consequences of this and its personal implications for co-op members were poignantly expressed by Jack Mpapea, Chair and stalwart of Lilepe Co-op at Thaba Bosiu, when I interviewed him in 2004. Old and grey now, Mpapea was responding to the question of why he left the co-op – which was still functioning at the time – and whether he would do it all again:

> I worked for a co-operative for more than thirteen years. Now I am exhausted with co-operatives – I would choose business, a straight business rather than the co-operative.
>
> I noticed that really, for the past fourteen years, I did all of this: here are buildings, here are poultry sheds, here is irrigation equipment; everything is in place. But at the end of the day I am going to be alone at my home. I won't take any of these things home.
>
> That is why I decided to leave that co-op, to go alone, looking for other opportunities. Now I have my own small business. If at all I can get some

funds somewhere – very little funds – I can be able to stand on my own. (Interview with Jack Mpapea 2003)

This is precisely the incentive problem that the Mondragon Co-op attempted to address with its innovative system of internal capital accounts for members. To become a full member of a Mondragon co-op, it is necessary to contribute the equivalent of one year's earnings to the capital of the co-op (which can be paid off over time as a low-interest loan). This is used to open an individual, interest-bearing capital account in the co-op bank. Each year, when profits are distributed, a certain minimum amount goes to reserves and a social fund, but up to 70 per cent of profits can be distributed to these capital accounts. Workers can withdraw the interest on these accounts annually, but can only withdraw the capital amounts in instalments when they leave or retire. This provides the co-op with a substantial capital resource-pool on which to draw, but workers are not faced with a choice between distributing co-op surpluses to themselves, or losing any future access to it by investing it in co-op growth. Instead, Mondragon's capital account system squares this circle.

In a thoughtful set of essays published by the ICA and entitled 'The Capital Conundrum for Co-ops', the dilemmas and tensions around capital access, structuring and control affecting not just worker co-ops but all forms of co-op are considered, in recognition of 'the philosophical and practical angst that co-operatives experience over capital' (ICA 2017 p. 21). It is not only Mondragon that has tried to innovate in this regard, nor is it only worker co-ops that face tensions and contradictions in relation to the character of capital in the co-op. Dismissing innovation that attempts to grapple with the need to balance the legitimate interests of co-op members with the social goals of co-operatives as 'degeneration' seems too glib a response to a problem for which there are pragmatic solutions.

Dilemmas of growth

The next issue ascribed to degeneration relates to the choices made when a co-op has the opportunity to expand: and the question arises whether to include new members or to employ workers as wage labour. Certainly, the emergence of categories of workers with limited rights and precarious conditions of work, as well as the development of co-ops as global players with subsidiaries structured as conventional companies – for example in both Mondragon and some co-ops in the Lega – illustrate real risks of degeneration in the fully pejorative sense of the word:

Mondragon multinational co-ops control 100 foreign subsidiaries and joint ventures, employing approximately twelve thousand workers, mostly in developing and post-socialist countries, where wages are low or markets growing. These firms are not worker-owned and their employees do not have the rights or privileges of co-op members. Even in the Basque country and in Spain, co-ops depend on significant numbers of temporary workers on short-term contracts. Only about one-half of Mondragon's businesses are co-operatives and one-third of its employees are members. (Kasmir 2016, p. 55)

So, degeneration is an issue. Yet the decision not to offer membership to new workers is not always a cut-and-dried case of a co-op losing its principles, with the issue in fact more complex than that.

The two main factors influencing the decision to place limits and conditions on membership include the issues already discussed above: firstly, the process through which co-ops find ways to institutionalise democracy in production and secondly the incentive issues linked to capital ownership and who benefits from prior investments. We explore the latter first:

> As a simplistic but illustrative example, suppose a pharmaceutical workers co-op were to reinvest $100 000 on laboratory equipment to screen exotic rainforest plants for a new cure for malaria. For the first five years, nothing is found; there is little return on the reinvested capital and research consumables spending reduces the co-op's net income. All the co-operators suffer financial hardship. In year 6, through the good luck and judgement of the co-op's scientists, a new drug is found and patented. After clinical trials, use on humans is finally permitted in year 14; the co-op's potential income increases by a factor of 100 overnight. Such is demand, that the co-op must take on new workers to meet it. In this case, the major component of the co-op's effective capital is its patent on the new drug ... A key question is to what extent should newer and future members get to share in the delayed, intangible capital created by risks, decisions and efforts of the older and past members? Now that the firm is a reasonably safe bet for the duration of the patent, who should reap the rewards? What about members who have retired or left at various times during the last 15 years? (Major 1996, p. 552)

Lilepe Co-op may not have been about to patent malaria drugs any time soon, but the issues raised here nevertheless also apply in marginal co-ops – as reflected in Mpapea's reflections. In addition, assuming that new members have equal voting rights, this will change the balance of forces in the co-op – in a context in which such new members may not recognise the prior sacrifices or claims of longer-serving members, nor the value of norms and internal processes that have been developed over time and that may have served the co-op well. Ironically, it is co-ops with the highest levels of direct democracy that are most at risk of being de-stabilised by the participation of new and inexperienced members in production decision making – as the experience at the Leribe Co-op and its subsequent collapse graphically illustrated. No doubt this is why, in many worker co-ops in the Italian Lega, workers must work for five years in the co-op before they can be considered for membership.

While critics may denounce this as a form of degeneration, Italian worker co-ops have achieved levels of success, stability and longevity that are hard to match. If Leribe Co-op had applied the same principle it might still be here today.

In sum, while the concept of 'degeneration' is used pejoratively, some of the forms of degeneration that have attracted that label can be seen instead as adaptations borne from experience, designed to align incentives and processes in the co-op as necessary conditions for long-term success – on terms that aim to protect and retain core co-op values. NUM's experience illustrates that these issues do not only affect successful co-ops in the developed economies, but impact on marginal co-ops in a developing context also: once such co-ops overcome the significant initial hurdles of survival.

A critical requirement for successful worker co-ops therefore does entail a long hard look at the institutional approaches associated with success and failure and a willingness to adapt the traditional co-op model in ways that address incentive failures within it: motivated by the desire to secure the sustainability of the co-op model rather than to abandon it. If all such institutional adaptation is dismissed as degeneration, this may in itself create a self-limiting constraint on the success rate of worker co-ops.

Worker co-ops do not, however, exist in isolation from other forms of co-op and the existence of a wider co-operative movement may be as important for their success as any of these internal incentive issues, not least because they provide access to capital and credit through co-op banks and to markets through the extensive reach of consumer co-ops. Certainly, in Italy's Lega, worker co-ops are a smaller part of a much wider movement in which user and producer co-ops provide the backbone: because while worker co-ops may struggle to absorb more than a handful of members, and an oversupply of labour can destroy their viability, user and producer co-ops get stronger the more members they have, because this enhances the economies of scale they can achieve. Outreach and membership growth are fully aligned with their business model. In the process, they extend participatory practices in communities and underpin the growth of a co-op movement as part of a wider social economy, complementing other forms of social organisation, civic action and solidarity: and also providing a supportive framework within which worker co-ops have a greater chance of survival.

In South Africa at the time, while no such wider co-op movement existed to provide support to nascent worker co-ops, conditions certainly seemed conducive to its emergence. Society was highly mobilised, solidarity was strong, and a myriad of forms of local organisation enabled the participation of youth, women, students and community residents. Arguably, the potential existed to translate this organisation and energy into a multiplicity of forms of local economic co-operation and mutual assistance. Instead, however, the post-apartheid period saw this organisation and energy de-mobilised; faith was instead placed in the power of the democratic state to deliver. It was a fateful error at so many levels; this was just one of them.

Meanwhile, for NUM, rising levels of retrenchments and job losses on the mines were heightening the pressure to create jobs in labour-sending areas – with the NUM Co-op Programme manifestly unable to respond at anything like the kind of scale – or success rate – that NUM expected to see. The heat was on to develop new approaches.

9 The Mineworkers Development Agency's Development Centre Strategy

The early days of the co-op programme took place against the backdrop of the final stages of a repressive state of emergency in South Africa; unimaginable as it seemed at the time, the end of apartheid was just around the corner. In early 1990, the ANC and other banned organisations were unbanned; later that year, the task of representing the democratic movement to meet Nelson Mandela as he finally exited from Pollsmoor Prison went to NUM General Secretary Cyril Ramaphosa. By 1993, Ramaphosa was leading the country's constitutional negotiations; within the democratic movement, the terms of a post-apartheid Reconstruction and Development Programme were under negotiation. A transition to democracy seemed plausible, if not yet certain. The idealised socialism of the imagination was not yet dead, even if the socialism of the Eastern Bloc was crumbling. It was a different era from the one in which the co-op programme had begun. It had new possibilities, new spaces within which to work and the promise of the transition to democracy ahead – with all the unknown territory this would entail.

Nevertheless, retrenchments in the mining industry continued unabated. In 1991, NUM initiated the first Mining Industry Summit, bringing together labour, the industry and government to negotiate a social plan to address the crisis of retrenchments in the industry. The outcomes were disappointing, with no commitment to limit retrenchments, and only a lukewarm response to NUM's proposal for a wide-reaching social plan to address the development needs of mining towns and mine labour-sending areas.

Meanwhile, by 1993, the NUM Co-op Unit had drawn the conclusion that support to worker co-ops was not offering a sufficiently effective strategy for creating jobs for ex-miners at scale. The numbers of people able to benefit relative to the costs of set up and of ongoing technical support were just too low, with success rates and returns to participants low also. The approach was an insufficient response to the challenges confronted. We needed to reach far greater scale.

Close involvement of NUM's National Executive Committee (NEC) members in mediating disputes at co-op level meant a high level of exposure to the challenges and to the limited gains this route offered to members. The NEC supported the view that additional, more-inclusive and more-effective strategies of contributing to the livelihoods of ex-miners and their communities were needed; we were tasked with devising these.

In strategic terms, it was, however, a step into the unknown. During the co-op programme, our purpose had at least been clearly defined. Now, without any pre-packaged 'solution' to offer, what were the economic alternatives in mine labour-sending areas? How could we impact at greater scale? Clearly, this required us to break from a role that created such a high level of dependence on ongoing and direct support to specific enterprises; instead, we needed to play a more catalytic role in dynamising local economic development, to unlock local skills, resources, initiative and agency in new ways. Through what organisational and institutional strategies could this be achieved?

It was in this context that a group of mineworkers were retrenched from Amcoal's Arnot Colliery. Their organisational innovation and the new forms of economic co-operation that they initiated played a significant role in shaping the approach to organising ex-miners and their communities that NUM then took, creating levels of demand for support for enterprise services that provided the basis for the establishment of development centres that followed.

Organisational innovation at Mhala

Amcoal's Arnot Colliery in NUM's Witbank Region was a particularly well-organised mine. Andrea Nzima was the union branch Chair, with fifteen years of experience on the mine and deep organising skills. He was also one of the NUM NEC members on its Co-op Sub-committee, to which the Co-op Unit reported. He had therefore been in close contact with developments in the co-ops and had been deployed many times to mediate co-op conflicts, particularly in Swaziland. He was a vocal supporter, within NUM, of the need to forge new approaches to development in mining communities.

When, in that context, Arnot Colliery was faced with retrenchments, he and others in the union branch took the initiative to innovate. They organised workers on the mine into 'district contact groups'. These groups met while they were still on the mine and discussed their liveli-hood strategies for the future and how they would invest their retrench-ment packages. They also created a communication network to stay in contact after leaving the mine. Andrea Nzima, Douglas Mboweni, Colin Ndlovu and William Nyathi were all from a string of villages in the Bushbuckridge lowveld, near Tulamahashe, that was then part of the Gazankulu Bantustan. Thirty-four of the retrenched miners from Arnot were from this area.

On their arrival home, they invited the community to a 'welcome home party' for themselves at which they slaughtered an ox and announced that they did not intend to return to the mines: they aimed to create jobs in the local community instead. They invited members of the community to join them in this endeavour.

The district contact groups set up at Arnot were then converted into village groups, which now included members of the community. These village groups decided to hire transport collectively to buy live chickens from a farmer some sixty kilometres away in Hazyview, on the assumption that they would be able to make a decent profit selling them locally. They were right.

The critical facilitation and organising roles in this process were performed by ex-NUM leaders, applying old skills in new ways. The work was done on a voluntary basis. Later, Nzima was paid a stipend and then became a Mineworkers Development Agency (MDA) employee, but those options were not initially on the table. Participation in the village groups was based on self-selection and each member decided their own level of involvement and risk and placed their orders for chickens accordingly.

While some participants ordered twenty-five birds a week, others took five or fifty. Some grouped together to build joint holding pens for their chickens, others did it alone. Some arranged to sell from a particular roadside site in rotation, others sold their birds independently. All of these choices and arrangements were made on the basis of decisions and reciprocities that participants defined for themselves and while they entailed economic co-operation, they did not require collective consensus. Each person decided their own level of risk, time and money and earned accordingly – and separately. The problem of 'democratic management' simply never arose. Within weeks, about forty people spread across six villages were earning incomes from buying and selling live chickens: more people than in any of the NUM co-ops.

Participants each paid R2 per bird for the hire of a truck from a local person. The birds cost R12 from the farmer and they could sell them for R18. They generally sold the birds within a day or two and so feed was based on leftovers and scraps rather than commercial poultry feed. They kept them at their homes and sold them locally, so other expenses were minimal. There was an active process of shared learning and mutual assistance in the groups, which met regularly to place orders and receive their birds.

For those people selling just twenty-five chickens a week, this meant a net income of R400 a month (about US$125 at the time). This was significantly more than any co-op member was earning at the time. Those able to sell fifty chickens a week were able to double this, which matched what many had been earning on the mines.

From NUM's side, there was no capital input or direct subsidy to the process. There was the time of organisers Stanley Mathebule and

Francis Dipholo and the largely voluntary time of the ex-miners from Arnot.

Meagre as they look, the incomes earned from selling live chickens compared favourably with the alternatives. The contrast with the worker co-op programme was stark. Here was a network of people – self-selected, self-financed, in business and earning better incomes than co-op members did: from an activity that was part-time, often taking up only about two days of the week. The barriers to entry were low and the returns on investment were rapid and reasonable. In the process, participants had crafted a form of economic co-operation that gave them collective economies of scale and mutual support but within a framework that also gave them flexibility to make their own choices about their level of commitment, investment, risk and return.

This could be described as a nascent form of agricultural supply co-op, in which farmers come together to create economies of scale in relation to their input supplies, but without the collective production dimension characteristic of a worker co-op. In this context, however, participants had simply used their own initiative to come up with a strategy of economic co-operation that worked for them.

As much by luck as by design, this first foray into micro-enterprise activity happened to focus on one of very few niches where entrepreneurs were not in direct competition with the large companies that dominate the South African economy and which produce the majority of basic consumption items. A vibrant market for live chickens from within poor communities had been overlooked by the big players. Yet in this market, consumers were willing to pay more for a live chicken than a frozen one. Partly, this was because few houses yet had electricity – and a live chicken stays fresh until you need it. There was also a cultural element. Later, at a meeting in Welkom in the Free State at which mine management were responding with scepticism to an NUM proposal to establish a poultry supply centre in the township, a mineworker made the analogy that, for white people, if guests arrive at their homes on the weekend, they will not offer them wine from a box, but will open a bottle of wine with a cork. For black people, he argued, it's the same: 'we will not cook a frozen chicken, we will slaughter a live bird for the pot – to show respect and hospitality'.

The approach developed at Mhala was rapidly replicated in other contexts, including in Lesotho. Trained and supported by Dr Ed Wethli and poultry officer Philemon Ralenkoane, MDA set up a network of poultry supply centres. The users of these centres organised themselves into the Basotho Poultry Farmers Association, which challenged unfair practices in the Lesotho poultry market at the time.

NUM then also began to facilitate access to micro-loans (financed by the Amcoal/NUM Fund) initially running this directly but later outsourcing it to an entity called the Rural Finance Facility. This enabled many participants to buy their first chickens. Given the lack of other investment required and the quick turnaround times, the impacts of high interest rates were mitigated and these loans allowed participants to rapidly ratchet up their scale. This went along with small business training, using a five-day business training module.

Within six months, the network of poultry entrepreneurs at Mhala was ordering a standard five hundred birds a week and the viability of localising the supply of chickens became apparent.

Andrea Nzima and his team then negotiated to purchase the use rights of a large, abandoned poultry farm in Mhala, owned by the Gazankulu Development Corporation and with the capacity to produce 1,200 birds a week.

This site, just opposite the Rolle Station railway siding, became the Mhala Development Centre, funded by the Amcoal/NUM Fund. Its poultry unit started at full capacity, breeding 1,200 day-old chicks per week into fully-grown birds and supplying the existing network of poultry entrepreneurs. It therefore had a minimum of start-up risk. Over time, many of the group members then set up their own outgrower sheds and started to order three-week old chicks through the Centre, taking them at an age when the key risks of mortality are over. This halved the turnaround time and doubled the capacity of the MDC's sheds. Next, some participants started to take day-old birds, ordered in bulk along with the Centre's own order.

So, a process that began with an apparently marginal retail activity was able to localise and expand production over quite a short time-frame, with unemployed people with no enterprise experience and few other formal skills able to make the transition from being retailers to being producers. While the returns varied according to scale, many were able to match the incomes earned on the mines at the time. Far more people in this one local economy were also participating and benefiting than the co-op programme had ever been able to absorb in an equivalent local context.

Development centres catalyse local economic development

Despite the early successes achieved at Mhala, MDA's vision was not to turn every ex-mineworker into a poultry producer. The experience illustrated two important things, however. Firstly, it demonstrated the scope for a mode of development organising that was based on a very simple form of economic co-operation, driven by self-selection on terms that involved not only ex-miners but any interested aspirant entrepreneurs in the community. In the process, it created local networks and support systems, along with contact points and the required critical mass for the delivery of services such as training and micro-finance.

Photo 11 *A demonstration of a mini-tractor at an open day at the Mhala Development Centre, Bushbuckridge, Northern Province; the large mural on the Centre could be seen for miles. Artist Andrew Lindsay worked with local artists at most MDA sites to transform otherwise drab low cost structures; 1993.*

Secondly, it illustrated the scope to use forms of economic co-operation at the local level to generate economies of scale that in turn catalysed new opportunities for local economic development. Once a certain minimum threshold of scale was reached, the Mhala Poultry Supply Centre became a viable proposition, enabling the localisation of production. How else might this logic apply and how might we use it to promote development in the local economy?

Building on this momentum required local knowledge and a local presence; this was to be the function of development centres, which MDA started to establish in mining communities where sufficient scale of demand from networks of entrepreneurs justified such a presence. By 2002, development centres were operating in the following places:

In South Africa:
- Kokstad, E. Cape/KwaZulu-Natal
- Mhala, Bushbuckridge, Northern Province
- Welkom, Free State
- Klerksdorp, North West Province
- Morokweng, North West Province
- Bathlaros, near Kuruman, Northern Cape

Figure 1 Services at MDA's development centres (adapted from Philip 2002, p. 15)

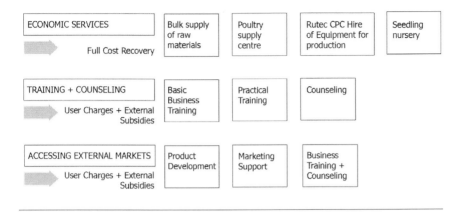

In Lesotho:
• Maseru, Lesotho

The different elements within the development centre concept – and the funding strategy for these – are illustrated in Figure 1.

These development centres provided a platform from which MDA attempted to promote diversification in the local economy, offering a mix of what were called 'economic services', and 'strategic services'. The economic services were services that could follow the poultry model: starting small but with the scope to build effective demand until they became viable business units, operating on the basis of full cost recovery, able to anchor the viability of the Centre as a whole and contribute to its core running costs, limiting the vulnerability of the centres to the vagaries of donor funding which were seen as providing an initial contribution, not an ongoing one.

Strategic services were defined as services that could operate on the basis of some level of user charge, but that would require ongoing subsidies. These were seen as driving innovation and access into external markets. In the first instance, however, the centres focused on supporting local production for local consumption.

The economic services offered several elements. These included a model of 'community production centres' developed by the Rural Technology Company (Rutec), which provided access to training, equipment hire and equipment sale for more than thirty different micro-enterprise options, including mini-bakeries and poultry units, moulds for non-standard cement products such as lintels, gutters and paving stones, tools for leather processing and the production of leather goods, T-shirt printing equipment, tyre-repair, ice-making, ice-lolly production, solar drying, peanut butter production, maize mills, oil presses, welding equipment, barbed-wire fence-makers and many others. These introduced small-scale manufacturing opportunities that were often completely absent within the local economy, but for goods consumed locally as well as for inputs into other economic activity such as construction.

Business supply stores were an important complementary element in relation to the community production centres, with the lack of local supply of any but the most basic raw material inputs for production activities acting as a constraint on diversification in the local economy. So, items such as brass buckles for leather sandals and belts or T-shirt printing inks are only available in major centres, with the lack of packaging supplies also limiting the formalisation of production activities. It is easy enough to make *atchar* (a form of relish) at a local level; but not so easy to find the plastic containers required to sell it in. The same applies in relation to egg boxes, peanut butter jars, foil caps and containers for yoghurt or fruit juice, screw-top containers for juice-pulp concentrate, bag-sealers for biscuits or dried fruit, or plastic tubing for ice-lollies.

Suppliers of these kinds of inputs are simply not geared towards the distribution needs of far-flung rural producers who need to buy in small quantities. While *spaza*[1] shop suppliers such as Metro Cash & Carry had started to do bulk breaking of consumer goods such as maize and sugar in some parts of the country, suppliers of production or packaging inputs were not yet doing the same (Abt Associates and Brij Consulting 1998).

Small-volume purchases made regularly from the nearest town meant exorbitant transport costs, with taxis charging not only for the passenger but for their goods also. It was this gap in input supply markets that the business supply stores at the development centres were intended to fill. Later, with funds from the De Beers/NUM Retrenchment Fund, MDA set up Ethaleni – a central buying company servicing all the centres in order to secure further economies of scale in this regard.

The centres also offered production equipment for hire on site which allowed people to experiment with production options at a minimum cost and risk, producing on a small scale and testing the market: creating a safe space for learning from doing.

Baumann reports how at Mhala Development Centre (MDC), a network of fifty to sixty small manufacturers of window and door frames emerged to take advantage of the growth in housing investment in the area:

> Many of these micro-enterprises got started via MDC. Aspirant steelworkers would come to MDC to learn how to cut steel rods, weld, manage a business and so on. Once in business, goods would be manufactured at MDC's site,

---

[1]   A small informal shop in a township or informal settlement, often operating from a private house.

using its welding equipment, electricity and transport, for which MDC would charge a fee. Once sufficient profits were accumulated, however, the manufacturer would invest in his or her own machinery, using credit and equipment-supply connections facilitated by MDC, and start manufacturing at home or on site, closer to the ultimate client, further reducing costs.

These manufacturers use steel bought from Nelspruit suppliers. MDC has played an important role by acting as a local warehouse and distributor for bulk steel, rendering it unnecessary for manufacturers to travel personally to Nelspruit. MDC's profits now come mainly from ongoing supply activities and commissions on credit and equipment sales. (Baumann 1998)

He describes a similar process in relation to cement products. Based on interviews with the Centre staff, he characterised the role of the Centre as follows:

MDC provides established clients with administrative, coordination, marketing, credit and risk-management services. For example, MDC tracks local construction opportunities and advises clients on how and where to tender. MDC also helps clients to arrange direct purchase of materials from suppliers and marketing of finished goods. Clients needing larger-scale credit are counselled and referred to institutions such as the Rural Finance Facility or AltFin. The impact of such services is hard to measure but invaluable. They serve to reduce transactions costs ... and risk by providing services for a number of enterprises in one place. This lowers the cost of doing business for each individual micro-enterprise. It would be expensive for each micro-enterprise to undertake such services individually. Through MDC, clients can get cheap information on tender opportunities. Similarly, MDC's marketing and supply services help to reduce the risk of unsold products.

As with MDC's informal credit arrangements, these services have evolved through informal local contact with target communities, supported by the wider network of experience in other MDA-supported initiatives. (Baumann 1998)

While the economies of scale and localisation of supply improved the potential competitiveness of local enterprise, the centres also played a less tangible role by facilitating information flows, which in turn enhanced the access of local entrepreneurs to tenders, to suppliers and to finance. In addition, the centres provided a level of formality that bridged the gap between the high levels of informality in the local economy and the protocols of 'anonymous exchange' required to make deals and secure terms with formal-sector suppliers in the core economy. This was a two-way process: for Baldwin Steel, who offered MDC a franchise as a consequence of the high volumes of steel traded, the Mhala Centre facilitated access to new markets for them also.

Ted Baumann was commissioned to do a case study of MDC in 1998 for the Department of Constitutional Development, as part of exploring different approaches to local economic development (LED) and summarises the MDC experience as follows:

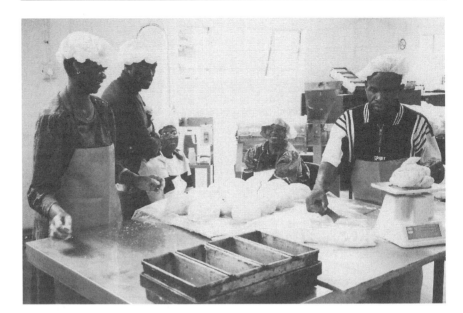

Photo 12 *Training in bread-baking and running a bakery at MDA's Klerksdorp Development Centre, North West Province; 2002.*

MDC is a useful example of an informal approach to community-driven LED. MDC has been successful because, for a variety of reasons, it has generated local solutions to local problems, based on local opportunities. The specific *solutions* may not be as important as the *processes* that generated them. The case suggests that in some instances it is not a useful approach for local governments wanting to promote LED to develop a check-list of 'do's and don'ts' to be implemented. Instead, local governments can learn to support what is *already happening* in 'civil society', rather than rely solely on 'creating' such processes. (Baumann 1998, p. 7, original emphasis)

In relation to a range of sub-sectors, the network effects at MDC created conditions – on a small scale in a marginal economic context – that nevertheless shared certain of the advantages of the kind of cluster effects identified and highlighted by Michael Porter, with the Centre catalysing the development of networks and of communities of practice, operating as a knowledge hub and a site for learning by doing (and learning by watching, which was where many entrepreneurs began) with exposure to unfamiliar technologies and techniques. Alongside this was the product development and marketing function – explored in more depth in Chapters 13 and 14 – and the scope for support to innovation that these strategic services held out.

It was at these seven development centres that MDA was able to offer the most integrated and extensive set of support services, but this still left vast areas across rural southern Africa where mineworkers and their communities were hard to reach, despite outreach by teams of trainers from the centres and also by NUM's Mobile Unit – a twenty-ton truck (with Sipho Nqwelo in charge) that included all the equipment typical of a centre and that did training on the mines during retrenchment processes and in rural areas.

Confronting marginal returns once more

By 2000, MDA had trained over 7,921 people over a three-year period (MDA Training Data-Base);[2] it also had a wider user-base than this for economic services such as the poultry supply stores or business supply stores. The shift from a project-establishment focus in the co-op programme to a focus on the delivery of economic services had certainly allowed a significant increase in the number of people serviced by the programme, including community outreach beyond just the mining constituency. Notable was the high level of participation by women and the families of mineworkers and ex-mineworkers.

In 2000, Caroline Pinder conducted a series of impact assessments on behalf of the United Kingdom (UK)'s Department for International Development (DFID) in South Africa. The assessment period was from 1 September 1998 to 31 August 1999 and covered a random selection of 20 per cent of clients trained at selected centres during this period (excluding Lesotho). Her notes on the logistical difficulties of the process reflect the programme's reach into deep rural areas:

> MDA's clients were found in some of the most remote and rural areas; the random sampling methodology took us to sixteen different districts in the Eastern Cape alone, reflecting the depth and breadth of MDA's penetration in rural areas. In most regions, there were some clients who could not be reached because rain had made roads impassable, reflecting also the conditions in which they engage with the outside world. (Pinder 2000, p. 14)

A total of 163 clients were interviewed. The process found that on average across the programme, 70 per cent of MDA's trainees has taken the initiative to use the skills learned to initiate or expand an enterprise or income-generating activity. A year after the training, 77 per cent of those who did apply the skills (or 54 per cent of total trainees) were still engaged in such economic activity.

This was the good news. More sobering were the insights into the depth of the challenges faced by many such entrepreneurs and the limited returns to effort that were the norm, in terms of incomes earned.

Assessing incomes earned is a highly vexed issue in all enterprise development programmes because, despite the best efforts of small enterprise development agencies to promote proper record keeping – motivated in part by the desire for accurate figures for their own purposes – these are rarely in place and are rarely accurate.

[2] No longer extant; data extracted 2001.

Figure 2 *Breakdown of MDA participants with links to the mining industry, September 1998 – August 1999 (Pinder 2000)*

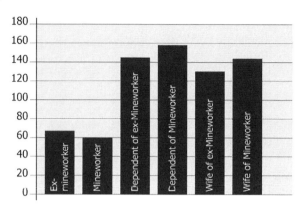

Figure 3 *Income returns to MDA participants (Pinder 2000)*

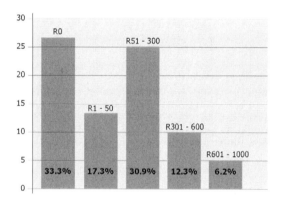

Figure 4 *Income per person compared by enterprise type (Pinder 2000)*

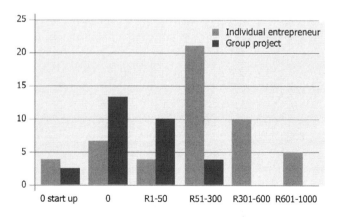

In addition, the same confusions typical in co-ops abound over terms such as 'net profit' and 'turnover' and over the distinction between income to the business and personal income to the entrepreneur. Even where enterprises do have accurate figures, entrepreneurs are often reluctant to divulge detailed business information and are as likely to exaggerate their returns as to understate them, depending on the context. There is therefore no way to adjust data for predictable distortions.

Duly qualified, the monthly income returns from income-generating activity were still shockingly low. Early optimism fueled by the returns from the sale of live chickens had not translated into a wider pattern of returns for micro-enterprise activity, despite examples of success – which often relied on close proximity to the full suite of services offered by a development centre. Low as these figures were, however, 50 per cent of respondents claimed that the income from their enterprise activities constituted *all* of their household income, with a further 11 per cent saying it contributed more than half.

Important as these incomes were for participants, they were certainly not providing a pathway out of poverty. Disaggregated by enterprise type, the evaluation also showed that the lowest returns of all were to group projects.

While MDA was no longer involved in setting up co-ops, 'group projects' had become a standard form of development intervention and many of these groups came to the centres for training and services. Often loosely defined as co-ops, these interventions at times appeared to have been designed to illustrate a worst-case scenario approach to development. All too often, an organiser from a non-governmental organisation (NGO), a representative of a foreign donor programme or a government official would arrive in a community and ask the question: 'Who wants to be in a project?' Perhaps some sixty people would come forward, mainly women. They would be arbitrarily allocated to groups; or a process of 'outing' the poorest of the poor would be undertaken. Access to grant funding or credit to start projects was often made conditional on group formation of this kind, but with ownership vesting more widely in 'the community' in an undefined way. The selection of business activities was often externally driven with little account taken of the competitive context in which they would operate. These community groups then started with little if any guidance on how decisions would be made, how finances were to be controlled, how work would be allocated and how surplus or profits would be calculated, with a set of expectations of some form of benefit from the enterprise raised in the wider community. This set the stage for later conflict as 'the community' demanded a share of such benefits – in contexts in which often there were none. What might appear from outside to be a hive of production and marketing activity with lots of money flowing in and out was all too often actually operating at a loss. Where donors specified that equipment in such enterprises was owned by 'the community', ambiguity was created over whose responsibility it was to repair, maintain or replace such equipment: at whose cost and to whose benefit? Often, projects had to navigate all of this complex terrain on their own. Many operated with no division of labour, sharing all tasks equally, with the purchase of inputs, production and marketing treated as serial, collective activities in which all members would participate. Small wonder that so many failed. When they did, explanations typically included the low levels of skill of participants; less well recognised was that, all too often, as big a problem lay with the poor business skills of the government officials and donors initiating such projects.

It was not, however, just group projects like these – nor other entrepreneurs supported by MDA – for whom the returns from entrepreneurial activity were low. Du Toit and Neves, for example, comment on the 'vanishingly small economic rewards' from the economic activities of informants in their research:

> [S]elling a few cooked sheep's heads – which require hours of arduous, dirty and unpleasant work – for R10 profit a head; selling, by the cupful, paraffin carried kilometres in the hot sun at a profit of a few cents per sale; selling individual pieces of chewing gum or single cigarettes or biscuits for 10c each; helping run a crèche all day, every day, for R200 [about US$27] a month; being paid R10 to R15 [about US$1–2] for a day's work plastering a mud hut in the Eastern Cape. All these activities seemed barely sustainable or profitable, yet they seemed to be the household's only means of getting their hands on some cash. (Du Toit and Neves 2007b, p. 38)

All of this begged the question of why people continued to invest time and energy in such activity. The rationale seems to include an emphasis on the social utility of such economic participation: keeping people – especially women – within networks of exchange and reciprocity at the local level and limiting their risks of becoming socially marginalised (Neves and Du Toit 2013). Economic participation signified that a contribution was being made to the household and the community, which mattered to people's sense of self-worth as well as to how they were seen by others.

In group projects, participation also provides a form of interface with external resources from the state or other donors and, for as long as the funding lasts, it is a welcome boost to local incomes. There are also disincentives for non-participation, with unwillingness to participate potentially signalling a disengagement from the patronage relationships within which the allocation of funds for projects were all too often associated.

The majority of participants in group projects were women – with women entrepreneurs facing a distinct set of constraints across the spectrum of forms of enterprise.

Figure 5 *Gender breakdown of training participants at selected sites, September 1998 – August 1999 (Pinder 1999)*

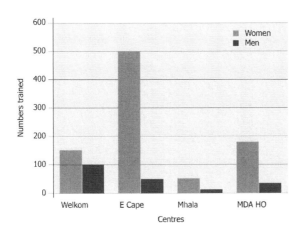

Extra hurdles for women

The majority of MDA's clients were women. In a Gender Appraisal focused on the impacts on women participants, a range of factors were identified that limited women in particular from engaging in enterprise or income-generating activity on a full-time basis, yet data comparisons tend to assume a return to full-time effort. Yet livelihoods were typically complex and few participants were solely dependent on the proceeds of the enterprise:

> They were engaged in a wide range of subsistence and survival activities (e.g. casual labour, working on their own and/or family plots) and this diversification of energies often inhibited the growth of enterprise activity as it meant larger orders were not sought for fear they could not be met within the time available to project members. (Pinder 2000, p. 30)

Partly, this spread of activities is about risk mitigation; but it is not always a matter of choice. Women cited the disruptive effects of compulsory traditional duties such as planting, weeding and harvesting in the chief's fields as constraints on their business activity and on business growth (Pinder 1999, p. 8)

To further complicate an assessment, the figures on income returns from enterprise activity did not capture the role played by in-kind contributions, to which participants had great difficulty putting a value:

> Initially, many people, particularly women in the focus groups, said they paid themselves nothing, thinking only of cash payments. Further questioning, however, revealed they often 'paid' themselves in kind, even if it was a

small amount (e.g. baking extra loaves for themselves). Others said they occasionally bought a large amount of food with the proceeds of the business and shared this out amongst themselves. (Pinder 2000, p. 24)

In certain instances, women preferred to receive payment in kind, going so far as to use project funds to purchase maize which they then distributed to members rather than paying out cash. As became clear, cash can be captured by other household members, while returns in food are more likely to be used to feed the family. It also emerged that there were incentives for women to keep their enterprise activities marginal:

> Women often do not want their businesses to 'grow' in the style of western businesses: as was mentioned by MDA's staff and some of the women, if they grow into large businesses their husbands want to take over, so it is not in their interest to grow; nor do they always want the increased responsibility of a larger enterprise even if that means greater income, as it increases their workloads still further and creates more conflict with their family responsibilities. (Pinder 1999, p. 16)

This issue was illustrated by the case of a woman in Elukwatini, Mpumalanga, who had attended training and had been running a thriving *spaza* shop. When MDA trainers and Pinder arrived to interview her, it transpired that her husband had taken over the business, in which she was now an occasionally paid employee.

The bottom line, however, was that despite some success stories, self-employment and engagement in enterprise activity was not yielding the kinds of results or returns required to make a real impact on poverty or unemployment. The returns were low and failure rates were high: even if worst-case-scenario interventions were excluded. If there had been such a thing as a theory of change at the time, we would have had to declare that its assumptions were flawed. But in what ways? Where did the problem lie? Why were returns so low? Why did such approaches seem to work in other countries but not here? What were we doing wrong?

So began another cycle of reflection and analysis, to try to understand why the outcomes were so disappointing – and what that should mean for the next phase of MDA's strategy.

Against the backdrop of war in KwaZulu-Natal

Retrenchments continued unabated and, in this period, NUM had negotiated the establishment of a jointly controlled development fund to support workers laid off from Eskom, South Africa's electricity utility. I was approached by a representative of these retrenched workers – we'll call him Jabu – to meet a group of them near a town then called Piet Retief. NUM National Executive Committee member Korde Manqina agreed to come with me.

Our directions took us off the tarred road into deep rural territory in northern KwaZulu-Natal, where an all-out war was taking place between Inkatha and the United Democratic Front (as a proxy for ANC support). When I'd taken down the directions, this important piece of geo-spatial information had escaped me.

Finally we saw the small trading store at which we had arranged to meet the former Eskom workers. It seemed strangely deserted. Manqina got out of the car to stretch when suddenly we saw two large casspirs (armoured vehicles) parked on the far side of the store – and a group of well-armed soldiers leaning against them.

Manqina was wearing an NUM T-shirt; not helpful under these circumstances. He is a large man, but he moved like lightning – getting back into the car and sliding down below the dashboard before I had even managed to get the car into reverse. By now the soldiers were looking in our direction. I waved and smiled and, although a white woman alone in a car must have been a little unusual in that part of the world, we were already back on the road before anyone thought of stopping us.

We were still in mild shock when, a few kilometres on, we saw Jabu walking along the side of the road with his brother. We stopped. He was incredulous.

'What are you doing here?' he said. 'I left a message at NUM Head Office that you must not come – that your lives would be in danger if you did!'

In those days, a group of receptionists managed NUM's incoming calls, with messages written down on a small form and then jabbed onto a sharp metal spike, where vast swathes would accumulate each day. No doubt this particular one was languishing there, with no-one thinking to escalate it to our attention. Jabu insisted we accompany him to his homestead before our return, where he presented me with a live chicken as a gift.

Some time later, when the local situation seemed calmer, I returned, accompanied this time by NUM staff member Peter Mthembu. At an initial meeting under a designated tree, workers told us that the local chief was willing to allocate them a piece of land and a meeting had been arranged with him for that very day, so that I could confirm their eligibility for funding from the Eskom Development Fund.

On our way to the tribal authority offices, in an area deep within Inkatha territory, they added an afterthought to the earlier briefing: if the chief were to find out that we were from NUM, then all of our lives would be in danger. They had therefore told him that I represented Eskom *management* and could I please pretend this was the case. All things considered, this was quite as plausible – on the face of it – as that I represented NUM. Oh – and could we please not use the word 'comrade', because it was a dead give-away.

We arrived at the offices of the traditional authority, high on a hill with views forever. We waited with about twenty elders in a small meeting room, on low wooden benches. When the chief and his senior advisor arrived, everyone fell to their knees on the floor. The chief was young, handsome and impeccably dressed in a designer silk suit.

I did not actually present myself as Eskom management, but as a representative of the Fund – which I was. Nevertheless, the assumption was clear.

In the course of the meeting, Mthembu translated for me. He was a soft-spoken man nearing retirement age and had recently returned from exile. He had been addressing people as 'comrade' for a very long time. So every time he started to translate, habit kicked in. 'Co... Co... Co......' he would start. All the workers' eyes were fixed on him in horror. 'Colleagues...' he continued. The relief in the room was palpable. And then again: 'Com...... com...... com...'

'Compatriots!'

When I finished my input – kept as brief as possible, obviously – the meeting was opened to questions from the floor. Hands shot up from amongst the elders. It turned out most of them had also worked for Eskom and had a string of grievances related to their Provident Fund monies and other issues, which they now expected me to resolve – in my new-found capacity as Eskom management.

'You really should join a trade union' is what I did not say.

10 Small Enterprise
IN THE SHADOW OF THE CORE ECONOMY

From the late 1990s, the policy discourse started to place increasing store on the scope for small enterprise to provide a solution to South Africa's stubbornly high levels of unemployment. In particular, there was an assumption that – enabled by access to micro-loans at commercial interest rates and a bit of grit and determination – the poor would be able to self-employ their way out of poverty. The attraction of this solution was clear: poverty could be solved through the market-driven efforts of the poor themselves, while leaving the core economy and its patterns of accumulation untouched, with no wider change in economic structures or patterns of distribution required. The banks could even profit from it.

Yet against the backdrop of this growing hubris, the Mineworkers Development Agency (MDA) was confronted in practice with the limits of such an approach. Despite the alacrity with which poor and unemployed people were using the services of the MDA centres and initiating enterprise activity, returns were, for the most part, low. Time and again, the explanation given to MDA by entrepreneurs was that there was 'no market' for their products. Closer inspection, however, found that all too often, there was no lack of such markets: they were just already taken.

The strategy of supporting local production for local consumption embraced by MDA's centres overlooked a crucial reality: that, distant as the commanding heights of the South African economy might appear from the vantage of its most remote and poorly developed rural margins, 'the local' was inextricably tied to the national and even global economy. In fact, we had made the same mistake that President Thabo Mbeki was to make some years later, during an address to the National Council of Provinces, in his description of South Africa as having 'two economies':

> The second economy (or the marginalised economy) is characterised by underdevelopment, contributes little to GDP, contains a large percentage of our population, incorporates the poorest of our rural and urban poor, is structurally disconnected from both the first and the global economy, and is incapable of self-generated growth and development. (Mbeki 2003)

Certainly, apartheid's migrant-labour policies and the bantustan policies that followed left stark legacies of economic marginalisation, reflected in the extreme spatial inequality that still today provides a proxy map for where the bantustans used to be, in relation to any poverty indicator one cares to choose. Far from representing a 'structural disconnection', however, these highly unequal outcomes reflect a history of dispossession, extraction and exploitation, with outcomes at each end of the spectrum linked together in highly interdependent ways and with the structure of South Africa's core economy casting a long shadow over economic initiatives on the margins in ways we did not fully anticipate.

A key feature of this economic structure is its level of concentration. At the point of transition in South Africa, just five groups controlled 84 per cent of all shares on the Johannesburg Stock Exchange (JSE): with Anglo American alone owning 43 per cent of the total (Rumney 2005, p. 402). Within this concentrated structure, characterised as white monopoly capital, ownership was a spaghetti bowl of crossholdings.

These levels of concentration were in part a result of the combined effects of sanctions coupled with the tight foreign exchange controls imposed by the apartheid government. These meant that South Africa's highly profitable mining and other industries were unable to seek out expansion opportunities across the globe; instead, they had to find investment opportunities – and markets – within the national economy, diversifying up and down value chains in every imaginable market segment, from beer to banks. As markets within the white population became saturated, the far-larger markets of black consumers became an obvious target.

The net effect was that, by the time apartheid ended, the vast majority of manufactured or agro-processed items in the consumption basket of poor people were mass-produced in the core economy and distributed efficiently to even the most remote areas. They still are. To a South African audience, the following products – and their associated brand names – are familiar examples of this penetration:

> Maize meal (Iwisa, Ace, White Star), bread (Albany, SASKO, Blue Ribbon), sugar (Illovo, Tongaat-Hulett), milk and dairy products (Clover, Dairy Belle), sunflower oil (Nola, Epic), flour (SASKO, Premier Milling), tea (Joko, Glen, Five Roses), coffee (Ricoffy, Frisco), peanut butter (Yum-Yum, Black Cat), margarine (Flora, Rama), beer (South African Breweries – SAB), fruit juices (Ceres, Liquifruit, Oros), canned goods (Koo, Gold Crest, All Gold), rice (Tastic).

Small producers not only had to compete on price in the face of the vast economies of scale enjoyed by these giants; they had to compete against brand loyalties and advertising, in a context in which aspirations for a better life ran high and branded goods were seen to signify exactly that. Even the most rural *spaza* shops started to have branded advertising: such as for Coke, Rama margarine, Iwisa maizemeal and Omo washing powder. For poor consumers, branded goods also offer consistency and quality assurance.

To compound the competitive challenges, many of the conglomerates (and large state-owned companies also) were involved not only in the production of end products; they were also the suppliers of raw material inputs required by their competitors.

So, at the time, before the mass rollout of electricity after 1994, candles were used for lighting in many rural homes. The local production of these was a popular small enterprise. The main supplier of bulk wax for candle production was Sasol, as a by-product of its production of petroleum from coal. As it happened, Sasolchem – a division of Sasol – owned Price Candles, South Africa's largest household candle manufacturer. Try as they might, small-scale candle producers were rarely able to produce household candles at a more competitive price – even taking into account the costs of distance involved in distribution of such candles into remote rural areas.

Wire products confronted a similar challenge, with steel mills providing the raw wire required for barbed wire and mesh fencing also producing these as finished products, leading to allegations from even medium-sized producers that the raw wire was priced to keep them uncompetitive (Staff reporter, *Mail and Guardian* 2011).

Another favourite was the production of school uniforms by sewing groups. At the time, the main supplier of the standard fabric for the ubiquitous black tunics worn by school-girls across the country was also involved in producing these same uniforms, leading to similar concerns. Certainly, sewing groups producing school uniforms failed with regularity. For other clothing, cheap mass-market stores were increasingly present in small rural towns.

Surely locally baked bread offered a business opportunity? In 2002, MDA counted over 800 mini-bakeries in the former Transkei that thought so too. Yet while these mini-bakeries had to buy in their flour, their competitors were part of vertically integrated supply chains that had an interest in maintaining the competitiveness of their large-scale bakeries. Would such supply chains really price the flour to keep small producers out of the market? Years later, the Competition Commission found they had been doing exactly that over at least an eight-year period (Ledger 2016, p. 71).

Yet surely, in rural areas, some advantages must exist for small-scale agro-processing opportunities? Not necessarily so. Agro-processing initiatives rely on some level of surplus production by local farmers, but there was little of this in former bantustan areas. Instead, the trend then was – and still is now – one of de-agrarianisation, with a high level of reliance on the cash economy for food. So, in the Mount Frere district in the Eastern Cape,

> for a vast majority of households that are involved in agriculture, food production plays only a supplementary role: 87% of households report that they are dependent on store-bought maize meal all year round, while only 5% report that they can produce enough maize for own consumption for three months in the year or more. (Du Toit 2009)

Even where households were engaged in agricultural activity, this did not translate into the production of surpluses, limiting the scope for this classic trajectory into value addition and upstream markets. In the absence of such surpluses there was also an absence of incentives to develop the kinds of co-ordination mechanisms that enable small-scale producers to achieve any real economies of scale.

By contrast, this trajectory into agro-processing was well established in white commercial farming areas, where decades of subsidies and support to large-scale (whites-only) agricultural co-ops provided effective co-ordination and support to farmers in relation to input supplies, storage and off-take agreements, with vertical integration into value chains.

Within former bantustan areas, any trajectory into agro-processing required support to the development of viable agriculture. Yet policy decisions in the immediate post-apartheid period did not help in this regard. So, for example, quite inexplicably, South Africa opted to remove tariff protections for agriculture on a scale that far exceeded the requirements of the World Trade Organization at the time, making South Africa the second-least-protected agriculture sector in the world, and significantly raising the bar for new entrants; a case of kicking away the ladder for black farmers, whether in the former bantustans or in previously white commercial farming areas (Ledger 2016, p. 12). Nor have co-ordination failures in former bantustan areas been overcome in the post-apartheid period. Despite certain exceptions, there has been a litany of failed state-led development programmes as a result of tractor services not delivered in time, of credit provision arriving too late for the planting season, of crops rotting because of a lack of storage, and more.

Meanwhile, in commercial agriculture, concentration has continued to intensify, with competitive pressures on farmers leading to increases in farm sizes. So, between 1998 and 2014, more than five thousand dairy farmers went out of business, resulting in an estimated loss of fifty thousand jobs:

> The majority of these have been smaller farmers. Dairy herd size has increased steadily over the last 20 years, and the milk market is now dominated by herds of more than 300 cows. This market structure has created a very effective barrier to market entry for small producers, and thus job creation in rural areas. (Ledger 2016, p. 69)

Concentration and vertical integration in the core economy had direct impacts on the scope for small-scale manufacturing and agro-processing in the economically marginal migrant-labour-sending areas where MDA's centres were located. Might opportunities exist, however, in relation to services? Certainly, the taxi industry was growing exponentially – often bridging the distances created by spatial inequality and ferrying passengers between the economic centres and the margins. Could such spatial inequality even provide some advantages for the services sector?

If consumers need a tyre repaired, or their hair cut, or their child cared for, they need those services where they are: the fact that such services are available more cheaply in a larger town is not necessarily of any assistance.

Although opportunities in the services sector were evident, the small scale of manufacturing activity in marginal areas had knock-on impacts. An important part of the services sector involves business services. To be viable, these require a certain minimum level of demand within a given local economy, with local manufacturing providing part of the market for such services. In the absence of the kind of critical mass required to support business services, this sector ends up largely reliant on personal services. At the same time, in a vicious cycle, limits on the dynamism of the business services sector can place a further constraint on the scope for other forms of local business development.

It was in this overall context that retail activities ended up being the dominant form of self-employment in South Africa – largely distributing branded goods from the core economy to the margins, through street trading, *spaza* shops and shebeens. These are rarely a channel for the distribution of goods produced by small or informal enterprises, instead extending the penetration of distribution systems for branded goods – and, increasingly, for cheap imported goods such as those from China.

However, even these small-scale and/or informal distribution channels have faced increasing levels of competitive pressure as the formal retail sector targets new markets, with South Africa's large supermarket chains playing an ambiguous role, for example in Mount Frere in the Eastern Cape:

> The ability of these supermarkets to provide access to relatively low-priced staples has complex local effects. On one level, this does enable those who have some access to cash to stretch their resources. On another level, their arrival has had profound impacts on the local productive economy. For one thing, the availability of cheap staples reduces the incentives for local agricultural production – not only because own maize is no longer significantly cheaper than store-bought maize, but also because access to store-bought maize does not impose the risks imposed on own production by the vagaries of the local climate and the risk of theft. Secondly, the coming of supermarkets has eviscerated the local trading stores that, before retail deregulation, formed the hubs of the local credit economy. Thirdly, local supermarkets compete with small entrepreneurs, squeezing them out of the service economy, while their supply chains bypass local producers. (Du Toit and Neves 2007a)

Despite the massive structural and competitive hurdles that new entrepreneurs faced, the picture was not all bleak. There were always some success stories and niches and opportunities overlooked by others: such as the bakery in Lusikisiki whose business model relied on selling fresh, hot bread at taxi ranks before the Albany trucks arrived from Umtata each day. Nor has the position remained static in the period since. The point is not that there were – or are – no opportunities at all, but that the nature of such opportunities was highly affected by concentration in the core economy and its competitive impacts in even the most remote contexts. It was a more uphill battle than anticipated, with any glib expectations that self-employment or enterprise development would offer an easy or scalable alternative to unemployment proving deeply flawed.

For MDA's centres to provide effective local support, an in-depth understanding of this competitive context was required, along with a recognition of the shadow that the core economy cast over even the most remote local economies. Yet this issue was (and largely remains) absent from the discourse. Instead, explanations for the disappointing outcomes from micro and small enterprise development strategies tended to focus instead on the characteristics of the entrepreneurs – their lack of entrepreneurship or skills – and on issues such as access to credit or regulatory obstacles (for example, see the Global Entrepreneurship Monitor's annual country reports at www.gemconsortium.org).

For MDA, however, grappling with the challenge of local economic development in this context meant understanding what these over-arching factors meant, looking for loopholes, exploring issues of co-ordination and the scope to create economies of scale, as well as looking at how local entrepreneurs might insert themselves within wider value chains. It certainly also meant reconsidering 'local production for local consumption' as the mainstay of local economic development.

At one level, in terms of local markets, this involved a sectoral shift, recognising the limits of small-scale manufacturing and exploring opportunities in relation to services and retail.

It also meant looking beyond local markets, because, for all the advantages these offer in terms of proximity and familiarity, local markets were comprised mainly of poor consumers for whom price and brand familiarity were often determinant – with local enterprises at the greatest disadvantage in meeting these specific characteristics. Yet, in a context of high inequality such as in South Africa, not all consumers are poor. What opportunities might exist in markets beyond the local context? What scope existed to target consumers with more disposable income? On what terms might producers on the margins enter such markets – and to what extent might such access draw new resources back into their local economies? Taken to scale, to what extent might tapping into wealthy urban markets even have potentially redistributive outcomes?

MDA's next stage of strategy was designed to explore these questions. So focused were we, however, on analysing and understanding our own strategic context that we overlooked the extent to which our work fell within the wider ambit of small enterprise development strategy internationally and, in that wider context, a paradigm shift was taking place that we could not ignore for long: even though we most certainly would have preferred to do so at the time.

11 A New Enterprise Development Paradigm

Internationally, by the turn of the millennium, a paradigm shift was taking place within the small enterprise support sector that crystallised into what became known as the market development approach to business development services (BDS) – later absorbed into a wider approach characterised as 'making markets work for the poor'. The paradigm was certainly a game-changer – which we could not ignore, because, despite some internal contestation, the UK Department for International Development (DFID) had become a leading proponent of the approach. As MDA was at the time receiving significant support from DFID for strategic services and for the Lesotho programme, we found ourselves directly in the line of fire in relation to these seismic shifts in donor strategy.

This chapter will explain this paradigm shift, in the terms that we were confronted with at the time. While the approach had deep flaws, the irony is that it opened our eyes to dynamics we had not analysed before and to insights we would not have had without the challenge function it performed. It certainly shifted the terrain of debate in the sector and there is no way now to close Pandora's box: the small enterprise development sector will certainly never be the same. In some respects it is better for it: although not necessarily in the ways anticipated. Yet it remains hard to measure at what price.

In essence, until this time, donors were willing to support NGOs involved in small enterprise development to offer a range of services that supported the development of small enterprises. The most common focus of donor support was on training, but support also went, for example, to product development and to upgrading small enterprise competencies to enable their participation in value chains, in a context in which value-chain analysis was also on the rise. While donor support to such services was common, donors also strongly encouraged NGOs to develop strategies for cost recovery from the delivery of such services, to contribute to their organisational sustainability in anticipation that one day donor funding would come to an end. In this context, sustainability was mainly defined as the ability to become financially self-sufficient in some way. In fact, donor funding was often contingent on a plausible exit strategy for the donor being built into the model.

By contrast, the BDS market development approach was strongly opposed to any donor subsidies to the delivery of business services and to development agencies playing any role in the direct delivery of such services. While the importance of a diverse range of business services was central to the approach, the argument was that donor support to the direct delivery of such services distorted the market for them in ways that crowded out private provision, thereby limiting the sustainable development of markets for such services. The focus of strategy should be on the development of such markets – not on the direct delivery of the services. Services – including training – should be delivered by private-sector players only.

By offering subsidised services and/or charging fees for such services, agencies became market players, it was argued: crowding out the emergence of private suppliers and limiting the scope for the development of a sustainable market for such services. If there was any role for development agencies at all, it was to facilitate the development of such private markets – and funding for such facilitation was acceptable, but funding for service delivery was not. Service delivery was out: facilitation was the new game in town.

This dramatic turnaround in the logic applied to the sector left many development agencies breathless and confused. What *were* we supposed to do? Did we have any role at all? Not necessarily, it soon became apparent. Private-sector development needed private-sector players, it was argued, and too often, NGOs simply muddied the waters, leaving only distorted markets in their wake.

For MDA, this logic cast the entire development centre model into question. The centres were based on a hybrid model in which their set-up costs were covered by donor funding, but in which, over time, successful local enterprise development was expected to lead to growing economies of scale, allowing them to cover their core operating costs. In MDA's view, grant funding in the early stages was justified in order to enable the centres to address various forms of market failure; as these were overcome, the centres would transition to a cost-recovery model.

Within this approach, MDA made a distinction between what were called economic services and strategic services. The former were seen as services that were expected to become fully self-sufficient over time.

By contrast, strategic services, such as training, assistance to product development and market facilitation were not ever expected to be self-funding on the basis of cost recovery from client users. The expectation was that some form of funding support was necessary. Full cost recovery was not expected to come from fees paid by small enterprises.

For the BDS approach, this distinction between economic services and strategic services was immaterial: MDA's involvement in both was wrong and could no longer be supported. The impacts of this on MDA will be explored in the next chapter. First, however, a little more justice needs to be done to the arguments underpinning what was, to MDA at the time, still largely incomprehensible.

The base document for the BDS market development approach was prepared by the Committee of Donor Agencies for Small Enterprise Development of the World Bank and is entitled 'Business Development Services for Small Enterprises: Guiding Principles for Donor Intervention, 2001 Edition' – rather appropriately referred to as the 'Blue Book' (hereafter the Donor Guidelines). It was the recognised foundation document for the BDS market development approach.

The membership of the Committee of Donor Agencies is a who's who of international donor agencies. According to the Committee, the search for a new paradigm in the small enterprise development sector was motivated by frustration by both donors and many practitioners at the lack of outreach, impact and sustainability of small enterprise support programmes at the time. 'Motivating the search for a "new paradigm" for BDS was the shared recognition that traditional interventions have failed to provide quality, affordable BDS to a large proportion of the target population of small enterprises' (Committee of Donor Agencies 2001, p. v).

This was coupled with a desire to emulate the successes believed to have been achieved in the financial services sector, which had seen a paradigm shift of its own.

Lessons from the microcredit revolution

In the 1990s, building on the experience of the Grameen Bank in Bangladesh, and experience elsewhere, the view developed that it was not the cost of finance that was the critical constraint in access to finance for the poor. Instead, it was argued, ample evidence existed that the poor were willing and able to pay exorbitant fees to informal money-lenders in order to access finance; yet they continued to be excluded from more affordable market-based forms of access. By subsidising interest rates for the poor, the development sector had therefore distorted the market for micro-finance in ways that meant the private sector could not compete, which was why they were not servicing this sector. Subsidies for a few were preventing the sustainable expansion of access, because the outreach of subsidised programmes would always be limited by the budgets available for such subsidies, leaving most poor people at the mercy of informal money-lenders. Hence the aim should be to facilitate broadened access to finance through market-based mechanisms, which would expand access to finance on a sustainable basis that did not rely on donors, and was also expected to make such finance more affordable than the rates being paid to the money-lenders. Everyone could be a winner, it seemed.

In this context, subsidised interest rates in micro-finance programmes targeted at the poor largely ended in the early 1990s. While subsidies for product development, capacity building and pre- and post-transaction costs still justified funding, interest rate subsidies did not. As a consequence, interest rates soared in programmes targeting the poor.

At the time, there was a widespread consensus that this shift had precipitated new dynamism and created expanded access to financial services. Critiques of this micro-finance revolution were still muted or non-existent. Milford Bateman characterises the enthusiasm of the time:

> Thirty years ago, the international development community was abuzz with excitement. The reason was that the almost perfect solution to poverty, unemployment, inequality and low growth in developing countries appeared to have been finally located. This solution was *microcredit* ... A widespread assumption quickly emerged suggesting that the microcredit model would, among other things, generate significant local employment opportunities, raise average incomes, empower women, reduce inequality and so, overall, create the basic foundation for sustainable 'bottom-up' local economic and social development. Not surprisingly, given such assumed benefits, microcredit was quickly and very centrally incorporated into the international development community's array of local development policies and programs, ultimately becoming the most important international development policy of all. (Bateman 2014, p. 92)

In a searing article that reviews the outcomes and impacts of micro-credit in South Africa, Bateman finds instead a poisoned chalice, concluding as follows:

> This article has argued that the microcredit model has played a calamitous role in the hoped for local economic and social development progress of post-apartheid South Africa. In particular, South Africa's scarce financial resources have been increasingly intermediated into consumption spending and, where 'invested' at all, into no-growth ultra-low productivity informal microenterprises and self-employment ventures. As in many other locations where such a financial intermediation structure has emerged, the end result in South Africa has been the deindustrialisation, informalisation, disconnectedness and primitivisation of the average local community and so a poverty trap has effectively been created thanks to microcredit. (Bateman 2014, p. 134)

Internationally, the impacts of microcredit have also come under increasing question. The January 2015 edition of the *American Economic Journal: Applied Economics* provides a comprehensive review of the evidence and in randomised control trials of six programmes it finds that, although micro-finance programmes contributed to increased business activity, this did not translate into increased incomes in any programme and, in two, contributed to reductions in consumption. This is of course the benefit of hindsight; it is relevant, however, because of the extent to which the micro-finance revolution was used as the template for what was proposed for the small enterprise development sector.

In the same way that the withdrawal of subsidies from credit markets was expected to result in the private sector moving into these markets, with products that were more expensive than subsidised ones but less expensive than the rates charged by informal money-lenders, the assumption was that if subsidies for business services were withdrawn, this would open the way for the delivery of services by private-sector providers, with small enterprises willing and able to pay for them.

So, the role of development intervention in the sector would shift from an ongoing and permanent role in service delivery to a focus on the development of markets for business services. As a consequence of such markets, access to business services would reach far beyond the few small and medium-size enterprises (SMEs) able to access subsidies, and the market-based nature of such service delivery would mean the services were sustainable – creating a systemic change in the environment in which SMEs operated.

For the debate to follow, two issues need to be flagged. Firstly, despite the different paradigm from which the insight came, the notion that the role of development intervention should not be trapped forever at the level of ongoing service delivery did resonate; and secondly, although the concept of systemic change used by the BDS trumpeteers was a really narrow one, it nevertheless placed it on the development agenda in the small enterprise sector – available for appropriation within a wider view of political economy, in a context in which the concept of systemic change had until then been notably absent within the small enterprise development discourse. Once opened, however, Pandora's box can be rather hard to close. With the idea that the role of development intervention is to create systemic change, the market development approach started to become interesting and to raise important new questions – but that is to jump ahead. At this early stage in the development of the paradigm, the focus was on creating markets for business services – and on little else.

Within the BDS market development approach, subsidies to service delivery came in for particular attack. The scourge of subsidies not only creates dependency, it was argued; subsidies have also distorted service markets in ways that have undermined the development of market forces:

> In many countries the net effect of years of government and donor-supported interventions has been to undermine the development of market forces. Products delivered at low cost or free to SMEs induce a debilitating dependency and a cynicism over quality and value; providers offered easy and generous terms by donors develop a taste for these inflated fees which often bear little relation to real economy situations; they become motivated to pursue donors rather than, for example, private sector customers or sponsorship.

Agencies have budgets that, above all, need to be spent – a predilection that may lead neither to considered actions nor to 'treading softly'. The result has been hugely distorted and largely dysfunctional markets, especially in low-income countries where institutions (including markets) are often more fragile and less able to resist the compelling pressures of hard donor money. Private sector BDS providers are inexorably 'crowded out'. (Gibson 1999, quoted in Hitchins et al. 2004)

Strong language was reserved for subsidies to small enterprise development, which were guilty of distorting markets and suppressing, crowding out and smothering the private sector:

Long term donor subsidies to the demand or supply of BDS are likely to distort BDS markets and crowd out the commercial provision of services, thus undermining the objectives of impact, outreach, cost effectiveness and sustainability that are the pillars of the BDS market development paradigm. (Committee of Donor Agencies 2001, p. 6)

Large government and donor programs have often suppressed private BDS markets or crowded out private suppliers ... If markets are to develop and serve low-income clients with the services they desire, they must not be smothered. (Miehlbradt and McVay 2002, p. 25)

[T]he provision of free or highly subsidised services may contribute to market failures and inhibit the availability of services to [small enterprises]. While these highly subsidised services may benefit the few who have access to them, in the long run, they may hinder economic growth, employment generation and poverty alleviation (Miehlbradt and McVay 2002, p. 30).

Instead, the Donor Guidelines presented the following alternative:

The ultimate vision for BDS ... is of a well functioning market with a diverse array of high-quality services that meet the needs of a large proportion of SEs [small enterprises] affordably. Thus, these Guiding Principles are based on a private-sector led, market economy framework which reflects:

- A fundamental belief in the principles of a market economy, where the State has a role in providing an enabling environment, in correcting or compensating for market failures and in the provision of public goods, but not in the direct provision of private goods that can be more efficiently provided by the market;
- The assumption that the majority of BDS are private goods and are thus similar in nature to any other service, so market rules apply;
- The expectation that, with appropriate product design, delivery and payment mechanisms, BDS can be provided on a commercial basis even for the lowest-income segment of the entrepreneurial SE sector.
(Committee of Donor Agencies 2001, p. 1)

These assumptions form the backbone of the approach; they also illustrate the essential flaws that bedevil its application in practice.

Flaws in the assumptions of the approach

At an overall level, a key weakness in the approach was, ironically, its weak understanding of markets in marginal areas, as later partly conceded in Hitchins et al. 2004. Commercial markets for business services can only arise as a consequence of a minimum level of enterprise activity in a local economy, in which sufficient demand for business services exists to sustain commercial supply. A market with a diverse array of business services requires a diverse array of businesses to service, and a feature of weak markets and marginal contexts is that the necessary economies of scale on the demand side are often absent.

This raises the question: how do you build a growing, vibrant, diverse, sustainable SE sector in marginal economic contexts in which the level of demand and/or the ability to afford key business development services cannot yet sustain the commercial delivery of such services? This was exactly the challenge that confronted MDA.

Yet the Donor Guidelines were confident that all forms of BDS 'can be provided on a commercial basis even for the lowest-income segment of the entrepreneurial SE sector' and that once 'distortionary' subsidies are removed, the private sector will fill the service gap – crowding in where, previously, they had been crowded out. By 2004, however, the BDS Update produced by the International Training Centre of the International Labour Organisation in Turin as part of its annual course on BDS noted as follows:

> A critical supply-side challenge is engaging providers in the programme and convincing them to serve SEs. Most implementers report difficulty in persuading private businesses that targeting SEs or improving services to SEs is a profitable business opportunity. (Miehlbradt and McVay 2004, p. 52)

The smaller and more marginal the enterprises, the less attractive they were as a target market, with a reliance on market-driven BDS leading to upward targeting by service providers, who had a tendency to gravitate away from the bottom end of the market for predictable market-driven reasons. In addition, in more marginal economic areas, the level of demand required to underpin the viability of such services often did not exist. What a surprise.

This would not have mattered as much if SE development was not simultaneously being promoted as a direct strategy for poverty reduction, which meant success was measured primarily by the progress made in the poorest and most marginal contexts: where market-driven processes faced the greatest obstacles.

The next key assumption in the Donor Guidelines was that the majority of business services are private goods and so market rules should apply. Actually, there had never been any dispute that most business services are private goods, nor any great tendency for donors to subsidise these or for development agencies to try to deliver them.

There was, however, a debate over whether *some* services had impacts that contributed to wider policy goals and hence to the public good in ways that might create a development rationale for incentivising their delivery in some way: with training and skills development being the most obvious in this regard. This debate took place through a proxy debate over whether there was any value in distinguishing between operational and strategic services. The Donor Guidelines conceded a distinction in order to refute it:

> A distinction is sometimes made between 'operational' and 'strategic' business services. Operational services are those needed for day-to-day operations, such as information and communications, management of accounts and tax records and compliance with labor laws and other regulations. Strategic services, on the other hand, are used by the enterprise to address medium- and long-term issues in order to improve the performance of the enterprise, its access to markets and its ability to compete. For example, strategic services can help the enterprise to identify and service markets, design products, set up facilities and seek financing.
>
> The market for operational services may already exist, since there is often articulated demand and willingness to pay for these services. In contrast, markets for strategic services for SEs have largely failed to develop and they are the focus of most donor interventions in BDS. (Committee of Donor Agencies 2001, p. 1)

This is an excellent definition of the distinction between the two. It seemed to lead logically to an argument that, while there is little rationale for subsidies to operational services, there may be a case in relation to strategic services, because these target the more medium-term and non-core aims of innovation, enhanced productivity, expansion, opening new markets or skills development, all of which contribute to wider economic policy aims. The strategic imperative of supporting these outcomes in the economy as a whole means that, even at the developed end of the private sector, such strategic services are often incentivised. The rationale for doing so is that the potential outcomes benefit not only a given enterprise, but contribute also to growth, job creation and/or human capital formation. This is the rationale for support inter alia to cluster organisations, to research and development, to export promotion, and to innovation systems.

In marginal markets, the issues in this regard are further complicated by threshold effects. So, operational services are largely recurrent costs, which means they require a more limited universe of users to be viable. Each new customer adds to the turnover base of providers and can be relied upon for repeat purchases on a consistent cycle. In addition, many operational services are generic and can service a diverse range of types of enterprise: for example, motor vehicle maintenance, freight or accountancy services. Once a given threshold of demand is reached, such services can be offered on a viable basis. There is an access frontier for business services that can be reached and breached, after which delivery of such services is a viable commercial prospect in a given local economy.

Strategic services, by contrast, are usually not recurrent; any one business may use a particular strategic service only once and such a strategic service is less likely to be generic. It therefore requires a far larger market in which a degree of specialisation has taken place for strategic services to be viable on purely commercial terms. This recognition is part of the rationale for cluster development. Without a critical mass of demand in a given area, however, such services will not be locally viable; yet bringing them in to remote areas from elsewhere is likely to be at a prohibitive cost, making such services unaffordable, reinforcing the competitive disadvantages constraining development in such areas and the likelihood of unequal development outcomes.

That distinction was not accepted at the time, however. Bear et al. 2003 argued that no distinction between operational and strategic services was relevant to the debate, while Hitchins et al. 2004 questioned whether strategic services are really necessary in weak markets at all:

> Development agencies have typically focused on services they perceive as sophisticated, strategic or developmental (hence the term business development services!). In weak economic situations – where commercial tasks are perhaps less complex and the operating environment presents more challenges – the presence or absence of often quite a basic range of services make a big difference to doing business. For example, pest control, email or mobile phone service points, equipment leasing or the maintenance of water or irrigation systems. Such practical and accessible services are often far more relevant and desirable to business on the margins than, for example, comprehensive extension, entrepreneurship or business management services. (Hitchins et al. 2004, p. 29)

Of course 'practical and accessible' services are a starting point in these areas. That is why such services were prioritised by development centres and defined as economic services that were expected to breach demand thresholds to run on a commercial basis. But, giving examples of strategic services intended to seem irrelevant in order to show that they have no role in weak markets is just disingenuous. In practice, as later chapters will demonstrate, the provision of strategic services can be vital in catalysing new opportunities that assist enterprise in marginal markets to break out of low-value poverty traps. Where such services remain beyond the access frontier for marginal enterprises, effective ways to bridge this gap remain a legitimate target for development intervention.

The next critical element in the assumptions was that the 'lowest-income segment' would be both willing and able to pay for the services they need – including strategic services. In this regard, a distinction was made between affordability and willingness to pay. Affordability was not considered a binding constraint for the poor (nor a legitimate concern of development strategy). Instead, willingness to pay was deemed to be the critical factor and the constraint to be overcome. Concern with affordability was routinely dismissed as the self-serving concern of donor-dependent NGOs wanting a continuation of subsidies to their organisations. In a paper on BDS, the issue of affordability – or capacity to pay – is addressed only once in a footnote:

> Capacity to pay is not tracked separately. Willingness to pay is a better proxy for motivation than capacity. Willingness is a precondition for a successful market transaction. Low capacity to pay is something that can be fixed – e.g. through credit or different payment terms. (Footnote in Field et al. 2000, p. 4)

Little credence was given to the notion that for many enterprises, there really might be affordability constraints for the kinds of strategic services that might unlock growth, especially where the threshold for the viable delivery of such services did not exist in a given local economy.

For the BDS market development approach, however, it seemed that all that stood between SEs and a wide and sustainable range of business development services was their own bad attitude.

New roles for development actors

In the context of this approach, new roles were also defined for development actors:

> Traditionally, donors and governments have intervened in BDS markets at the level of the BDS transaction: directly providing services to SEs via public BDS providers, or permanently subsidising services delivered by other BDS providers. In the old approach, donors and governments have tended to substitute for underdeveloped BDS markets, possibly crowding out existing or potential commercial providers of services. (Miehlbradt and McVay 2002)

Government's role was to exit from direct service provision, and rather to focus on building market-enhancing institutions that reduce information asymmetries, reduce transaction costs and enhance competition in markets, as advocated in the World Bank's World Development Report 2002. In this regard, the BDS market development approach drew from North's work on institutions (e.g. North 1990a, 1991) and from New Institutional Economics – but on terms that tended to equate any direct state role in enterprise support with market distortion, evoking the alternative of free and unfettered markets, as if these lay within some kind of easy reach, with history just an innocent bystander on a level playing field.

Instead of direct service delivery, the role of development agencies was to act as facilitators or catalysts for the development of markets for business services and, while subsidised services to entrepreneurs were not acceptable, subsidies to stimulate or develop the market for such services could be:

> Subsidies may be justified in the short term as an investment in the development of BDS markets (e.g. through development of new products and models). However, even temporary subsidies can create distortions and are justified only if their market development impacts outweigh their distortionary effects. Therefore, donors must exercise care in the application and duration of subsidies. (Committee of Donor Agencies 2001, p. 6)

The role of market facilitation could be funded, as long as such facilitation was not an ongoing function in a given market and was time-bound, targeted at systemic change in markets, and had clear exit strategies. Organisations should not, however, function as both service providers and facilitators, and would have to choose whether they were in the market, or were facilitating the development of the market. They could not do both.

In this process of redefining these development roles, the emphasis donors had placed on the need for development agencies to cover at least some of their costs through the delivery of services was removed – as was any donor concern with the organisational sustainability of such agencies.

Instead, sustainability was to be measured by the extent to which the facilitation role was able to catalyse systemic change in business services market, leading to expanded demand and supply of such services on market terms, with this the new measure of sustainability. What this left unstated, however, was the question of organisational sustainability, of how to build effective organisations with the high-level skills this new facilitation role required. For the advocates of the approach, this concern with organisational sustainability was seen as simply parochial and self-serving.

Development agencies were therefore confronted with a clear choice: between playing a fully funded facilitation role, which in practice implied complete donor dependence in a fickle donor environment, or converting to operating as a purely commercial provider and kissing the donors goodbye: a tempting option, indeed.

Markets, power and inequality

> For some critics, the notion that (amoral) markets can serve (moral) developmental objectives is anathema – even if they are the basis of market economies – therefore 'debate' here is about more than BDS market development alone. (Bear et al. 2003, p. 21)

The debate was certainly about more than BDS markets alone; but the morality or otherwise of markets was really not the point. Instead, the problem was the absence of any recognition of the role of power, politics and history in shaping the rules of the game and framing whose interests they serve.

The market development approach placed a lot of emphasis on the need to remove distortions in order for markets to work for the poor. But the limited framework within which distortions were defined assumed a blank slate and a level playing field; it assumed that unfettered markets were feasible – and that they would have some kind of innate tendency to work for the poor. The approach seemed simply blind to the weight of history involved: to feudalism, colonialism, conquest, land appropriation, slavery, patriarchy and patronage, for a start. These 'distortions', further shaped by contestation of many kinds and with varying outcomes, live on in the social relations of the present. In this context, where does market distortion start and end? And how can these distortions be addressed without engaging the social and political dimensions underpinning them?

As argued in Philip 2003, power relations past and present influence the patterns of demand, supply and the terms of exchange: not only on the macro, global level, but in any given village – or household – too. Yet there was scant evidence of reflection on these issues in the discourse. Instead, the BDS market paradigm seemed to promote an uncritical genuflection towards a notion of markets that was devoid of social context and content, as if markets operate in a privileged domain outside of social forces and relations, and are innocent of any but beneficial social impacts.

In addition, insofar as the approach remained narrowly focused on the internal functioning of particular markets and on tinkering with distortions internal to the workings of such markets without engaging these wider issues, then it was at serious risk of re-enforcing inequalities and empowering elites – with adverse consequences for the poor.

In South Africa, the ways in which social relations and the history of political power have informed the structure of markets is glaring, as are the ways those market structures continue to play a role in shaping the reproduction of poverty and inequality – despite the opportunities for wealth creation and growth they may simultaneously hold. In South Africa, North's notion of 'path dependency' (1990a, pp. 98–9, 103–4) is writ large in the way in which patterns of wealth, ownership and poverty are being reproduced despite the best (and second best) efforts of policy. Markets cannot be made to work for the poor without confronting wider distributional issues, or the nature of the endowments with which players enter the game.

12 Market Development – or a New 'Anti-Politics Machine'?

The market development approach to business development services discussed in the previous chapter turned the existing small enterprise (SE) development paradigm on its head. Within the Mineworkers Development Agency (MDA), we railed against it. It was anathema to our world view and to our strategies. Yet despite the flaws described, the Business Development Services (BDS) market development approach posed important challenges to how development in the sector was understood and done and to the terms of the debate since. Despite our resistance and reservations, we learned sometimes unexpected lessons from the process.

Firstly, despite its narrow initial focus, in which the development of business service markets became the new all-encompassing purpose of development intervention in the sector, it did lay the basis for a far more concerted focus on the role of markets in development. Surprising as this may seem today, a context in which SE development had become a focus of poverty reduction strategies meant the dominant paradigm (in South Africa at least) was often devoid of market analysis. MDA was arguably ahead of the game in its level of focus on market dynamics at the time, in particular, on how the structure of the economy was impacting on the competitiveness of small entrepreneurs and limiting the scope for self-employment to act as a pathway out of poverty. Yet, in the sector as a whole, an understanding of market dynamics was often absent from the discourse. For example, livelihoods approaches then gaining traction in the social sector often lacked any analysis of how markets might be impacting on livelihood opportunities, with livelihoods seen as a category of economic activity operating in some kind of parallel universe largely unaffected by market structure or market forces. So, while we certainly argued about how markets were understood, there was no dispute about the need to do so.

Secondly, the BDS market development approach focused attention on the market effects of development intervention. Until then, the focus of impact assessment had been on the effects of intervention on those SEs that were the direct beneficiaries. Looking at the market effects of development agencies as market players meant stepping back a level and recognising how intervention might be changing a given market context. Until then, the role of development agencies had tended to be seen as market-neutral rather than as having potentially systemic impacts on how markets functioned – for better or for worse.

Thirdly, linked to the role of development agencies was the role of subsidies in development, how they were used and the potential for them to have negative effects. While the focus of the market development paradigm was on subsidies to service delivery, MDA centres were grappling with a policy context in which subsidies given directly to start-up enterprises in the form of grants were indeed having certain negative impacts on existing local enterprises, because, for as long as these donor-funded enterprises survived, their access to grant funding skewed their cost structure in ways that meant they could undercut other local enterprises funded from savings or loans. While the grant-funded enterprises often did not survive for long after their funding ended, this was often long enough for them to put other local entrepreneurs out of business. So while the early absolutism with which subsidies were rejected by the BDS trumpeteers was misplaced, the notion that subsidies could impact on local markets in unanticipated and negative ways, and the need for mindfulness in their use, was not.

Fourthly, the approach cast the limitations of 'service delivery as development purpose' into relief. At the time, the sector was in the grip of the logic of cost recovery, with sustainability measured by the extent to which development agencies could cover their own costs from the delivery of services to poor people, and with access to donor funding dependent on a reasonable prospect of achieving this in due course. Service delivery – rather than systemic change of any kind – had become the proxy purpose of development. Despite its narrow focus on BDS markets, the approach did at least put the issue of systemic change back on the development agenda, where it should always have been.

Finally, the focus on facilitation as having a catalytic role in development brought the catalytic function back into focus in development praxis – even if through an unexpected door. Instead of doing the same things over and over again, this challenged development agencies to act as the agents of catalytic change. This was an important shift in role scope – even if it left many unanswered questions about how organisations could fund such a role without complete donor dependency.

So, while the paradigm certainly brought challenges to MDA's praxis, it also brought new insights. What this meant for MDA's development centre model is scrutinised below, with the conclusions not only drawing attention to some core contradictions in the BDS market development approach – but in MDA's development model also.

Re-examining the role of economic services

The Mineworkers Development Agency's rationale for delivering economic services through development centres was twofold. Firstly, they were intended to address market failures by filling service gaps in the local market that could catalyse wider local enterprise development. Secondly, as economies of scale grew and these became viable business units, these were intended to underpin the sustainability of the centres, making them less vulnerable to the ebb and flow of funding for those development services that did require subsidies. So, in the way the centres were conceptualised, a distinction was made between those services that could become viable and operate on a commercial basis, which were referred to in MDA as economic services, and services such as training, counselling, product development and market facilitation that were seen as strategic services able to unlock wider enterprise growth, but that needed to be resourced.

Mhala Development Centre (MDC) was MDA's textbook case. Like all the centres, it had a business supply store providing a range of business inputs to local entrepreneurs as well as offering equipment hire. The role of the poultry centre has been described, as well as Mhala's role in the steel fabrication sector. A similar role was played in relation to the construction sector, as Ted Baumann describes:

> As with steel fabrication, MDC initially provided training, equipment, materials and space for centre members to begin producing cement blocks on site ... the actual production process was gradually transferred to independent micro-enterprises off-site and MDC became a raw materials and equipment supplier, maintaining stocks of cement and other requisites for easy purchase and/or hire.
>
> For many of its larger clients, MDC is now gradually moving away from this direct wholesale role towards that of a purchasing agent and administrator. Increasingly, MDC facilitates transactions between manufacturers (in Nelspruit and beyond) and local contractors, levying a small surcharge for the service. (Baumann 1998, p. 12)

The examples in the poultry, steel fabrication and construction sectors all illustrate the way Mhala's role changed over time in relation to the needs and development of entrepreneurs in each of these different sectors. Within these change processes, Mhala's role incorporated all the different development roles that are at issue in this debate – with the Centre providing subsidised services in the early stages, building to a point of full cost recovery from the delivery of those services, then moving finally into a facilitation role, linking demand and supply – in relation to changing needs and opportunities and the changed competitive context in a given sector.

In each case, the services offered by the Mhala Centre changed the nature of opportunities in the local economy, which in turn created new conditions. These new conditions then displaced the need for the original services – with increased economies of scale creating the necessary conditions for market mechanisms to kick in on sustainable terms. Once this key point was reached, a form of systemic change in the structure of the local market was achieved and the access frontier shifted. In the process, the needs of entrepreneurs and the opportunities in the local economy changed also.

In these examples, MDC adapts in ways that respond to the growing scope and scale of local economic activity and that draw increased added value into the Mhala local economy. While the MDC plays a pivotal and direct role initially, it plays a declining and increasingly facilitative role as the sector grows. These are good development outcomes. In each of these sub-sectors, a level of market change was achieved, in ways that developed their own local momentum once a certain level of scale was achieved. Rather than the binary choice the BDS model attempted to impose, MDC achieved change in local market conditions by playing a hybrid role. From MDA's perspective, this role was not distorting local markets, it was having market development effects.

The first part of the strategic rationale for the centres was that the delivery of services would contribute to overcoming market failures that were constraining the expansion of local enterprise activity. Some success could certainly be claimed in this regard. The second part of the strategic rationale was that some of these services would become commercially viable over time and that these would contribute to the financial sustainability of the Centre as a whole. It was in this latter regard that outcomes were more ambiguous.

The success of the poultry centre in supporting local entrepreneurs translated, over time, into declining returns for the centre itself, with its functions displaced by the local enterprise activity it had catalysed. It closed in the end. In addition, while the MDC might have been able to replace revenue from the sale of steel with fees for a linkage service between contractors and suppliers, such transitions are not necessarily equivalent in value or seamless and they placed the business model of the Centre at risk.

In practice, there was a tension between playing the more dynamic facilitative linkage role and the imperatives of running viable local stores – and other enterprises. This formed part of an ongoing tension between the wider developmental role and potential of the centres and the narrower imperatives of organisational sustainability, from which the salaries and the continued employment of staff was derived. These tensions were manifest as contradictions in the incentive framework of the centres at an organisational level.

Rather than being incentivised to encourage the emergence of a range of different forms of linkages to suppliers and to competitive sources of supply in the local economy, the business stores had an objective competitive interest in maintaining their own pivotal role in the process, because the sustainability of the centres and the jobs of their staff depended on doing so. Legitimate as these organisational imperatives may be, monopoly control of a service that is strategic for local economic development is not a good development outcome. Insofar as that monopoly control relied on subsidies to the centres, this could certainly be construed as a problem.

This was an objective tension that existed in the roles expected of centres, which centre staff managed in different and often highly creative ways. As the Mhala example illustrates, the staff at the MDC tended to prioritise the role of local development facilitators, even where this may have undermined the immediate interests of the store, to the chagrin of Connie Shumba, the Institutional Support Manager in MDA Head Office, whose unenviable task it was to optimise the financial performance and sustainability of the centres as business entities.

These contradictions came into focus when competition developed in the local economies in which business services operated – as it always did, over time. At Mhala, for example, Colin Ndlovu, ex-miner from Arnot and one of the original Mhala group, runs a poultry business called Bambanani that came to far exceed Mhala's capacity. Mhala claimed this as one of its success stories and so it certainly was; but the success in the local poultry sector of this and other poultry enterprises supported by the MDC also displaced the need for Mhala's Poultry Supply Centre over time. Ndlovu's business grew to a scale of sixteen thousand birds a month, compared to the MDC's one thousand two hundred birds, on the same model of supplying local networks of sellers and part-producers.

Similarly, while the business supply store played a key role in the early days of the MDC, a review of stores conducted by Sam Vilakazi, MDA's Acting Institutional Support Manager, reported in 2002 that 'the store is completely dead due to stiff competition in the area' (Vilakazi 2002). For the business supply stores, competition came both from local entrepreneurs, often trained by the centre, as well as from national operators who were expanding their outreach.

In Bathlaros, for example, the business supply store thrived as one of the more profitable stores until local and national competitors entered the market and the Bathlaros business supply store was, in the end, unable to compete and closed down, but not without a prolonged fight.

In some areas, the expansion of supply networks may well have happened anyway. In others, the centres arguably played a path-breaking role in building the minimum volumes required for viable local stores. The threshold at which such market entry was feasible differed, however, for local entrepreneurs and the national players who started spreading their networks into such areas. These national operators had all the advantages of high levels of concentration and national economies of scale, as well as equity to invest – in a context in which the difference between a situation of market failure and the point at which business services become viable is sometimes equivalent to the cost of capital – particularly with the prime rate above 15 per cent, as it was in this period.

The need to capitalise a business with loan finance raises the threshold at which it is possible to overcome market failure on market terms. For local entrepreneurs, the barriers to entry and the threshold of business viability is therefore higher – all things being equal – than for established operators with equity to invest in new markets. As a consequence, in contexts of high inequality such as South Africa, any really profitable local market opportunities often close to local entrepreneurs before they even open up, with the large national players having a significant cost advantage in relation to their cost of capital. This is an important mechanism through which market-based development processes reproduce inequality and exacerbate concentration: because new entrants without capital are always at a disadvantage in relation to players with equity to invest. So who exactly is crowding out whom in these markets? Capital subsidies to new entrants were deemed a market distortion – while the consequences of the raw and racialised processes of appropriation that underlie asset inequality in South Africa were not. Existing endowments reproduce inequality of access in markets, providing a form of market power that keeps insiders in – and new entrants out. Making markets work better for poor people has to include new ways of creating access to capital and to equity, exploring forms of ownership and partnership that lead to different distributional outcomes – or the local economic development game will simply be played with loaded dice as usual, providing new opportunities for the strongest players, deepening concentration and crowding out alternatives.

Cost recovery: another anti-politics machine

In several instances, the centres had followed a trajectory that was not anticipated either in MDA's own model nor in the classic BDS model. They had played the role of direct service providers in a context of market failure; the existence of a secure supply – such as in relation to poultry – had created a demand-side response which should in theory have secured the centre a sustainable future, but which had, instead, lead to the emergence of local market competition that rendered the role of the centre redundant within these particular markets. It was not planned that way, it may not have been the most efficient way to achieve market change, it certainly was not considered acceptable by the BDS market development pundits, but, in its own way, the result was the development of sustainable local business service markets in particular sub-sectors in these local economies. In this sense, the centres played a market development role.

In the process, as the examples illustrate, a central tension had emerged between the role of the centres as change agents in the local economy and the need for them to achieve economic sustainability by operating as service providers, with the primacy of cost recovery introducing a tension that went to the heart of the development rationale for the centres. This was foregrounded when an Output to Purpose Review commissioned by DFID in 2001 (and undertaken by two leading proponents of the BDS approach) took the view that MDA's centres were indeed distorting local markets and recommended that the development centres should either be fully commercialised or should close.

In relation to strategic services such as product development and market facilitation, full cost recovery was not an option. Yet, from MDA's perspective, these were investments in wider market linkages and access to value chains that were necessary to shift local enterprise options into higher-value markets and out of the low-value local markets in which they were trapped. From our perspective, these interventions qualified as part of a market development approach: but the argument did not wash.

This reduced the centres to fee-based training service providers and business supply stores. In the debate that followed, the question was less whether centres could survive commercially on this basis – some could and some could not – than at what cost this would be in relation to their development roles.

In practice, the business performance of the centres varied widely and it also fluctuated at each centre over time, with management capacity a critical and challenging issue. At the time, trends in the South African labour market meant that the kinds of management skills required to run complex business entities such as the centres were at a premium nationally and the chances of getting or retaining such skills at the margins was a constant constraint, with MDA's Institutional Support Unit having to invest significant time and energy in upgrading management capacity and governance at the centres: a crucial function funded by DFID at the time.

However, while the performance of different centres was variable, in practice, all business units did well simply to cover their own costs. They were operating in weak markets and so, even where the magic threshold was reached where commercial supply of services was feasible, margins were low. Nowhere – not even at the fully self-sufficient Lesotho Development Centre – were the economic services ever able to cross-subsidise development activities or strategic services. The reverse flow was a more likely one – with funds for development purposes underpinning the competitiveness of what were intended to be commercial activities. In addition, these commercial activities absorbed significant management time at the centres and from MDA Head Office. Instead of the business units being a means to a wider developmental end, wider development resources were at times being used for business purposes, with cost recovery increasingly becoming an end in itself.

Where full financial sustainability was achieved, as at the Lesotho Development Centre, it came at a price, as its Manager Mapota Molefi describes:

> You know when that sustainability thinking came about, we were under a very heavy pressure, we didn't even know what to do. We thought the management [MDA] will say, no, we have failed, we should just close this centre because it is not sustainable. At the same time, we said, what are we going to do if this centre is closed? Because of that, the relationship between MDA and the centre was not good, because of that pressure, it was a very heavy pressure. When someone comes to us and says, 'Let's see how is the centre – what is the performance of the centre?' Well it was hell, it was heartbreaking just to hear that.
>
> It took us some time to realise that, no, these people are right. I still remember Connie [Connie Shumba, Institutional Support Manager]. Really, truly speaking, I was a little bit frustrated when she came, because you know, Connie would just demand so many things. 'Can I have the report that's talking about that and that and the financial report and what and what...' Just because of that sustainability element, but in the end we realised that well, MDA was right, the centres were supposed to show that they are there to stay, they are there to support the target group, there to see to it that the people who are working for the centre are getting something. So once we realised that – well our lives changed completely. We said, no, they are right, we must pull up the socks. What I do as a centre manager, MDA pushes me, I push you. But it was tough, you know, really it was tough. (Interview with Mapota Molefi, 10 December 2004)

Molefi was asked whether the pressure to achieve sustainability targets affected the business strategy of the Centre and its ability to target ex-mineworkers. He responded as follows:

> [Whistles] It affected us a lot! We didn't even think of the mineworkers, once that came about; we thought we'll do whatever we do to anybody who comes to us and buy, we don't care whether it's an ex-mineworker and the charges that we gave to the people were very high, we had to change everything.
>
> We targeted the people from the government, as far as the accommodation block was concerned; the people from the sports, people from private organisations, we didn't even think of the poor people from the villages, who would just come and say, 'I want one bag of wax, the price is very high'. We knew that the prices were high. We would just say, no, it's no more R200, its R400. Ja, it affected us a lot, because, let me say, the target group – you forget absolutely about the target group. So that means our strategy changed completely. (Interview with Molefi, 2004)

The primacy of cost recovery pitted the survival of the centres against their development purpose. As each centre approached the end of its initial three-year period of operating subsidy and faced a context in which its organisational survival depended on the business units and in which staff salaries differed quite substantially across centres on the basis of their business performance, these tensions intensified and so did the tendency to target away from ex-miners and the poor.

The kinds of grassroots networking, organising and facilitation of economic activity in rural local economies that had characterised the early village-based support processes – and that MDA's staff were unusually skilled at – was time-consuming and did not yield fee-based returns. These were neglected. The development role of the centres was impoverished. While MDA and centre boards exhorted centre managers to retain their focus on the development agenda, the imperatives of achieving financial sustainability continuously trumped this focus – because no market-based incentives recognised these roles and in the absence of any other form of funding, these were the only incentives left on the table.

Susan Barton was the manager of the Mhala Centre in 2000–01. When asked about this tension, she said: 'There was no tension. Chasing turn-over targets was all-consuming – how else would we pay salaries at the end of the month? There was no time for anything else' (interview with Susan Barton, 18 August 2005).

This in turn created an explicit and growing tension with NUM, which expected MDA's centres to provide a range of development support functions and to give priority to the NUM constituency. But returns from servicing the NUM constituency were often highly erratic, linked to unpredictable retrenchment processes, with the low skills levels amongst ex-miners tending to yield poorer impact returns than other local constituencies. Proof of impact was an important criterion in an increasingly competitive funding market-place; so even in relation to funded activities, MDA's centres were starting to target away from our own constituency to achieve better performance outcomes.

In this context, the full commercialisation of the centres would exacer-bate this mission drift. After consideration of many different variants on the centre model, MDA rejected the recommendation that the centres be fully commercialised and that those that could not achieve this should close.

Instead, the MDA Board approved a resolution to convert the centres from subsidiary companies into branches of MDA, with a mandate to act as local development facilitators and to exit from direct service delivery (MDA Board Minutes, 26 February 2002). The centre infrastructure would continue to provide a development hub at local levels, with the intention of reducing transaction costs for local entrepreneurs, but the aim was to outsource the delivery of services to a mix of private and non-profit partners at each centre, with MDA providing the core infrastructure and focusing on the development facilitator role – with significantly reduced costs and risk as a consequence. MDA's 2002 Annual Report explains further:

> At the same time, with bills to pay and costs to cover, centre managers were more inclined to concentrate on the sale of cement than on identifying new business opportunities for clients in the area, or attending local development forums. They were also likely to promote their own training options rather than to encourage a more diverse range of opportunities for ex-miners. By setting the centres up as businesses, we created an incentive framework that potentially undermined the delivery of our core mandate; and created conflicts of interest between the interests of the centre as a business and the interests of our constituency. (MDA 2002)

This intended shift was, however, a substantial change in organisational logic that proved to be a bridge too far. While at a national level MDA could rely on core funding from the Mineworkers Investment Trust, in turn funded by the Mineworkers Investment Company, the centres had been expected to cover their own core costs. In practice, the facilitation model was never effectively resourced in a wider funding environment in which the logic of full cost recovery remained dominant. Yet predictably, reliance on full cost recovery lead to a reduced development role for centres and often, their slow demise.

The experience of the quest to achieve organisational sustainability from full cost recovery leading to upward targeting in business centres was not unique to MDA. During the 1990s, business centres were set up on a widespread basis all over the world, and are still around today. Many have been set up with very similar sets of aims as MDA's centres, except some aimed for full cost recovery from the start (Sievers et al. 2003). Many shared MDA's experience, with their strategic goals locked in mortal combat with the imperative of cost recovery as the necessary condition for organisational survival.

A report from the International Labour Organization (ILO) reviews the performance of sixteen centres set up by the United Nations Industrial Development Organization (UNIDO) in Romania, centres set up by Swisscontact in Peru, the Philippines and Indonesia; by USAID in the Russian Federation, by the Inter-American Development Bank in Argentina, Colombia, Costa Rica and El Salvador, and 136 centres set up across Europe by the EU's PHARE programme. Across the board, the quest for organisational sustainability went hand in hand with upward targeting, resulting in centres competing with private-sector providers. A characteristic comment applied to the case of UNIDO's business centres (BCs) follows:

> After the sponsors reduced their financial support, the three BCs responded by offering more diversified services and targeting larger companies. This meant that sustainability was achieved by targeting larger enterprises and not

the SME clientele. As long as the centres focus solely on providing business development services to SMEs, full cost recovery is recognised by UNIDO to be impossible. (Sievers et al. 2003, p. 5)

In the ILO's conclusions, they note the following:

BCs differ from traditional donor interventions in that they tend to be market-led institutions. They put more emphasis on working under market conditions and on developing services that can be self-sustaining. As in micro-finance, this has also led to a stronger emphasis on BC institutional sustainability than on the ultimate impact on the client. (Sievers et al. 2003, p. 39)

For development agencies, the focus on cost recovery pits the organisation against its own purpose, leaving no space for the kinds of change-agent roles required to effect systemic change. This is a new kind of 'anti-politics machine' in development. While Ferguson's (1990) concept of development as an anti-politics machine was aimed at bureaucratic state-driven development, market-driven development processes dependent on achieving cost recovery similarly bypass poor people – with the 'development from below' that Ferguson posed as an alternative still all too tenuous and elusive.

Development dilemmas

The BDS paradigm focused attention on the market effects of development intervention in a way that was new. This focus on the effects of development centres in their local economies, coupled with the effects of market pressures on the centres, helped clarify contradictions – or at least tensions – in the core development rationale of the centres. Yet, while the BDS approach was focused on the extent to which the centres, as development interventions, were supposedly distorting local markets, it inadvertently highlighted the extent to which the market-driven imperatives of cost recovery were distorting MDA's ability to achieve its development purpose.

In marginal contexts, risks are high and viability will be a challenge for even the best-performing businesses. In this context, the potential to cross-subsidise other forms of development activity from commercial activities will be rare. Not only that, it is in fact just as likely that business losses will place more than just the business services at risk, reversing the direction in which cross-subsidies flow, with the consequent diversion of development resources into chicken feed.

By pegging the sustainability and success of the centres to the ongoing viability of services such as business supply stores and poultry centres, the centres were locked into an incentive structure based on a permanent place in local supply chains, for which changes in the local economy and in the nature of market failures within it were potentially threatening. As a result of the dynamics outlined above, both Mhala's store and its poultry centre declined in viability. Was this a sign of failure? It all depends on whether the success criterion was the sustainability of the Centre as an organisation, or was related instead to its success in catalysing shifts in the local economy that removed the market failure identified.

In addition, the imperative of financial sustainability also created an entirely rational, market-driven tendency to target away from the poorer segments of the community and to disinvest in playing the wider development or change-agent roles necessary to achieve systemic change – an anti-politics effect that drained the developmental content out of the roles played.

Yet despite recognition of all of the above, there remains little doubt that as a result of participating in these markets, MDA staff were far more street-wise, canny and creative about how these markets worked, and how they needed to be changed, than many market-disconnected enterprise development practitioners operating in similar environments, whose approaches to enterprise development often had no such insight – and no such success, either. Perhaps this is only an issue in South Africa, because of the scarcity of entrepreneurial experience in the period under review: but the fact that the centres operated as businesses – to the best of their ability – and had to grapple with the nature of market constraints and how to overcome them on a daily basis made them better enterprise advisors, embedded in the local market context, with an increasingly fine-tuned understanding of what worked and what didn't. Such skills remain all too rare in the enterprise development sector in South Africa.

In addition, despite an incentive framework in which the best interests of the centres objectively meant driving out the competition, this was not actually what typically happened in practice. In relation to the poultry unit and supply of steel, for example, MDC progressively exited in ways that enabled the development of local alternatives to the supply services that the Centre had initially provided.

Was there not scope to allow the insights into these market-change dynamics and the incentive issues they raised to contribute to more informed and mindful strategies in this regard – rather than simply exiting from any market-based roles? Is there no scope to mitigate the anti-developmental impacts of a full-blown cost-recovery model with core funding, while keeping the depth and discipline that comes from being locked into market realities at some level? Could the change-function role played by market-based activity in a context of initial market failure not have been supported, in ways that incentivised exits from that role at the appropriate stage?

At the time, the door was firmly closed to any discussion of a hybrid model, with a binary choice between a fully commercial service-delivery role and what was defined as the role of 'market facilitation' – the shiny new concept in the sector. Facilitation was defined as a catalytic function, focused on achieving market change at a systemic level.

Despite the ambivalence we certainly felt at the binary nature of the choices presented at the time, facilitation – defined in this way – is potentially a much more interesting developmental role than being locked into ongoing service provision, particularly if this role can move beyond the narrow confines of business service markets to embrace a wider political economy of markets and market systems. The question, however, is how this role should be played and how these outcomes can be achieved. In the process, the role of organisations – and the importance of their survival – comes back into the picture in new ways.

Across a spectrum that includes Karl Polanyi, Douglass North, Ha-Joon Chang and Mushtaq Khan, theories of economic and institutional change place emphasis on the extent to which change processes are a function of contestation within markets and within societies and on the crucial role of forms of organisation and association in such change processes. Hand in hand with that goes the long-term and incremental nature of the processes that yield institutional change: 'It is the interaction between institutions and organisations that shapes the institutional evolution of an economy. If institutions are the rules of the game, organisations and their entrepreneurs are the players' (North 1994, p. 361).

For North, organisations are made up of groups of individuals bound together by some common purpose to achieve certain objectives: this definition includes firms, trade unions, family farms, churches and political parties, to name a few (North 1994). The point is that it is primarily through the role of a multiplicity of organisations that the kind of contestation necessary for institutional change takes place: this is the level at which change becomes 'systemic'.

This being the case, the existence of forms of organisation and association that are able to represent, support and/or advocate on behalf of diverse sets of interests in society – including the poor – is clearly a critical factor in achieving sustainable and systemic change in the terms on which markets work and in whose interests they work.

Once again, the role of trade unions provides a rare example of the least resourced and powerful players within a given market using organisation to change the terms on which that market functions. The extent to which trade unions have been able to influence labour markets around the world – limitations and setbacks notwithstanding – derives at least in part from the fact that trade unions have become a permanent feature of the organisational landscape, able to stay the course, developing deep institutional memory and insight into their sectors and the levers of power and influence within them. Where the scale of membership allows them to be self-funding, trade unions have also been able to escape the grip of dependency on external funding, giving them an independence and long-term organisational trajectory that has been critical to their ability to influence the rules of the game over time.

What analogous examples exist within other market contexts? Certainly, producer associations, agricultural and other forms of co-operative play such roles; despite significant differences in context, there are also lessons from the alliances formed by small producers in the context of Italy's industrial districts. While cluster organisations can simply end up representing the strongest voices in a given cluster, they are a form of economic organisation with scope to influence the rules of the game. Nor is it only representative forms of organisation that count: so do entities such as MDA's centres and other forms of support organisation providing resources within marginalised local contexts that can build networks, create economies of scale, negotiate with power brokers and amplify local voices.

Yet, despite the centrality of the role of organisation and its depth and breadth in effective change processes, the discourse in this area is thin. What *are* the forms of organisation through which change processes favouring the interests of the poor in a given market are best expressed and asserted – and in resource-poor contexts, how are such forms of organisation sustained? This critical question – with implications beyond simply the domain of market-change processes – remains largely unanswered. Relying on the erratic goodwill of donors does not do it and, as we have seen, cost-recovery models target away from the poor. So through what institutionalised mechanisms can societies correct the imbalance in influence and power that arises from the dearth of forms of organisation able to engage in the kind of contestation likely to shift the terms of access and the returns from market participation onto more equitable trajectories?

While these questions focus on the roles of players within markets, the concept of facilitation was presented as a change-function role played from outside of markets: a kind of 'honest broker' function, in which the facilitator is an external agent, representing the interests of the poor in markets as a matter of purpose – in a context in which that purpose is quite often defined by a donor logframe rather than by expressed demand from organised constituencies of poor people within such markets or forms of support organisation rooted within such communities.

Facilitation is also defined as a transient role, with a great deal of focus placed on exit strategies. This transient 'silver bullet' dimension of a facilitation role is considered a legitimate focus for donor funding, while the core costs of organisations are not. This emphasis is influenced by a context in which exit strategies have become a prescribed part of programme design. As a consequence, strategy – and what is deemed to be successful – is driven by a different set of imperatives for donors from the organisations or agencies driving change and institutional development from within a given society where, by contrast, certain roles and support functions may be legitimate and necessary in the longer term and may need to be embedded, even if their exact functions adapt and change over time.

This tension is highlighted by an attempt to clarify the nature of 'systemic change' in Nippard et al. (2014) in which, in relation to each of a defined set of stages of facilitation, the question against which systemic change is measured is: 'what would happen if we left now?' If the answer is that the change would endure, then systemic change has been achieved. By contrast, what about a question that asks: 'what could happen if we stayed?'

The contrast between these two questions highlights the dichotomy between the roles of insiders and outsiders that needs to be recognised. Donor organisations are not typically from the society or community in which they operate; they do not expect their role to be permanent and, inevitably, this informs the strategies it is appropriate *for them to play*. The problem arises, however, when this donor discourse frames the overall development discourse in a society – in which strategy cannot be about coming or going, but about what *ongoing* local trajectory of organisational and institutional development is needed to transform the dynamics of access or power or market structure and how such an ongoing trajectory should be institutionalised and resourced.

According to North: 'Organizations are a response to the institutional structure of societies, and, in consequence, the major cause of the alteration of that institutional structure' (North 1990b p. 390). If institutional change is a function of the role of forms of organisation in society, then the existence of relevant forms of organisation is a critical development concern; with their ability to influence outcomes also likely to be a function of their resilience and longevity, with institutional change typically achieved in incremental and cumulative ways. This links in turn with the work of Mushtaq Khan, who argues that, at the level of political economy, it is the relative power of organisations in society that influences the distribution of benefits. Presumably, this does not just apply at the big-picture level, but at every level at which contestation takes place. For Khan, a critical dimension of the power of organisations relates to their 'holding power': to how long they can hold out in actual or potential conflicts against other organisations or the state (Khan 2012, p. 8).

A similar analysis informed important dimensions of the struggle against apartheid in South Africa – with a multitude of forms organisation built to contest every sphere of social and economic life, and with the development of such organisation recognised as a necessary condition for social and economic transformation. Where did that understanding – and praxis – go?

The absence of organisational depth in poor and marginalised communities and the inability to resource such organisation in ways that allow 'holding power' reinforces institutional biases in society that favour the more organised and resourced, often correlated with those who hold economic power. In the process this deepens inequality: rendering the task of making markets work better for the poor elusive indeed.

For as long as the critical problem of organisational sustainability is left unanswered, the generic 'poor' are left to rely too often on donor-funded consultants contracted without their knowledge or consent to facilitate change on their behalf – in contexts in which such consultants too often have scant knowledge of local markets or the local political economy. This is the de facto model through which much of the facilitation supported by donors has been funded.

So, while the anti-politics effect of 'cost recovery as development' is clear, the shift to a facilitation model has largely ignored the issue of organisational sustainability and ushered in a rise in the use of development consultants – an anti-politics effect if ever there was one. Yet the concept of facilitation with its focus on systemic change and on a catalytic role for development agencies has nevertheless provided an important break with the dominant discourse in which service delivery had become equated with development purpose.

The challenge is to find a way in which to embrace this catalytic change-agent function in ways that simultaneously support, embed and resource the growth of diverse forms of organisation in marginal contexts, that enable them to develop 'holding power' – and that do not treat the issue of organisational survival as simply the self-serving concern of the staff in affected support NGOs: as was certainly the aspersion cast at the time.

Meanwhile, as we grappled with these issues and their implications for Development Centres, MDA was also attempting to apply our earlier insights into the impacts of the structure of the economy on local opportunities; in particular, on the need to move beyond a focus on local production for local consumption and to find ways to break into external markets instead. Our attempts to do so had already begun when the paradigm shift discussed in this chapter forced us to look in new ways at what our role in such processes could and should be. Did the case for the provision of 'strategic services' hold? Could we test the concept of a market facilitation role? And in what ways might we support innovation and new product development? It is to these issues that the focus now turns.

13 Breaking into Higher-value Markets in the Craft Sector

In many parts of the developing world, the easiest entry point into market-based activity is for people to make and sell goods they use themselves and know their neighbours need. In South Africa a highly centralised corporate sector was already mass producing almost every manufactured or agro-processed product that poor people consume, with distribution systems reaching the most remote corners of the country. This limited the opportunities for small-scale producers targeting local markets in poor communities, where they struggled to compete in relation to either price or brand recognition.

South Africa's high levels of inequality mean that not everyone is poor, however. Different market segments have different levels of disposable income. At the time, the emergence of a black middle class was starting to change the traditional segmentation of local markets and South Africa's re-entry into global markets also held the promise of new opportunities. So how could entrepreneurs access these wider markets – on terms that would yield better returns?

The Mineworkers Development Agency (MDA)'s strategy shifted from a focus on local markets to explore how best to meet this different challenge. Until this point, support strategies at MDA's centres had been framed spatially, aiming to support diversification in local markets and tackling common obstacles facing local enterprises in a multi-sectoral way. Accessing higher-value, external markets required greater sectoral specificity, however, and put participation in value chains on our radar.

Market development and value chains

In the wider enterprise development discourse, there was a shift from the narrow focus on business service markets described in the previous chapters to an approach called 'making markets work for the poor', (commonly abbreviated as M4P) and focused on market systems, defined widely to include not only buyers, sellers and others directly involved in exchange, but also the institutions, rules of the game, organisations and enabling-environment factors shaping the terms on which exchange takes place.

There was certainly plenty of contestation over what this new M4P approach might mean, with early formulations fitting rather squarely into the hegemonic neo-liberal consensus of the day. Over time, however, a range of inputs from different disciplines brought more analytical nuance to whether – and if so how – market development processes might best assist the poor to benefit from economic development and growth: with recognition, in some quarters at least, that markets cannot be understood in purely economic terms:

> Markets also exist in a social space and are deeply embedded in a set of non-market, social and political institutions. The way in which people and the poor in particular, participate in markets is conditioned by economic, political, social and cultural factors which must be incorporated in the analysis. (Johnson 2005, p. 5)

Johnson describes the features of a market that works for the poor:

> A market which *works for the poor* is one which expands the choices available to poor people and produces market outcomes that benefit the poor. These outcomes include job opportunities with attractive wage rates, better returns on goods sold and greater affordability of products and services. Over time the participation of the poor in these key markets should increase. In terms of contributing to pro-poor growth, the key indicator will be the average rate of growth of the incomes of the poor. From the perspective of the poor, the important criteria are improvements in:
> - Access to important markets and overcoming any forms of market exclusion
> - Affordability (for purchases)
> - Returns (for sales) including wages from the sale of labour
> - Choice and
> - Risk reduction.
>
> (Johnson 2005, p. 11; original emphasis)

The approach also recognises that increased integration in markets can have contradictory effects:

> [T]he intensified competition resulting from greater market integration may be a two-edged sword, bringing simultaneous positive and negative effects. For example, markets may bring greater production efficiency and lower consumer prices, but also livelihood loss for existing producers. (Johnson 2005, p. 15)

At the same time, there was a growing discourse on the innovation and productivity-enhancing impacts of networks and clusters, with a largely spatial focus, as well as on forms of co-ordination within firms and between firms, in increasingly global value chains. Such value chains represent a more explicit form of economic co-ordination than arms-length market relationships, developed to limit risks and transaction costs in increasingly complex global markets.

Different sets of relationships and forms of governance exist within such chains – with implications for the spread of benefits and for access to such chains by smaller players or new entrants (Humphrey and Schmitz 2001). More relational value chains are contrasted with more hierarchical ones. The latter includes those in which producers are captive to product specifications set by the buyers – a form of privatised central planning in which producers simply do as they are told. By contrast, there are also value chains in which it is in fact the producers that drive design and development of both the product and the value chain, from below. In essence, governance is about control within the chain, with critical areas of control wielded in relation to the following issues:

1. What is to be produced, or product definition;
2. How it is to be produced; this involves the definition of production processes, which can include elements such as the technology to be used, quality systems, labour standards and environmental standards;
3. When it is to be produced;
4. How much is to be produced;
5. Price.

(Summarised from Humphrey and Schmitz 2001, p. 4)

In practice, the decision to try to bridge the gap between marginal producers and higher-value external markets meant participating in value chains: was there scope to do so on terms that were not just exploitative?

Venturing into value chains in the craft sector

In 2000, MDA set up a small Marketing Unit headed by Tessa Teixeira, with Cyril Turton and Jacob Monoge. They were tasked with identifying where rural areas would have a competitive advantage over urban areas. Craft activities, using a mix of existing and new skills, with potential applications and markets across the craft, homeware, jewellery and fashion industries, was identified as one such opportunity.

MDA aimed to experiment with the development of strategies that bridged the gap between rural producers and higher-value markets, to increase producers' income returns. In the process, MDA needed to set about understanding the operations of this market, the key role-players, its supply and value chains, constraints on market access for producers – and how to change the terms on which rural producers were able to participate.

MDA was in fact a latecomer to the craft sector. The Department of Trade and Industry (dti) had already identified it as a focus area; a sector strategy was in process, which defined craft as follows:

Craft refers to the creation and production of a broad range of utilitarian and decorative items produced on a *small scale* with *hand processes* being a significant part of the value-added content. The production of goods uses a range of natural and synthetic materials. (Department of Trade and Industry, 2005, p. 3, original emphasis)

As the dti noted, the craft sector had a long history of being at the receiving end of charitable, welfarist and developmental interventions, with 'the project' a well-known phenomenon.

At MDA, we had little experience in facilitating market linkages into sophisticated urban markets. To understand the demand side of the equation, in February 2001 MDA held a conference called 'Bridging the Gap between rural producers and high value markets', with a follow up in 2002. The conferences included a spectrum of participants, from more explicitly development-oriented organisations to large-scale, upmarket retail outlets, along with producers and designers.

In fact, MDA already had some early exposure to the difficulties of bridging the gap, in the co-op programme. In the early 1990s, MDA worked with a group of widows whose husbands had been killed in mine accidents, in a village near Butha Buthe in Lesotho. The women were knitting cream-coloured, pure wool jerseys with a Lesotho hut motif. MDA took samples of the jerseys to Johannesburg and secured orders.

Then we waited; and waited. Both we and they had overestimated their production capacity. The first completed jerseys arrived in mid-summer – brought to Johannesburg by a group of women who travelled by taxi with the jerseys in huge garbage bags. Although the jerseys that had been used to source the orders had been cream-coloured, these jerseys had been knitted in black, green and red. Instead of pure wool, the jerseys were knitted in pure acrylic. The group had travelled to Durban to buy wool to produce the order and had chosen the acrylic wool because it was cheaper.

It was a terrible moment of truth: because despite all the skills, time and labour that had gone into producing these jerseys, it was clear that the women had not understood the value proposition of their product in relation to the aesthetic of the market they were targeting ... and, as MDA, we had failed to grasp the extent of this gap in understanding. As a result, several months of labour were largely wasted.

Producers targeting their home markets understand the value proposition in relation to quality expectations, pricing, packaging and design. The feedback to help them do so often comes directly from the end consumer. With all its limitations of scope and scale, the local market is familiar.

Not so external markets. Most rural producers have little knowledge of the market for which they are producing – of its expectations or what it is about what they produce that is valued, let alone how rapidly changing trends might affect them. Joseph Mathe, the Chief Director in the Department of Arts Science and Technology, gave his perspective at the conference:

> Bridging the gap can be a tough task. I recall being phoned by someone in the United Kingdom, a South African living there now who was trying to facilitate access to markets there for local craft. She had placed an order with a particular group for some products, let me not say what, and she had specifically ordered them in white. The delivery didn't come and it didn't come and she was getting highly impatient. Finally, the order arrived, but instead of the products being white, they had all been done in blue. When she contacted the producers, all up in arms, they were surprised and responded by saying: 'But blue is also nice!' (Joseph Mathe at MDA's Bridging the Gap Conference, 2001)

This was typical. While retailers were criticised for not supporting local products and producers, the retail sector had its own view of the difficulties and risks in sourcing supplies from South African crafters. Many believed they had gone the extra mile to support local and rural producers, often at too high a cost, as the constraints on the supply side translated into a litany of tales of late delivery, poor quality, wrong quantities and more.

Bright House was at the time a contemporary homeware and furniture store with outlets in Johannesburg and Cape Town. Adrienne Sparks from Bright House offered her perspective:

> When a retailer spends time and money in developing a product with a group and then invests in promotion and marketing of this product, they need to know that delivery will be reliable; they need the quality to be consistent with the samples they have promoted and the correct quantities to be delivered in order to fulfil the expectations they have created for their customers. If this does not happen, then they have lost money: and they are unlikely to want to repeat the experience. Unfortunately, many of us in the sector have had these kinds of problems and under these circumstances, any business will give preference to suppliers that are reliable. (Adrienne Sparks e-mail correspondence, 3 December 2002)

Yet for their part, crafters had to deal with a wide range of external constraints, including poor roads, lack of telecommunications and much more. These, and internal technical and managerial skills shortcomings, were all compounded when rural producers tried to access external markets.

Problems such as late delivery can be attributed to logistical and management difficulties. Lack of consistent quality and the failure to produce accurately against specifications have more to do with not understanding the value proposition. It's an occupational hazard for producers targeting markets outside their experience, exacerbated by rapidly changing trends in the craft sector, where the role of design and product development is so important. It is also an example of the risks of exchange where there is a lack of accurate measurement and specification of what is being exchanged. So, NUM's Johannesburg buyers assumed that what they were ordering were pure-wool, hand-knitted, cream-coloured jerseys and what the Lesotho co-op believed it had contracted to supply were hand-knitted jerseys.

Contract enforcement limits risks

If things go wrong, then without clear contractual terms, neither side has much recourse. This heightens risk – and disincentivises both parties from entering into an exchange.

Little did we realise at the time, but at the heart of this issue was the shift from local, informal transactions to 'anonymous exchange', the term coined by that patriarch of economics, Adam Smith. Anonymous exchange was a consequence of growing specialisation and division of labour within society. This required the emergence of new forms of contract and new institutions to ensure transactions could be enforced:

> Those who disliked the Age of Commerce contrasted it with a happier past when workers had permanent masters who looked after their welfare, what was made locally was consumed locally and exchange was not just an anonymous act but a rich social ritual with extra-economic resonance. (Quoted in Desai, 2004, p. 22)

Mitigating the risks associated with anonymous exchange has driven the development of contract law, with the growth of institutions to reduce uncertainty underpinning the rise of the services sector in advanced capitalism. Such institutions influence which markets work and whether and how enterprise on the margins can participate in them. According to North, with a growing division of labour and increased specialisation in society,

> societies need effective, impersonal contract enforcement, because personal ties, voluntaristic constraints and ostracism are no longer effective as more complex and impersonal forms of exchange emerge. It is not that these personal and social alternatives are unimportant; they are still significant even in today's interdependent world. But in the absence of effective impersonal contracting, the gains from 'defection' are great enough to forestall the development of complex exchange. (North 1991, p. 101)

> Without contract enforcement mechanisms, transaction costs will reflect the risk of the other party defecting on the contract. North argues that throughout history, the size of this risk premium limited the development of complex exchange and therefore the possibilities of economic growth (North 1990a, p. 33).

Remote as such economic theory may have seemed then, the experiences of market participants trying to bridge the gap into external markets graphically illustrated the issues arising from anonymous exchange; in particular, they underlined the need for the parties involved in a transaction to be able to rely on a set of arrangements that mitigate their risks. For example, will the buyer pay? Will the supplier deliver the quality expected? For local producers, gone are the comforts of knowing where your customers live if they owe you money. For the buyer, gone is the knowledge that if sellers cheat, their reputation in the community will be at stake. Likewise, the reciprocities and meanings of many forms of local exchange, where transactions are not only economic, but have a relational and social content, vanish.

Anonymous exchange introduces risk and the need for mechanisms to limit that risk. Formality – or legal status – is just the start. For buyers in formal-sector markets, business transactions are also governed by a set of institutions and rules of the game that they take for granted. The interface with rural enterprises that do not play this game, or appear not to understand its rules, is not only insecure but it is sometimes administratively impossible because key signifiers for a transaction to be recognised do not exist. At the most basic level, this includes agreed ways of recording the transaction, including an order note, invoices, bank account numbers, letter-headed receipts and, if not an e-mail address, then at very least a physical address. Without these, neither company auditors nor the South African Revenue Service will recognise the transaction.

Anonymous exchange means the end of informality; or at least far higher levels of formality and compliance with accepted business practices than face-to-face transactions require. Without established ways of doing things or institutions to mitigate the risks, the interface between rural producers and external markets needs extensive facilitation and intermediation. Yet few things are as controversial in the sector as the role of intermediaries, who are inextricably linked to real and perceived exploitation of rural producers and issues of pricing.

Costs, risks and intermediation

Clearly, abuse by intermediaries – often referred to as 'middlemen' – does happen. However, confusions over pricing and what constitutes fair trade in the sector are rife. At the Bridging the Gap conference, a producer gave as an example of exploitation a retailer adding a 50 per cent mark-up on products and was drowned out by a chorus of retailers saying this was charity and that 100 to 150 per cent mark-ups were the norm if retailers were to survive. The fairly consistent rate of business failure in the niche retail sector shows that business survival is tough for retailers too, as Adrienne Sparks from Bright House argued:

NGO structures must get over the 'exploitation' word. In the real world South African producers are competing against the Far East and India in the handmade craft industry. Pricing of product has become such a sensitive issue and exploitation is a word that is used far too frequently. Producers should be taught about competitive markets and how to tackle them, rather than fearing that every purchaser is there to exploit them. Everyone has to work hard for their money and this should be part of every producer's consciousness when entering into manufacturing. Retailers can only sell a tablemat for a certain maximum price. If they can't cover all their costs out of this price, they will just have to look for another product or another supplier. (Adrienne Sparks at the MDA Bridging the Gap Conference, 2001)

Many producers in marginal markets are used to selling directly to end-customers and not to seeing their product with a retail mark-up added. As Bronwyn James of the Lubombo Spatial Initiative pointed out at the conference, this lack of understanding of pricing and marketing also characterised the view of the National Parks Department and other government departments at the time, manifested in attempts to promote craft through local craft markets and national and international trade fairs. Despite the advantages of such event exposures, the distinction between trade shows targeting buyers and retail craft environments has not always been reflected in pricing policies, with implications for ongoing relationships in supply chains in the sector. Eugenie Drakes from designer craft outlet Piece explained it further:

> Many of the players in the sector do not understand business or the retail sector and, in the process, in the name of promoting craft, they actually undermine the sustainability of the producers. It's the 'missionary' approach again and it's manifest, for example, in relation to pricing practices.
>
> As a retailer, when I look at the Ubuntu Village, it was built for the sole purpose of promoting craft at the World Summit: for foreigners, for dollars, for hard currency buyers. Why then are they selling at wholesale prices? At less than what they sell to me, when I've still got to add a mark-up? They're undercutting me, they're competing with me: and yet I am their bread and butter; I am their sustainable market. And they are then bringing people onto that stand supposedly to train them to understand the market. They're training them to hang themselves; in my opinion, it's crazy.
>
> [...]
>
> Several institutions had product at the Ubuntu Village that was selling in the retail section at less than the price which we as retailers have to pay for it. It was ludicrous. What happens as a result is that retailers will not touch that product. Why should we? We can't compete on price; we're being undercut by the producer and, as a result, they just blew their market. (Interview with Eugenie Drakes, 20 January 2003)

Since the Bridging the Gap conference, there have clearly been changes – at the dti's One of a Kind exhibitions at Decorex each year, crafters now have wholesale and retail prices displayed next to their products. As explained above, in the name of cutting out intermediaries, event-based marketing has sometimes actively circumvented and displaced other players in the supply chain – inadvertently putting access to more sustainable market linkages at risk.

Few role players take as much flak as intermediaries in this sector. Many of them feel aggrieved at what they see as misconceptions and unrealistic expectations, and a failure to understand their role:

> Yes, there are buyers who use the imbalance of power and lack of pricing skills amongst producers to buy at very low prices: but we're only going to stop that by empowering rural producers with the knowledge and confidence to place a value on their products and by getting more organised as a sector.
>
> Without the much-maligned 'middleman', rural craft simply doesn't stand a chance of making it into wider or urban markets. This intermediary role is key and it is costly. The person playing this role has transport costs, travel between dispersed rural producers is time-consuming, they are often playing an unrecognised role in providing design and marketing feedback and they often can't on-sell all the product they buy. This role has high costs and if we expect it to be done out of solidarity alone, we will never grow the potential of this sector. It's time to get real. (Tessa Graaff, Montebello, at the MDA Bridging the Gap Conference 2001)

Oscar Ngcobo from Gone Rural is such an intermediary. He left a corporate sector job in Johannesburg to work with a network of about two hundred beaders in KwaZulu-Natal. His mother is a beader and he is a 'by-product of what he is doing now', because his mother made him help ever since he was small. He uses international exhibitions to get orders and both buys and commissions work. Ngcobo illustrates the financing risk intermediaries take:

> As you might well know if you've been in this sector, the banks finance a commodity so, where they see risk involved, they tend to stay away – they want to have collateral guarantees, of which I understand, from a business point of view, you can't just give money with no guarantee that you're going to get it back. So I understand where they're coming from; I just wish they would understand where I come from. (Interview with Oscar Ngcobo, 7 August 2005)

In 2005, Ngcobo supplied 17,000 units of beaded bracelets and necklaces to the large department chain El Corte Inglese in Spain:

> A classic example, I had this huge order which I had to execute from Spain, last year. Because it was a huge order, which I've never had in my career, ever since I've been involved, I had to take a mortgage against my house. I came through it, even though they were sceptical whether I was going to do it, because it's a black-owned company and I could understand they didn't want to take a chance, the representative from the company from Spain. Their representative over here, he was wary of whether I was going to meet the order. I said, 'Please, take a chance with me'. I pleaded with him and at the end of the day, he was so impressed, because I was three weeks ahead of schedule. (Laughs.) And of which, you know, the credit has to go to those

women because they rose up to the occasion and we were able to fulfil the order and it was unbelievable.

I had to pre-finance the raw material, as well as also to pay the women for what they've made, otherwise I wouldn't have been able to do it – I had to keep them going to have the funds to pay them for what they've made. Otherwise if I were to say to them that they must work but they're only going to get money after I've processed the order, it would not have achieved our objective. (Interview with Ngcobo, 2005)

Accessing external markets usually requires being part of a supply chain in ways that do not apply in local markets. In a supply chain, value, costs and mark-ups are added with each link:

When I was buying products from India and marketing them to the retail sector in the UK, I expected to pay a fair price to producers in rural India; and then pay a fair price to the agents who collected, packaged and freighted the products on my behalf. I then had to add my own mark-up to cover my costs and make a profit on the warehousing, marketing and distribution role I played in the UK; and the retailers who bought from me expected to do the same. So from the time the products left rural India to the time they reached British consumers, four mark-ups had been added. This isn't exploitative: it's simply what a supply chain looks like. Everyone in it has to be able to get a fair mark-up for their role and contribution or they can't be expected to do it: and it isn't sustainable. (Interview with Susan Barton, 18 August 2005)

The escalation in price in even the fairest of trade tends to come as a shock if the producer at the one end of the chain sees the price tag at the other. Supply chains can be complex and value is added at different points. In trying to link rural producers with external markets, it is often assumed that a finished product from rural areas is delivered to a shelf in Sandton or New York:

There is a lack of understanding that, in a supply chain, it is not just finished products that are bought. The fact that there are markets for the production of the raw materials for finished objects and that many of these materials are available in rural areas and are in demand by other producers, seems to be overlooked by the agencies initiating rural craft projects. (Adrienne Sparks e-mail correspondence, 3 December 2002)

More accessible entry points into supply chains may be overlooked. Sparks provides the example of sisal, needed by many craft producers, in northern KwaZulu-Natal.

With longer supply chains comes a need for more role specialisation – or more intermediaries – yet there is an expectation that rural producers should rather play multiple roles. Erica Elk from the Cape Craft and Design Institute (CCDI) reflects on how CCDI is addressing these issues:

Intermediaries are critical; and we've been trying to trumpet their role. The expectation that the crafter must be the designer, the product developer, the producer, the marketer, the agent and the exporter is just not realistic. The intermediary actually has a critical role to play. So let's engage with them and bring them into the picture and get the producer to value their input. Intermediaries come with intelligence; they know what the market is buying and what they can sell product for. So there is a shift but there are still people who hold onto this thing that people are being exploited. And of course it does happen, but let's deal with it by engaging it in this way. (Interview with Erica Elk, 7 August 2004)

Access to export markets

Bridging the gap between Cofimvaba (a small town in the Eastern Cape) and Cape Town is hard enough; targeting export markets is far more difficult. Yet in the late 1990s, much policy emphasis and support was on leap-frogging national markets, to support participation in international trade fairs and export marketing of products from selected producers. Yet exporting takes the difficulties of anonymous exchange to new levels:

> Going into the US market, any item has to be labelled 'Handmade in South Africa'. For every article that is not labelled, Customs will impose a fine and they will flag that importer, which will result in every shipment of theirs that comes in being stopped and searched. There's a searching fee involved and a time delay involved.
>
> [...]
>
> In addition, every time a shipment goes in, there's a $250 customs fee for checking it. So this also means that for an importer, consolidation of product is vital. The more product you can include in a shipment, the lower your unit cost for each item.
>
> Then, the way you explain the product on the invoice affects whether it is dutiable or not. For example, a cushion cover could go in at 0% or 26% or 55% duty: depending on how it's worded, what code it's given, what category it goes into. You've got to do that homework here: it's up to us here.
>
> You also need to know: do you need a certificate of origin for your product? If you need one, you've got to ensure that it's done correctly. With skins for example, it's got to have a veterinary certificate, a certificate proving that the skin used in the product was got legally, it wasn't poached, it wasn't this, it wasn't that. If there are feathers on the product, it could be a problem with Food and Wildlife.
>
> [...]
>
> I will do all this for my customers, for people who are buying from me. I will make 100 per cent sure the documents are right, the product is OK, and it involves a huge amount of time and research, because each country has its own dynamic. (Interview with Eugenie Drakes, 20 January 2003)

Where marketing strategy for rural producers has exports as an aim, the full weight of international trade debates over tariffs and phytosanitary standards comes into play; and there is an even greater distance in the value proposition, market intelligence and design trends – and longer supply chains with more intermediary roles.

For Ngcobo, despite the difficulties in exporting, international markets have provided easier access:

> There is demand but what normally happens is that people feel safe buying from a white person, unfortunately, if you talk about retail shops in South Africa. That's the reality. That's the fact. (Interview with Ngcobo, 2005)

The informal rules of the game can be as intractable as the formal ones. In accessing export markets, not only buyers experience the anxieties and risk of anonymous exchange. At an International Buyers Day facilitated by the dti, a representative from craft producer Wired related that a French company had wanted to place an order for twelve thousand beaded lights from them. They wanted them in a matter of weeks, but were not prepared to pay a deposit. Yet simply purchasing the lights required to produce the order was going to cost this small company over US$10,000. The risk was too great and they turned the order down.

From rural through national to global markets, new institutions need to be created that mitigate the risks of exchange. Without appropriate insurance, the banks would want their own risk mitigated before providing finance against such an order and there may not be enough Ngcobos in the sector to take that level of risk to break into the exponentially larger international markets.

The Cape Craft and Design Institute also brokered partnerships between producers and Woolworths and this brought new challenges along with opportunities:

> Our experience with Woolworths is that they're very strict around process issues such as workplace safety and quality assurance to ensure that products are food safe and standardised; and they're willing to support the producers in this respect. They have production engineers in-house who are willing to work with the manufacturers to get those things in place. So that's very positive if you can get into Woolworths and get that type of support to help your business. But price is critical; they have particular price points and can only fit things in at those price points so there was a lot of hard negotiation. (Interview with E. Elk, 7 August 2004)

This kind of design input and technical support provided by retailers and buyers is key in bridging the gap and is a local example of the kind of investment taking place in global value chains, seen as a necessary cost to mitigate the risks of such exchange. This is also an example of the potential benefits for small firms that rise to the occasion in meeting set labour and environmental standards. Productivity is raised and access to new markets is opened, improving local economic development and reducing poverty.

Producers, however, need to have some foothold into the value chain. Such relationships come with their own sets of issues around exclusivity, intellectual property, pricing and power relationships. Producers risk becoming 'captive' within that chain; but as their level of tacit knowledge rises, the switching costs for the buyer rise too and, with this, the potential for a greater mutual dependence and a shift in the balance of power. The Lesotho stonecutters provide a perhaps unlikely example of such a relationship.

MDA and market facilitation: The stonecutters of Lesotho

Bridging the gap needs to be positioned within a wider market development framework, with strategic intervention on both the demand and the supply side at the level of the craft sector. While MDA's Bridging the Gap process catalysed some new interactions in the sector, MDA was never placed to play an overall sectoral role, in the way CCDI, for example, is doing in the Western Cape. CCDI's growth and development and the remarkable improvements in the quality, design and links to market in the craft sector highlight the importance of an intermediary role.

MDA did, however, start to explore facilitating greater market access for producers. A brief case study of one small initiative, and the outcomes five years later, illustrate these wider issues for a very marginal group of producers.

MDA Lesotho had developed links with several stonecutting quarries in Lesotho, where members had formed themselves into co-ops and joined the Basotho Mineworkers Labour Co-operative (BMLC). The MDA Lesotho office proposed that working with these enterprises could pilot ways of bridging the gap and test product development and marketing roles for MDA's Marketing Unit.

Christabel Jackson describes the first product development workshop, led by artist Drew Lindsay:

> Drew came up with the catchphrase of 'let the stone speak to you'. So we would take all kinds of natural shapes and colours and see what you could do minimally to the stone to make it into something useful, like put a hole in it for a candle. That's where we started. We just tried different things – round bowls, rectangular containers, candlesticks. The masons wanted to make things very fussy, with lots of natty little curves and grooves on things and we had a kind of instinct to keep things minimally decorated. (Interview with Christabel Jackson, 2002)

With samples from this process, the Marketing Unit went into the market in Gauteng, traipsing from trendy interior design stores to garden outlets and trade fairs.

Initially, the stonecutters doubted they could break into Johannesburg markets with products they couldn't imagine, and the groups had to be incentivised to participate in the production of samples, for which orders were then secured. They were paid what they would have earned from block production for the duration of the product development processes – and a free lunch, which clinched the deal.

Over a year, the orders increased, priced to bring better returns than to the building blocks. MDA wanted to extricate itself and Jackson set up a business linkage for the masons close to home – in Ladybrand, through local architect turned homeware designer Nicol Grobler. Grobler markets a range of products to homeware and garden centres, as well as to other homeware producers, who use these as base elements for their products, adding further value. This linkage endured for well over five years after MDA exited. Grobler describes his role in the marketing as follows:

> I go around physically seeing people and finding people ... Most of them will never come out and explain to the people exactly what they want, so you need someone like me; and for that – it isn't financially extremely viable for me but it is, I cover my costs, but it's not a big money-spinning part of our business. (Interview with Nicol Grobler, 14 May 2004)

Grobler explains that he has to know the product, the group's capabilities, and how fast they can fulfil orders. The group manages quality, but in his presence:

> Quality control: they do it themselves and they do it well. I'll arrive and say ok what have you got for me and they'll bring it out of holes and plastic bags and things – because there's no storage and many times, stuff gets damaged on weekends. Then they'll start checking, there's one guy that goes around, checking dimensions. They don't even have a flat area to put anything on, they have a piece of steel – like an old piece of railway line or something – that's flat enough: then they'll put the sample next to it and check the height and dimensions. Many things are made hollowed out to a certain dimension so a candle can fit in; and I trust them with that, they hardly ever make mistakes. (Interview with Grobler, 2004)

A key part of Grobler's role is interpreting design trends to which the co-op members would otherwise have little access:

> Sometimes I find it hard to explain to them what it is I need. For example, we had orders from the Seychelles, one of the top décor designers, for chunks of rock on castors, as stools. Then I had to explain that this drum has to be as high as this table and this diameter – what's it going to be used for? Because it needs a stepped ridge on the inside so when it's upside down, a steel plate can fit in there, so the wheels can be attached to the steel plate without being visible and exactly so much above the floor. Then I explain to them, it's like something you put your beer on, fancy people in Johannesburg want something to put their beer on and oh, ok fine, then they understand. But

otherwise – what is this funny pattern for? What is the purpose of doing it like this? (Interview with Grobler, 2004)

The stonecutters are not producing final products for market. The intermediary role played by Grobler includes value addition of various kinds, sometimes through work done in his own workshop and sometimes through on-selling stone products to other intermediate production workshops. Like Ngcobo, Grobler takes financial risk as an intermediary, by buying up stock. Pricing is done by agreement:

> I ask them to make a price first and if I think it's not going to work, we start to discuss how long will it take one person to make this thing; they work on about R35 a day, so if it takes you the whole day to make one of these things, then it costs R35 [about US$4.5], basically ... Many times they'll come up with a price and I say ok I'll go and try it. And sometimes it's the reverse and they come with a very cheap price, but I try to be fair.
>
> I do think the stonecutters might be shocked to see their products at two to three times the cost that they are paid, but it is an expensive process and we do have costs also. I have other labourers here to make steel stands, to do the other work, to put bubble wrap over it and take it to JHB [Johannesburg] – those are expensive things to do. (Interview with Grobler, 2004)

Grobler comments on being the sole agent, and the issue of exclusivity:

> It's quite sad, in a way and dangerous for them. Although I think I'm privileged also, but it puts them in a situation where if something happens to me or I decide to move off or the business shuts down – which I don't foresee – it leaves them very vulnerable.
>
> My products – I told them I would not want them to sell any of the stuff I design with them to anyone else, because that would be unfair. But I've never felt that they're doing that in any case. (Interview with Grobler, 2014)

The group is not barred from producing for other buyers – as long as they do not produce Grobler's designs. In an interview, two representatives of the group, Thabiso Motume and Mathabang Majoeng, indicated that before MDA initiated the product development process, the market consisted of the government and individuals, buying blocks, but this was unsatisfactory. Both were adamant they could earn more now than from simply producing blocks. Also, there are greater volumes and a more consistent market, which turned the stonecutting into consistent work and consistent income.

The wholesale price of the homeware products yields a better return for the masons than the price of blocks sold directly to the end users. Members are paid on a piece-work basis. For each completed piece, a 'small amount' goes to the group bank account and the balance is paid to the individual.

Although concerned at their dependence on Grobler, they are positive about the relationship and the opportunities it brings. The following were their final comments on what working with the stone means.

TM: We feel proud.

MM: Especially because stone was something that had been neglected for a long time.

TM: People in the past used to say if you were working with stone, it means you were from the prison. But, however, we worked hard until now people actually realise you can get a living from stone.

(Interview with Motume and Majoeng, 14 May 2004)

Bridging the gap into external markets

The focus of MDA on bridging the gap between rural producers and higher-value markets in the craft sector highlighted a range of issues relevant not only to the craft sector, but also to understanding the comparative risks and rewards in targeting either local or external markets, and the strategic choices entailed. The nature of insertion into markets will have distinct implications for the types of strategies that can be pursued, and returns that can be expected, involving a set of trade-offs that provide a conundrum for development strategy.

While barriers to entry are lower in local, informal markets, opportunities to compete with the small-scale production of basic consumer items are limited. There are some success stories, but the framework conditions mean that for many, this pathway is a poverty trap. What opportunities do exist tend to be in retail or services.

Access to external markets is not, however, an easy alternative: barriers to entry are far higher. The first lesson learned is about the role of intermediaries. Far from being the scourge of the sector, they are the key to bridging the gap, the link into wider markets and value chains, providing feedback and translating critical market intelligence for producers.

This relationship can be dependent and exploitative, but it can be reciprocal and empowering, liberating producers from the limits of local markets. Policy has tended to try to circumvent and substitute for the role of market-based intermediaries, with the substitute mechanisms – including state-funded retail outlets – too often having no real access into the wider markets they promise, nor the specific and specialised knowledge and skills required to adapt product design to market needs, spot opportunities, set prices, negotiate terms and clinch contracts in markets on different continents. Instead of circumventing and substituting for market-based intermediaries, the priority is to find ways to build the required threshold effects for their role to be viable, to support risk-reduction mechanisms and to broker appropriate partnerships in which there is a fair share of benefits.

The second lesson is that the gap is rarely bridged in one leap. Moving beyond local markets means entering various supply and value chains. This allows specialisation, which can reduce the complexity of the entrepreneurial challenge. Opportunities can start at the level

Figure 6 *South Africa's enterprise development conundrum*

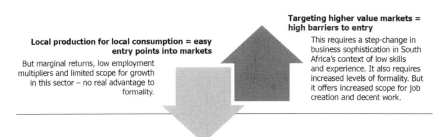

Targeting higher value markets = high barriers to entry

This requires a step-change in business sophistication in South Africa's context of low skills and experience. It also requires increased levels of formality. But it offers increased scope for job creation and decent work.

Local production for local consumption = easy entry points into markets

But marginal returns, low employment multipliers and limited scope for growth in this sector – no real advantage to formality.

of raw material collection from the wild for use further up the supply chain and include partly finished products. The value addition done locally can focus on labour input and on components when the local context provides a cost advantage, leaving inaccessible and high-cost inputs – such as designer packaging – to be included further up the chain. It helps when the raw material input is 'free' from nature, as with sisal, stone, marula and recycled materials, for example. While resource-management issues arise, and there are risks of being trapped in low-value-addition roles, these examples allow for labour to be the largest cost factor at local level, reducing risk and start-up costs and optimising poverty reduction.

Access to external markets often invokes all the challenges of impersonal exchange, including of measurement, specification and contract enforcement. Institutions that can bridge these gaps by mitigating the associated risks, including appropriate forms of insurance, need to be created. Not only formal institutions play this role. Participation in value chains means repeat transactions and access to networks in which trust, reciprocity, skills sharing and risk sharing come back into the picture in new ways.

For an enterprise to transact across distances of any kind, a certain level of formality is required. This may imply legal registration; such registration is likely to be necessary but not sufficient, however. What matters is that the enterprise is able to interact and transact within the framework of business 'rules of the game', which may vary from one supply chain to the next. The invoice, the receipt and the bank account are a necessary start, but food safety requirements, labelling and labour standards follow. The standards set in global markets are increasingly replicated in national markets. Rather than by regulation, these are increasingly driven by consumer demand and private-sector practice. By all means cut unnecessary red tape, but focusing narrowly on deregulation misses the point. Integration into supply chains and access to wider markets requires upgrading the capacities of enterprise to meet business norms and rising sets of minimum standards as a necessary condition for transacting.

Finally, in terms of the support environment, the Cape Craft and Design Institute offers an interesting contrast to MDA's development centres because it has managed to survive to the present day as a hybrid organisation. It has grant funding for core costs, freeing it to engage in a market development role, without the unbridled pressures of full cost recovery. This has allowed it to grow and adapt its role as the sector has grown in sophistication. Strategic services such as design input, product development advice and access to high-tech equipment such as laser-cutters and 3D printers on a partly subsidised basis have been catalytic in opening new product and market opportunities for producers, with growth effects. In its early days, simply securing orders for crafters from within the local retail sector was a major feat. Today, designer craft is integrated into homeware, fashion, jewellery and art markets, with an increasing export footprint. What is less clear is whether core funding will last when only development interventions that show 'sustainability' on the basis of full cost recovery are valued – regardless of the demonstrated sustainability and economic added value of their interventions.

Gwede Mantashe and the health bars

By the late 1990s, Gwede Mantashe (later to be Secretary General of the ANC) was the General Secretary of NUM – and also Chair of the MDA Board. From time to time, I really needed to meet with him to get his input and advice, but achieving this always required patience. I would arrive at NUM with issues and agenda items I considered important, only to find them trumped by a mine accident in which many lives had been lost, or an unprotected strike that required his full attention – to save the jobs of workers who all too often hadn't taken the union's advice. On one such occasion, I had at least made it into his office. He was, however taking a call. By now, NUM was sufficiently large and legitimate to attract the predatory attentions of miscellaneous profiteering opportunists. The man on the other end of the line was trying to offer Mantashe free health bars, in return for his endorsement of these for use on the mines. This was how Mantashe's end of the conversation went:

'No, I cannot endorse your bars. I would advise you to contact the workers' food committees in the hostels at each mine and to submit your bars for their consideration.'

......

'No, I will not accept a box of free health bars.'

......

'No, no, no.'

......

'No, I am not even willing to try them.'

And then, exasperated:

'OK fine. Bring me your health bars. I will try your health bars. I will not like them at all. And I will recommend that mineworkers *reject* your bars!'

He slammed the phone down. Our meeting began.

14 Marula
PRODUCT INNOVATION & VALUE CHAINS

In addition to the craft sector, the Mineworkers Development Agency (MDA) was also engaged in product innovation in the commercialisation of products derived from the indigenous marula fruit, harvested from the wild as a non-timber forest product (NTFP):

> Brought to public attention by Ben and Jerry's rainforest crunch ice cream and the Body Shop's range of exotic moisturisers, non-timber forest products have – for the last two decades – been widely promoted as a contribution to the sustainable development of tropical forest resources ... Non-timber forest products are seen as having the potential to achieve dual conservation and development goals by increasing the value of forest resources to local communities. (Schreckenberg et al. 2006, p. 1)

While marula grew prolifically in communal areas, it had not been commercialised to any significant extent. A rare opportunity therefore existed to catalyse new markets for products derived from this indigenous fruit, bringing a new source of income into poor communities from a potentially significant asset that until then had been hidden in plain view.

The marula, or *Sclerocarya birrea*, sub-species *caffera* is an ancient African tree that grows prolifically in a belt that stretches from northern KwaZulu-Natal across the lowveld into Namibia and all the way to Zambia.

Outside this belt, it is known for two main reasons: for the entirely apocryphal stories of elephants drunk on fermented marula berries stumbling around the veld, and for Amarula Cream – a liqueur sold in over one hundred countries and produced by Distell.

Within the marula belt, people have relied for centuries on the many qualities and uses of this prolific tree, including its fruit, kernels and wood, with homesteads also protected from the hot African sun by the shade cast by these massive and magnificent trees. The marula fruit has more vitamin C than oranges, its kernels are a source of protein in the local diet and the cosmetic properties of its oil have been known in these areas for centuries. Marula also has profound cultural significance within ritual systems as well as within traditional medicine. Festivals are held in honour of the marula fruit to celebrate the harvest; this includes the custom of *Xikuha*, in which households present marula beer to the village headman, following which the community celebrates together; the ritual of *Kuphula*, in which marula beer is offered to ancestral spirits, and the tradition of *Xirwhalo*, a gathering during the harvest season, at a household where marula beer has been brewed, that can take several days, after which the celebration moves to the next household (Shackleton and Shackleton 2005, p. 17).

Many homesteads have at least one marula tree within their boundaries. In an inventory of marula incidence and yields in Bushbuckridge, covering four villages, associated communal lands and two protected areas, Shackleton et al (2002) found that 78.9 per cent of households had *S. birrea* trees in their homesteads and 58.2 per cent had them in their fields.

Mhala Development Centre (MDC) is located squarely within the marula belt. Andrea Nzima, the local MDA co-ordinator proposed that Mhala Development Centre should embark on a product development process exploring the commercial use of marula products.

The involvement of MDA in this process began before our engagement with the 'making markets work' approach and it certainly did not qualify as 'facilitation'. Instead, MDA was a direct player within the value chain, in fact catalysing the development of that value chain on the basis of new product development, unlocking previously untapped value from an indigenous resource and with the chain reliant on the participation of thousands of rural women. Was it the best way to approach this challenge? There is no facilitation-based counterfactual against which to test this: but it certainly held lessons about the interaction between product development and market development processes that are relevant across paradigms.

These processes began under the auspices of Mhala Development Centre, but were later transferred into a company called Marula Natural Products (Pty) Ltd (MNP), which was a subsidiary of MDA. MDA transferred 30 per cent of the equity in MNP into the MNP Trust, initiated by MDA to represent wider community interests in this indigenous resource; MDA's intention was also to reserve some of the equity for the purposes of securing a private equity partner in due course as part of the commercialisation process.

At this time, despite extensive local use and an emergent informal trade in marula beer, commercial markets for marula products were very limited. A sub-sector analysis of the industry undertaken at the time identified that there were really only two formal commercial players in the marula market in South Africa at the time:

- Distell
- Mhala Development Centre (MDC)
  (Mander et al. 2002)

Given Distell's market capitalisation of over R4 billion, it and the MDC represented the elephant and the ant. Yet while the global penetration of Amarula Cream might seem to reflect a high level of commercialisation of the marula fruit, there are only actually very small quantities of marula in Amarula Cream and all Distell's marula needs were supplied by a company called Mirma in Phalaborwa, which sourced the fruit from a few local villages. For MDC, the development opportunity was to significantly expand the ways in which this prolific but under-utilised resource could benefit local communities: with no necessary tension between it and Mirma.

Yet such a process of commercialisation was not without wider risks, including concern at the possibility of 'trading away tradition'. 'Those embarking on the commercial development of NTFPs must balance carefully the benefits derived from commercialisation with those derived from subsistence and traditional use, in order to minimise negative impacts on livelihoods and culture' (Wynberg et al. 2003, p. 204).

The risks of commercialisation included reduced reciprocity associated with the free exchange of marula products, risks of increased privatisation of what is currently a communal resource, as well as reduced use of the resource as part of subsistence. Concerns were also raised that, as opportunities grew, more entrepreneurial groups might squeeze the poor out of the supply chain (Wynberg et al. 2003, p. 204). Yet these risks also had to be measured against the potential benefits to local communities – and the desirability of undertaking such a process with a development lens on these issues.

Mhala Development Centre embarked on the product development process by exploring whether traditional marula beer – widely and wildly drunk during the brief fruiting season – could be stabilised and commercialised.

At that time, the mines were outsourcing the running of the beer halls that were a part of mine life on all the mines. MDA was involved in an initiative at Premier Diamond Mine in Cullinan in which retrenchees were taking over the beer hall, which they named the Lapologa Chris Hani Beer Garden,[1] in a form of joint ownership between an Employee Share Ownership Scheme, representing the retrenchees, and the NUM branch at the mine. On behalf of NUM, MDA was considering a wider strategy of mine beer hall takeovers, and the plan was to sell marula beer to mineworkers through such a network: a nice tied market.

MDA entered into a research and development partnership with the Foodtek division of the Council for Scientific and Industrial Research (CSIR), working with food scientists Dave Harcourt and Morewane Mampuru.

---

[1]   This translates as the 'Rest in Peace Chris Hani' Beer Garden. Chris Hani was the General Secretary of the South African Communist Party, assassinated in 1993 in an incident that threatened to derail the transition to democracy – but did not.

Photo 13 *An ex-miner puts the finishing touches to the mural portrait of Chris Hani at the Lapologa Chris Hani Beer Garden at Premier Mine, Cullinan, Gauteng; 1993.*

At the 1997 NUM Congress, all eight hundred delegates were issued with a sample bottle of marula beer, labelled 'Vukanyi'. Taste trials were also done at the Lapologa Chris Hani Beer Garden. Contrary to our expectations, it was soon clear that targeting this market posed unanticipated problems. Mineworkers from parts of the country where marula does not grow were unfamiliar with it and didn't like it; those that knew it well wanted it to taste like traditional home-brewed beer, which the bottled version did not. In addition, far from being willing to pay a price premium for it, the latter group were used to getting it for free at home and certainly expected it to be cheaper than their favourite commercial brand, Castle Lager. Not even Vukanyi's beautifully-designed gold labels made the difference. We were confronted once more with the intractable challenges of volume, price and productivity ratios – and once again, we found ourselves in a market that was already occupied by a powerful monopoly player within South Africa's core economy.

Our strategy changed and our target market shifted. The MDC is ten kilometres away from the Kruger National Park and is surrounded by upmarket game lodges. Surely tourists in this 'external' but adjacent market would pay a premium for an exotic local product? MDA piloted this opportunity using a micro-brewery located at the CSIR, producing 3,500 litres for test marketing purposes (MDA Annual Report 2000). A small but reliable number of game farms did indeed place orders: but the volume requirements were not high enough to translate into the kind of volume supply necessary to offer a significant new source of income in the community. MDA was still in search of strategies able to reach the kind of scale that could do so.

Along with the beer and as part of targeting the game lodges, MDA tested the possibility of packaging marula kernels, labelled 'Timongo Nuts', to augment the indigenous experience. Tests run at the CSIR, however, found high levels of a carcinogen that causes liver cancer in the kernels once these were packaged in plastic – whereas in communities, their storage in open containers had no such effect. Just one example of why consumers do actually need to be protected by regulatory controls and standards in the food industry – the pressures for business-friendly cutting of red tape and deregulation notwithstanding. Timongo Nuts stopped right there (Correspondence with Dave Harcourt, 1997).

Meanwhile, however, the CSIR had developed a method for stabilising marula juice as an unfermented product which had not been done before. This opened a completely new set of opportunities.

In addition, a lucrative market for marula oil had also been identified. During this period MDA joined Marulanet, a loose network of NGOs scattered across Namibia, Zimbabwe and Botswana involved in commercialising marula products. On behalf of this network, a French NGO, the Centre for Research, Information and Action in Africa, Southern Africa Development Consulting (CRIAA SA-DC – later called Phytotrade) commissioned research into the properties of the oil. This alerted MDA to the potentially high commercial value of marula oil in the cosmetics industry:

> The oil is rich in Oleic acid, which is an essential component in the maintenance of healthy skin. It is a high-value oil appropriate for body and facial products, with natural alpha-hydroxy properties as well as natural sunscreens. It is also tremendously stable, outperforming all known natural liquid oils. (Barton 2001, p. 3)

Marula kernels were extracted manually from their hard nut casing and cold-pressed using oil presses on site. MNP's labour-intensive juice pulping process was designed to leave the nut undamaged so that quotas of nuts could be returned to suppliers pro rata to the weight of berries they had supplied, with the supply of the kernels back to MNP providing a secondary income stream:

> The aim was to contribute to people's livelihoods throughout the year and not only for three months. Plus, from the perspective of sustainable use, it made sense to optimise the returns from every berry. Research into uses for the peels should follow. (Interview with Susan Barton, MNP Manager, 18 August 2005)

Allowing a contribution to overheads from a diverse range of products across the year – rather than having these loaded solely onto the marula fruiting season – was equally important to MNP's viability.

Photo 14 *Women involved in the marula programme at Mhala at the launch of Vukanyi, MDA's marula beer product, at Lapologa Chris Hani Beer Garden at Premier Mine, Cullinan, Gauteng; 1993.*

By 2002, approximately 2,400 people in 42 villages were part of MNP's supply network; this rose to 4,000 participants by 2004, with the numbers varying in response to demand.

There was also significant variation in the volumes supplied by households, with a value range of R9 to R1,106 (about US$1–100) per household, per month, depending on the amount of effort applied and up to R1,900 (about US$246) for the sale of kernels out of season (Shackleton and Shackleton 2005, p. 11). This research was also undertaken in a period in which volume requirements from MDC were still rising:

> Although not a large amount, the timing of marula harvest at the beginning of the school year makes this extra income extremely important for the paying of school fees, clothing, and the purchase of food and household goods, particularly in areas with high levels of poverty. (Wynberg et al. 2003, p. 204)

Income from marula was never expected to be the sole source of household income but, instead, to assist large numbers of women to supplement existing livelihood strategies – with 99 per cent of the money earned from marula in the hands of women (Mahlati 2011, p. 110).

Institutions framing marula use

Historically, the management of communal farming areas and woodlands has been a function of the local tribal authority. In this region, people are fined for cutting down trees in communal areas without permission:

If found cutting down a tree that bears edible fruits, people are fined. The fines are as follows: Chief Khosa Jonilanga (Jongilanga Tribal Authority) – R500. Chief Nxumalo (Amashangana Tribal Authority) – R500 and confiscated the cutting tools (axes and saws and pangas [machetes]). Chief Chiloane (Sehlare Tribal Authority) – R300 and Chief Mnisi (Mnisi Tribal Authority) – R300. Charges for the permit range differ from one Tribal Authority to the next. Permits start from R1.00 for 10 poles. (Chiloane and Phala 2002)

However, the inability of tribal authorities to police this has led to increased degradation of the resource. During this period, MDA entered into a partnership with the Department of Water and Forestry (DWAF) to promote community forestry and the propagation and effective management of marula in the Bushbuckridge area, identifying the following problems of woodland management:

In the last ten years the woodlands have been even more degraded and people blame democracy.
    The cause of this partly lies with the chiefs and the local councillors who are competing for power in the communities. They use their power to give people access to land and natural resources to win the support of the communities. This competition is resulting in poor decisions being taken regarding the woodlands and is causing even more degradation
    [...]
    In this period of change and the resulting lack of clarity on roles, mandates and legislation – and in the way people interpret democracy (freedom) – any prior system of natural resource management has broken down. People take advantage of this confusing situation and get access to land or natural resources either through the chief or the local government depending on which one they think is more likely to grant them their request. However, in most instances they ignore both authorities and simply occupy and clear the land and collect natural resources without permits. It is this freedom that is causing problems. People say now there is freedom, they can do what they like and collect anywhere and collect as much as they like. (Chiloane and Phala 2002, p. 19)

With supply to MNP spread across forty-two villages, the risks of putting pressure on this resource did not seem high, even taking into account existing use and, indeed, towards the end of the period under review here, Shackleton and Shackleton (2003) found that commercialisation was not directly competing with or threatening domestic and subsistence needs and was instead providing a welcome source of income for the households involved, with only some 19 per cent of the total fruit gathered and used by households being sold.

While the potential for conflict over the resource remained an issue for concern, even villages that shared open-access areas reported no conflict at this stage. 'The only problem was that they were scared of snakes or lions and other dangerous animals' (Chiloane and Phala 2002). Below, MNP's Mademezulu Njoni explains initial resistance to commercialisation from tribal authorities:

Photo 15 *Mademezulu Njoni, CEO of Marula Natural Products, with a tub of marula kernels at the MNP office at Mhala Development Centre; with another mural by Andrew Lindsay and local artists; 2002.*

When we introduced the buying of fruit, the chiefs said: 'Then you want to introduce death in our communities, because marula is God's given fruit and you can't trade it'. But people are hungry. People are hungry. And when you look at that, it brings in a lot of other issues, gender issues, because the people who are hungry much more are the women and children. And they are the ones who are supposed to be brewing the juice for free and giving it to the men to enjoy and drink freely. But now the women are very much empowered, they are saying 'No! We are selling.' Somehow, poverty can change structures and, maybe, the way that things are supposed to be done. (Interview with Mademezulu Njoni, 8 August 2004)

Over time, these attitudes shifted, as it became evident that commercialisation strengthened conservation, leading to a convergence of interests in relation to conservation, strengthened systems of community and tribal authority management of marula and increased marula propagation at homestead level:

The tribal authorities and chiefs have realised that the only way of sustaining these trees is by commercialising them and putting some money value on them, because that's the only way the trees can get respected.
    [...]
    So now the chiefs are working with us in so many ways. They are more receptive to what we are introducing to these communities and we involve

them, because we believe it helps, because a lot of people still believe that what they get from the chief is the right thing ... We have involved them in our structures and the CDFs [Community Development Forums] and the municipalities.

They participate in the marula village committees and we want them there, it helps a lot. It's a good channel of communication. If we leave a message for the villagers with the chief to say that there's going to be a meeting, that message disseminates. (Interview with Njoni, 2004)

The marula committees were incorporated into the community development forums being established by newly elected local government councils, reflecting the reality of dual power in rural areas, with policy contestation over the relationships between these and traditional authorities. The ex-miners played an important role in mediating this tension. Both Andrea Nzima and Douglas Mboweni from MDC were by then elected councillors active in the establishment of community development forums.

The following responsibilities were defined for the marula committees:
- Transfer information to other community members
- Inform people of the collection dates and collection points
- Inform people about quality and quantities required
- Work closely with other committee members and collectors
- Weigh kernels and fruit to be sold by each collector
- Quality control of the fruit (not too green or too ripe) and kernels
- Solve problems and conflicts around marula collection and selling
- Conduct and attend meetings
- Write minutes and reports, filing and record keeping
- Encourage collectors to be patient and tolerate problems and be on good behaviour (they insult the people from DWAF and MDC when there are problems).

(Chiloane and Phala 2002)

In the first two seasons of fruit collection, MNP faced significant logistical challenges, including weighing the crop and paying suppliers at each village collection point, with delays at any one collection point leading to frustration further down the route.

New roles and relationships had to be defined but, over time, the role of the marula committees was institutionalised and the number of community liaison officers employed by MNP declined, as the committees took on more responsibility. The opening of bank accounts allowed a great leap forward:

What we also did this year is that we transferred the money into their bank accounts ... You cannot believe it! We requested the communities to open bank accounts and we asked the suppliers to collect a rand each to open that account and keep it alive, and it worked. It's a community account, not an individual account at the moment. So each village has their own account; we pay into the village account and with that account the village pays the individual. It is amazing.

HIV/AIDS takes its toll

At Mhala in this period, the Human immunodeficiency virus (HIV) and Acquired immune deficiency syndrome (AIDS) pandemic formed an integral part of the backdrop against which development intervention took place. MDC (and later MNP) manager Susan Barton describes it:

> We talked about HIV openly: staff and clients at the centre. Tinswalo hospital did free HIV checks in the area and we talked about whether to have them; some staff did and knew their status; others declared that they never wanted to know. I remember one staff member's open relief when he told us that he'd tested negative. The women who worked on marula were also told about the HIV screening clinics in the area and were handed female condoms and we all had a big laugh about them. I know the women discussed it whilst marula nuts were being crushed; the myths around HIV – such as that it could be cured by having sex with a virgin – were also discussed because I remember the conversations we had after a nine-month-old baby was raped in the area. (Susan Barton, correspondence with author, 2016)

Then the administrator at MDC (we'll call her Gladys) fell very ill. She wouldn't see a doctor and was resistant to discussing her illness, but we feared the worst. The symptoms seemed to fit. She became weaker and weaker. Stigma in the community was very real: her father threw her out of the family homestead for being ill. Her mother left with her. She would not stop work; it was her means of livelihood and her link to life. It was also a supportive space. By this stage, she actually had to be carried to work and placed at her desk: a bundle of bones, like a little bird.

Finally, she told Susan that she had seen a doctor and had been diagnosed – and it was *not* AIDS. She had a rare blood disease and had to have a series of blood transfusions but it should not prove terminal. We celebrated. Those of us who had assumed it was AIDS were mortified at having misjudged the situation. It highlighted how fear of the disease could have unanticipated consequences – preventing people from seeking medical help for preventable illnesses.

Then Gladys died; and it turned out it had been AIDS after all. Right to the end, the levels of stigma associated with the disease meant she would rather invent a diagnosis than confirm the real one – or get treatment for it.

Despite having thrown her out of his home when she was ill, her father felt entitled to claim her employee death benefit. He came to the Centre, brandishing a gun, demanding that then Centre Manager Thandi Hlatshwayo pay it over to him. That did not happen.

And now, with the introduction of the Mzansi account,[2] people will be encouraged to open their own accounts, so that we can transfer directly into those accounts. It will also be very helpful if we get a consistent supply, because then each one will know that each month, there will be a consistent amount coming into their account.

When we heard about Mzansi, we thought 'Wow! This is our solution!' We knew nothing about this Mzansi account that was being set up, it was co-incidental and what was amazing was to discover that while you're working on one thing, other people are working on something else that is part of your solution. (Interview with Njoni, 2004)

Challenges of commercialisation

Marula created a unique opportunity for poor communities because it had never been 'colonised' or propagated commercially, despite (or perhaps because of) its prolific availability on communal lands.

> This context made the private sector nervous. They couldn't quantify the scale of the resource and, because it is located on communal lands, access to marula meant working through tribal authority structures and communities and, in their terms, ownership relations were unclear. These concerns and perceptions represented a significant hurdle to overcome. (Interview with Barton, 2005)

In addition, according to Njoni (who became CEO of MNP in 2003), the private sector in the food industry is used to dealing with 'machines, ploughing, planting and contracts'. Dealing with communities that are highly dispersed 'has not been the game of the private sector'.

> For them, it takes a lot of time – and it does take a lot of time, it's very true ... for over five years now, each season, we still go to communities and remind them: the kind of fruit that we want; that they mustn't cut trees, the regeneration process, the administrative process ... So the private sector would be very ... lazy, if I have to put it that way ... to go into communities to talk to these people because, to them, they are too scattered and they don't understand, and it's taking a long time and it's too risky and all of that. (Interview with Njoni, 2004)

Through the organisation of marula committees, MNP was able to create a local institution with the legitimacy to co-ordinate access to the marula resource. Agreeing terms on which a particular set of village members were sanctioned to utilise an open-access resource in communities was no easy task. In the process, a new form of economic co-operation was also institutionalised, creating economies of scale that enabled entry into wider supply chains for the first time. Although not

---

[2]   After 1994, as part of the Financial Sector Charter, the banking sector commited to make banking more accessible to communities by opening low-cost transaction accounts – known as Mzansi accounts.

called co-ops, the marula committees aggregated supply in the same way that supply co-ops would do, generating volumes and strengthening their bargaining position in value chains – in this instance, in a value chain being constructed from below, with the marula committees a necessary condition for making this possible.

The marula committees were an institutional innovation organising suppliers at village level. MNP then provided the interface between these structures and the requirements of the commercial world – acting as an intermediary between these worlds apart and navigating the rules of the game that apply in each. Such intermediation provides a mechanism to bridge the gap between players who do not play by the same set of rules: whether this is between formal and informal, or in relation to the more complex differences in ownership, control and use rights that exist between communal tenure arrangements and market-based systems – with this form of intermediation mitigating the risks of exchange for both parties.

This critical intermediation role involves building forms of organisation and relations of trust with communities on the one side, in ways that recognise the rules of the game within which they function, at the same time as providing, on the other side, the formal contract certainty, quality assurance, predictability of supply and other signifiers necessary to mitigate the risks of exchange for private-sector players. Contractual certainty and these other signifiers are however necessary but not sufficient. Few risk-taking business decisions are ever taken without issues of trust being part of the calculus, and innovation certainly involves risk.

The functional roles played by intermediaries in value chains are well recognised: aggregating supply and providing quality assurance, forms of pre-processing, transport linkages and/or marketing facilitation. Where they are bridging the gap into value chains for marginalised producers, there is an additional more implicit role: providing an interface between different rules of the game and strengthening the trust calculus necessary to clinch deals and forge new forms of partnership between players not used to interacting with each other.

As we soon discovered, there is also a huge gap between demonstrating the theoretical properties of a product and securing a commitment to commercial product development and marketing of such products. In general, product development of NTFPs takes five to ten years; it took six years of engagement with CRIAA SA-DC before the Body Shop decided to integrate marula oil as a base ingredient in their make-up, which is distributed to over fifty countries in the world. This finally provided a core market against which suppliers could start to deliver (Shreckenberg 2003, p. 13).

Long lead times can sabotage the commercialisation process because of the costs and risks involved, skewing advantage towards established

players and significantly limiting the scope for new entrants to capture
the gains from this investment, with a six-year gap between the delivery
of samples and the first volume orders usually simply unbridgeable for
any start-up producer – or poor community. Nor is it possible to limit
those costs and risks by simply providing product samples to potential
buyers until they place an order:

> Of course the private sector is interested in the properties of your product but
> that is actually just the start. I've had buyers bowled over by the properties of
> the marula, but that has still not translated into follow-up orders. No private
> sector company is going to invest in a research and development process
> that will last for several years if they are not confident that a secure and
> consistent supply of the resource will be available at the end of that period.
> They won't invest in product development on the basis of samples that
> have been developed in a lab; they won't even start a product development
> process unless they are confident that there is a supply chain that can deliver
> the volumes and quality they will require if they decide to go ahead in the
> future. But without markets in place, how can a supply chain be in place?
> That's why a pre-commercial production phase was necessary. (Interview
> with Barton, 2005)

This intractable problem is at the heart of the commercialisation
challenge and significantly limits the ability of poor producers to enter
such markets. It was the reason why MDA opted to go into a pre-commercial phase of production, despite the lack of secure markets at the
time – playing a catalytic development role where the risks precluded
a simple market-driven process. This meant that marula committees
were established, berries and kernels were bought in and pilot-scale
production was initiated at risk, because it was clear that no-one in
the private sector was willing to buy an idea or invest in new product
development simply on the basis of samples of marula oil or pulp
produced in laboratory conditions. It was a strategy that worked. It also
enabled an iterative learning process:

> The very difficult thing in product development will always be what comes
> first. It helps that we've gone into production first because we've learned a
> lot: you find out that while you are producing, you are learning about the
> other side, the market and what they require – for instance quality issues,
> consistency issues, capacity issues – you learn about the marketing side of
> things, their minds and their thinking, in that world. (Interview with Njoni,
> 2004)

In addition to supplying the Body Shop, MNP secured markets for
the oil with Tropitone, as an ingredient in their suntan cream; with
US cosmetics company Arch as well as with Rain. Later, MNP also
launched its own set of hand and body creams. Yet by the end of the
period covered here, the combined volumes for all these contracts
remained below MNP's capacity to supply, limiting the scope for the oil

to support income generation on any significant scale. Instead, it was marula juice products that forged ahead.

Markets for Marula Mania – the juice

Marula fruit ferments extremely quickly; when the CSIR and MDA developed a process to prevent fermentation, this opened the door to the fruit beverage market for the first time:

> The initial plan was to set up a processing plant. When we ran the numbers, it was almost impossible to make a profit; because you had a three-month period in which you are producing and a nine-month period in which equipment is standing; but you would have to service that debt for nine months. (Interview with Boris Kamstra, 23 March 2006)

MNP needed to find a commercial partner with existing capacity to pulp the fruit. As luck would have it, Mhala is not only adjacent to game farms, it is also close to the main commercial farming region supplying sub-tropical fruit such as mangoes and litchis to the fruit beverage market on a mass commercial scale. Although just across the recently dismantled bantustan border separating Gazankulu from these white commercial farmlands, Mhala was in effect smack in the middle of a regional fruit-pulp processing cluster. Yet spatial, racial and social barriers limited access to these networks and MNP initially had no luck finding a commercial partner to pulp their fruit. 'Their view was that they cannot waste their time with us. When people believe they are too big it takes a lot of time for them to understand that they can help you to be at their level' (interview with Njoni, 2004).

Boris Kamstra, business consultant to MNP, was however able to facilitate a link with a large independent fruit-pulping company called Bronpro Processors (Pty) Ltd in Hazyview:

> The secret that unlocked Bronpro was that they had a citrus line that was standing unused during the marula season and aspects of that line could be adapted to cater for the marula. It's all about getting risk and exposure as low as you possibly can and optimising the equipment you have, so immediately the potential opportunity from marula was attractive to them – they said, OK, we probably only have to sink about R50,000 into capital equipment to do this – we'll do it.
>
> In addition, the major asset in these processes is your freezer farm. You have to process twenty-four hours a day in season and then freeze it, and freezer capacity is hugely expensive. But if you have a number of fruits going through at different seasons, you can rationalise those costs. Bronpro had spare freezer capacity. (Interview with Kamstra, 2006)

Bronpro took the risk, adapted their equipment and placed an order for fruit with MNP – in a context in which they too had no market for marula pulp. They were, however, a major player supplying a wide range of fruit pulps to the industry and had longstanding business relationships with processors further down the chain. They succeeded in marketing the concept of a new juice to a company called Fruit Time, who agreed to develop the first commercial marula juice product, which was retailed in 2002. At this point, the larger market players started to take more notice:

> Ceres are a lot more thorough and less entrepreneurial in their approach, but as soon as they realised another player had brought a marula juice product onto the shelves, they sat up and took some interest.
>
> Samples were continually going up and down from Bronpro to Ceres, but it took them two years before they finally said: 'OK, we'll run a trial'. It's that interim period that's so difficult, because you have to hold sufficient inventory to be considered serious – no-one is going to develop a new product if they know there's only five tons of inventory available; that doesn't make sense.
>
> So you have to be able to hold that position. Bronpro sat on half a million rands-worth of inventory for three years – it finally all went out at the end of last season. (Interview with Kamstra, 2006)

Ceres (a subsidiary of South African Breweries at the time) brought out a mixed juice product called Marula Mania under its Liquifruit label as well as an alcoholic marula Liqui Cooler. Bronpro supplied the fruit pulp, based on fruit supplied by MNP.

Initially, the fruit pulp was semi-processed and stabilised on site at Mhala Centre and then sieved and supplied to the manufacturers by Bronpro. When volumes increased from the initial ten tons in 2002 to 450 tons in the 2006 season, Bronpro adapted its machines to handle the full pulping process, with MNP providing the fruit directly (interview with Kamstra, 2006). MNP continued to produce a high-quality juice onsite in this period, to fill its own ten-ton freezer capacity and to service growing demand from lower-volume niche markets.

MNP had a unique offer that was not easily replicated. While Bronpro did buy from some independent marula suppliers at their factory gate, MNP remained their largest and preferred supplier. The longer such relationships last the more tacit knowledge is created and the greater the switching costs for both parties. The critical issue is how costs and risks are shared in the process. In this instance, Bronpro offered technological know-how and carried the costs of holding inventory in their freezers during the market development process. Without this, it is unlikely that access to wider markets would have been possible.

Such risk sharing cannot be assumed. In Namibia, in the early years of the Eudafano Co-op's contracts to supply the Body Shop – and despite the Body Shop's commitments to fair trade – suppliers from poor communities in Namibia were effectively pre-financing this global value chain, with a lag of six months and even a year between them supplying the marula kernels and finally being paid (Schreckenberg

Photo 16 *When the first marula juice product was launched, MNP provided samples to all the women involved in collecting the fruit. Here MNP staff set up in preparation for the event in Bushbuckridge, Mpumalanga; 2001.*

2003, p. 23). These differences illustrate the extent to which the spread of benefits is a variable outcome and a function of negotiation and power, which in turn influence the informal rules of 'fairness' in a given context. The terms of trade are a social construct.

According to Kamstra, Bronpro's involvement 'is a commercial proposition, totally and absolutely'. The selling points were that marula juice is organic and natural in a market seeking new flavours. In addition, as a global brand, Amarula Cream had helped pave the way into international markets.

Entering international markets posed new problems, however. In 2002, Bronpro secured a large order for marula juice from a German company. However, because marula was not registered as a food product in Europe prior to 1997, it could not be marketed in Europe without being proved safe for human consumption by the European Food Safety Authority in terms of European Commission Regulation No. 258/97 on novel foods and food ingredients. Distell generously provided supporting documentation to assist MNP and Bronpro in their attempt to appeal against this requirement on the grounds that Amarula had been marketed in Europe before the regulation, but this was rejected because the quantities of marula in Amarula are so small compared to the juice.

Getting marula juice approved as a food product and crossing other regulatory hurdles involved in accessing European markets took over two years and substantial expensive legal and specialist expertise. The way was however finally cleared for marula juice to be exported into Europe, based on organic certification. Then a US company expressed interest and MNP had to tackle the requirements of the US Food and Drug Administration: more years, more legal fees. Meanwhile, the South African market continued to grow.

Innovation that works for the poor?

In relation to marula juice, MDA catalysed the creation of a value chain from below. In the case of the oil, MDA was part of a wider process. The juice was a high-volume market, the oil a high-value one. In both cases, links were made between poor communities and national and global value chains, at levels of scale that enhanced the positive impacts on poverty at the same time as requiring new forms of local organisation.

The marula committees drew on skills and practices rooted in grass-roots community organising approaches, impacting at a community-wide level on the governance and management of this indigenous resource. At the same time, this created a new form of economic co-operation, which in turn enabled the economies of scale required for the commercialisation process. The process also shed new light on the role of intermediaries in bridging the gap between marginalised producers and wider opportunities and the dynamics and pressures that come with participation in a wider value chain. Yet despite these gains, there was no shortage of vexed and unresolved issues.

The first one related to how, whether and to what extent MNP should continue to receive donor or public funding to support the product development and commercialisation process. This was linked in turn to debate over the extent to which innovation constitutes a public good – as well as whether the intermediary role of bridging the gap for marginal producers into wider markets merits this designation.

Schreckenberg (2003) argues that, while innovation should be treated as a public good, manufacturing and marketing processes should function on a commercial basis. Conceptually clear as this may be, MNP's experience illustrated the messier reality that innovation is an outcome of an iterative process of learning from doing – and from marketing. The technological changes and adaptations required for effective commercialisation were driven by the scale imperatives and problem-solving requirements imposed in the production pro-cess, but driven by the needs of other partners in the value chain and market feedback. Research and development play an important role, but translating these into a commercial process and proposition happens in the pressure cooker created by business imperatives. A neat distinction between innovation and production and marketing processes is therefore hard to make.

Since the period under review, there has been a massive increase in policy support for the role of innovation systems in unlocking growth, and a much greater recognition of this as a public good, and a recognition that the gains from investment in innovation can rarely be captured by a single firm – with this deterring firms from carrying these costs. This dynamic was evident in the marula context. While MNP and Bronpro had some level of first-mover advantage, they shouldered the risks of innovation, in the process opening the door to followers whose costs and risks were much lower. When MNP began, marula products did not exist in the South African market. Today, marula-based cosmetics and beverages are relatively widespread.

For MNP, the more immediate implication of this debate related to the question of at what stage it should be expected to operate on a fully commercial basis, without any form of subsidy from donor or public funds. With the windows for donor funding closing, MNP started to approach development finance institutions (DFIs) in search of equity partnerships. We traipsed from one big-name DFI to the next, only to be turned away time and again. I recall sitting in posh offices in Midrand, being lectured by a fund manager from the National Empowerment Fund on why, despite the national and global markets already being serviced at the time, MNP was too high risk for two specific reasons: because of its reliance on marula committees for the supply of the raw material, and because the raw material was sourced from communal lands.

While MNP survived on a commercial basis for several years after donor funding ended – and still survives today – there was a catch: its limited capital and cash-flow resources made it extremely vulnerable to deals in which the short-term survival of the enterprise took precedence over the staying power needed to negotiate terms that would secure the benefits of the innovation undertaken and its associated intellectual property for poor communities. As this illustrated, it is in the early, insecure stages of business development that market pressures can make producers become 'willing captives', ceding intellectual property rights or entering terms of exchange to secure a market in the short term, at the expense of longer-term rights and returns.

This in turn was linked to the complex issue of intellectual property in a context in which deep indigenous knowledge of the properties of marula already existed in communities. Could MNP capture the intangible value of this collective indigenous knowledge, rather than ceding it further up the chain? Was MNP or even the community-based MNP Trust the right vehicle to do so, when there is much wider community ownership at stake? Yet how should these rights in indigenous knowledge be expressed and defined when the marula belt stretches halfway up sub-Saharan Africa?

Much as these rights need to be protected, how this is done can raise the bar for commercialisation so high that value can never actually be realised – a risk well illustrated by the complexity of various forms of legislation to protect indigenous knowledge. Thus far, there is a risk that the institutions deemed best able to act as the custodians of such knowledge are not well equipped to support commercialisation processes. The logic of indigenous knowledge protection also often rests on tying such knowledge to narrow tribal and ethnic roots when neither ethnicities nor traditional knowledge exist in the pure forms needed for this to have juristic effect. Yet lack of clarity over the potential for such claims is likely to act as a significant disincentive for private investment. Meanwhile, debate over these issues has not stopped marula trees from being propagated in Israel as a commercial proposition.

Finally, there was real debate about MNP's location in the value chain and whether this ceded too much value further up the chain. Was MNP locking communities into a low-value poverty trap in the supply chain? Was this actually just an example of making the poor work for markets?

It was argued that instead of providing fruit pulp and raw oil, MNP should be producing finished products such as its own line of marula cosmetics and its own line of juices to capture value addition at the level of the final branded products.

The critical issue was one of scale. Participating in existing value chains allowed for an exponential increase in volume requirements, which translated into a proportionate increase in the incomes going into poor communities. It was once Ceres agreed to produce 'Marula Mania' that MNP was able to extend its supply networks to include four thousand women in forty-two villages – with the prospect of further growth. Entering into competition with Ceres would, by contrast, have required significant capital investment in production and marketing facilities – yet with marula as the only product line and with a fruiting season of only three months in the year. It would have been extremely hard and probably impossible to do this on a competitive basis – quite apart from the fact that MNP did not have the capital available for such an approach.

In relation to the oil, while MNP did later develop its own line of soaps, moisturisers and body lotions, the volume of oil required to do so was very small. If the goal was to benefit communities on as large a scale as possible, then volume of supply was the critical driver. Going further up the value chain with finished products might secure better returns for MNP as a company, and create a handful of potentially decent jobs, but it would mean significantly lower volumes of supply would be required with less benefit to local communities. This was the trade-off; it was certainly an issue of contention within the governance structures of MNP.

Inequality will get you in the end

Finally, ways in which markets reproduce inequality and their distributional impacts were highlighted by a DFID-funded international study, 'Winners and Losers', that explored success factors in the commercialisation of non-timber forest products. A study of the commercialisation of marula in South Africa and Namibia by Mander et al. (2002) was a part of this wider study that included a comparison between Distell and the Mhala Development Centre in relation to the marula juice value chain:

> There is great differentiation between the current returns to the two largest commercial operations in the sub-sector (Distell and MDC). The Distell operation is estimated to run at a profit of R388 000 [about US$50,000] per annum while MDC is estimated to have operated at a loss of R36 396 [about US$4,700] in 2001. The profitability of the Distell operation is attributed to their success in securing a market, while the MDC operation has yet to establish a secure and reliable market for the quantities of marula products they are generating. (Mander et al. 2002, p. vi)

There's no dispute that Distell was making a profit and MDC was making a loss at the time this study was done. It did however seem to us that implicit in the conclusions drawn was that Distell was the winner and MDC the loser: despite a comparison between MDC in its pre-commercial phase – before contracts with either the Body Shop or Bronpro were in place – with Distell's established operations. While this may not have been the intention of the authors, the report certainly impacted negatively on the project at the time.

Yet the ostensibly neutral comparison made between Distell and the MDC, devoid of any political economy, created the impression of a level playing field, implicitly endorsing the status quo as a reflection of the outcomes of a free and fair competitive process, or some kind of Darwinist process of natural selection in the economic sphere.

To put this into context, Distell is iconic in what it represents in South Africa. It was formed from a merger of Stellenbosch Farmers Winery and Distillers, owned by the Rembrandt Group. The Rembrandt Group was formed in 1945 and was a symbol of the rise of Afrikaner capital in the South African economy in the apartheid years; a product in many respects of the policies aimed at converting the political power of the National Party into economic power – a central part of the apartheid project.

A shareholder in Distell is KWV, another South African icon. KWV – originally Koöperatieve Wijnbouwers Vereniging – was a wine cooperative and part of the network of white farming co-operatives that were the heartland of the political power of the agricultural sector in the apartheid years. In 1996, when KWV opted to convert from a co-op to a company, the Minister of Agriculture attempted to block this conversion in court, arguing that KWV had benefited significantly from state support over decades and that its assets – estimated at over R1 billion – could not so simply be privatised by its current members.

It was argued that KWV had benefited from statutory levies on wine and spirits that had been reinvested into its reserves, as part of a wider process in which white farmers benefited from tariffs, investment in infrastructure development, tax rebates and incentives, subsidised credit, drought relief schemes and more. By contrast, black farmers in the same period had been forcibly removed from their land – and into bantustans such as Gazankulu, where Mhala is located.

This political economy lives on in the structure of the economy and in the endowments that players bring into the market, and their scope to play the game in that market on 'winning' terms. To say that the profitability of Distell is attributed to their success in 'securing a market' is to somewhat understate the factors that placed Distell at a market advantage in the marula sub-sector by comparison with MNP.

The contrast between the decades of support to Distell and the dominant development logic of a rapid transition to full cost recovery by MNP could not have been more stark. Yet once again, this short-termist cost-recovery logic pitted MNP's survival against its purpose, with its ability to hold onto intangible brand value and intellectual property within the value chain at risk as the short-term price of market access and market survival: with better-endowed players poised as always to capture the opportunities instead.

Bringing history into the equation is generally treated as distasteful in market development debates. Even where history is acknowledged – and in South Africa it is hard to overlook – the current structure of the economy tends to be accepted as the given and immutable framework within which a market logic must now be given precedence going forward. Yet the application of a market logic to this context simply reinforces and deepens the inequality that history has embedded, reproducing the same patterns of winners and losers. This is a variant strain of Chang's (2002) 'kicking away the ladder' to maintain existing structures of economic power.

15 Implications for Enterprise Development Strategy

The central focus of this book has been on the quest to build effective strategies to support the development of enterprise on the margins, in South Africa's mine-labour-sending areas, to create jobs and to reduce poverty. Across fourteen years and several different phases of the Mineworkers Development Agency (MDA)'s programme, in a period that also straddled South Africa's transition to democracy, it is sobering just how marginal enterprise on the margins remained and how miserably low the returns usually were. Certainly, the ball can (and no doubt will) be thrown into our own court: in every phase, there was learning to do, mistakes made, strategic errors of omission and commission. Yet more than a decade later, surveying the field, a few things are striking. Firstly, many of the lessons we learned in this process remain very relevant to small enterprise (SE) development strategy in marginal contexts today. Secondly, it's clear that, unique as MDA's experience may have been, strategies promoting enterprise development in South Africa still often find it hard to achieve meaningful reductions in poverty.

At one level, this should come as no surprise. Yet the expectation that poor people can and will be able to self-employ their way out of poverty at significant scale – self-funded through micro-loans at commercial interest rates – remains deeply embedded in the policy discourse and the public imagination. Certainly, when the story outlined here began with the dismissal of forty thousand mineworkers, the expectation existed even in NUM that enterprise development activity – co-ops in particular – offered a feasible pathway back into employment for a significant proportion of this group. In the face of unemployment figures that have remained stubbornly high in the decades since, it really matters if the default assumptions about what it will take to change this are flawed.

As described in Chapter 10, strategies of enterprise development in poor and marginalised communities have had a tendency to under-estimate the economic implications of South Africa's high levels of structural inequality, including in particular the structure of the economy, the impacts of concentration and also of spatial inequality. The structure of the South African economy certainly also impacted on the wider region in which MDA's programmes operated. These constraints have a very specific set of implications for enterprise development strategies and for their scope to impact on employment creation and poverty reduction. The wider economic structure within which enterprise development strategy takes place will always impact on options and outcomes, with contextual variations: yet in the global discourse on small enterprise development, this issue is all too often absent.

These conclusions reflect on the lessons learned from grappling with this reality, the shifts in strategy over time and what this means for the place of enterprise development strategies within the wider agenda of employment creation and poverty reduction, before the final chapter returns briefly to the bigger-picture themes of markets and society.

From worker co-ops to economic co-operation

MDA's experience of enterprise development began with the co-op programme. While all forms of enterprise on the margins face complex sets of challenges and choices, these are compounded in worker co-ops or in other analogous forms of collective group enterprise.

Co-ops and collective enterprises can succeed; the problem in South Africa is that the sets of conditions required for them to do so are often absent in the very contexts in which they are most strongly incentivised.

In the early stages of NUM's engagement with enterprise development, worker co-ops were seen as prefiguring socialist forms of ownership and control and providing a form of social protection for workers against the impacts of the market. However, while the collective and democratic character of ownership and control within a co-op may mitigate certain negative features of work organisation associated with conventional employment, the co-op form provides no protection from market pressures for the enterprise as an entity, which still has to compete and engage within wider markets, with the tendency for worker co-ops to fail or degenerate often ascribed to such market pressures. And so our engagement with market issues began.

While the existence of market pressure on co-ops is common cause, the NUM co-op experience highlighted that the ability of worker co-ops to adapt to such pressure is circumscribed by a set of skewed internal incentives specific to the co-op form. Douglass North's analysis of economic history looks at how incentive structures at an institutional level in societies predispose them either to growth or to economic stagnation; it has been argued here that the incentive structures within worker co-ops predispose them to failure if they cannot adapt. Simply attempting to cushion the effects of markets on worker co-ops does not deal with these internal incentive issues, which require adaptations to the traditional co-op form and to the co-op principles – adaptations partly reflected in the shifts in these principles adopted by the International Co-operative Alliance in 1995 and also reflected in approaches taken in, for example, the Italian Lega and Spain's Mondragon Co-ops. Yet contestation over these issues has continued to be a feature of debate in co-op circles. It has however been argued here that it is where co-op movements have embraced adaptations to the classic model – often described pejoratively as 'degeneration' – that co-ops have thrived at a scale that allows them to become meaningful economic players within a wider social economy.

From a South African perspective, misplaced expectations of the scope for worker co-ops to create jobs at scale has continued to inform development strategy, particularly in the most marginal areas where the prospects for success are the most constrained. Worker co-ops offer an inspiring alternative of collective ownership and self-management, but they are the most complex of all forms of co-op – perhaps of all forms of enterprise. Promoting this form of economic organisation to people with no prior work experience (let alone enterprise management experience), and in the absence of any wider form of co-op movement or tradition, sets these co-ops – and participants – up for failure.

Meanwhile, there has been a dearth of concerted support for other forms of co-operative organisation, despite their stronger track records and the significant social – and employment – benefits they can bring. In particular, this relates to forms of user co-op that provide economic services to their members, which can include consumers, independent small producers, retailers and farmers. Evidence suggests, for example, that where South African traders and *spaza* shops are out-performed by foreign entrepreneurs, it is often because the latter have proven more adept at organising collective buying schemes that give them the shared advantage of economies of scale. Similarly, agricultural co-ops can play a vital role in supporting the viability of smallholder farmers – without collective production as a necessary condition for this.

These user co-ops and other forms of economic co-operation and association may fall short of the collective production ideal that inspires worker co-ops, but they provide a mechanism through which small-scale economic actors are able to assert their presence within markets on different terms: to create economies of scale, to negotiate a more equitable distribution of benefits and to change the balance of power within markets, in order to exert economic influence on the rules of the game within which they operate – with the potential to have a more systemic impact on the structure of a given value chain or market, on the way it works, and the terms of their inclusion in it.

Whereas worker co-ops often struggle to absorb more than a handful of members, because an oversupply of labour can threaten their viability, consumer co-ops, savings groups, agricultural co-ops, co-op banks and many other forms of co-op get stronger the more members they have.

This is why these forms of co-ops are so important in building a co-op movement – as the more than eight million members of co-ops in Italy's Lega demonstrate. At this scale, even though their primary purpose is not job creation but the provision of services to their members, they can in fact also become large-scale employers. To build such a movement, it is necessary to embrace and promote diverse forms of economic co-operation that respond to collective local needs: strengthening networks and linkages as part of a wider social economy and complementing other forms of social organisation, civic action and solidarity.

The 'projectising of poverty'

The conflicts and disputes that characterised the social history described in Chapter 3 illustrate a wider development reality that applied throughout the process, which is that, insofar as any form of development intervention succeeds in reducing poverty, such intervention will have distributional consequences, with the impacts on poverty invariably uneven, with winners but also sometimes losers. In turn, the distributional effects of development intervention will impact on power dynamics at local level, over the distribution of benefits and over ownership: not only of any assets or opportunities created but also over who is able to claim political ownership of any development gains made. In this process, the scope to mobilise a sense of relative deprivation within a given community can, in certain circumstances, translate into acts of local economic sabotage that appear to have little purpose other than to level the local playing field once more. This political economy of local development dynamics is all but ignored in the outputs-based discourse that dominates the sector: yet is a central determinant of outcomes.

These dynamics apply in particular at the project level, where development intervention brings new resources into resource-starved communities. As a result, the terms of intervention are likely to be contested and may cause conflict. No matter how inclusive the process is in one community, the adjacent community may well feel excluded. This is a critical weakness of project-based approaches, heightened where such projects require externally driven processes of participant selection (rather than self-selection) and when these same projects are presented as having some kinds of community-wide benefit or public character that raise expectations that are not met.

A lesson therefore is that the more development intervention takes place in a zero-sum context in which some benefit greatly and others not at all, the greater the likelihood of conflict. Yet this zero-sum effect is typical of the way in which income-generating projects or group enterprises have been promoted in many contexts in South Africa – and often still are. Where a development agency (or local government) plays a direct role in establishing enterprise projects, for which beneficiaries are then selected, lack of clarity over ownership, governance and the distribution of benefits tends to bedevil even viable initiatives. Such projects also typically offer at most limited and localised impacts.

As Judith Tendler has argued, the 'projectising' of poverty and of social policy (2004, p. 121) also lends itself to elite capture and patronage. Attempts to mitigate this by targeting the poorest, often through complex processes of 'outing' them in their communities, can have their own perverse consequences. Tendler also argues that the projectising of poverty keeps the attention of public policy at this level, at the expense of more systemic solutions – reflected in special project funds and ribbon-cutting exercises, with a rigorous review of outcomes all too rare.

Such approaches can also have unanticipated market effects. When grant funds are provided to establish local enterprises, the chances are that there are already a handful of self-employed entrepreneurs engaged in the same economic activity: probably informally, perhaps from their backyard, capitalised with their own savings or a micro-loan, on their own or maybe employing a few people. Then the project enters the same market: operating at a much larger scale, often with ten or twenty members and capitalised with new equipment and working capital grants.

The project may not survive for long after its grant funding ends, but until then it will compete with other local producers and its access to grant funding will give it a competitive cost advantage as well as a scale advantage over entrepreneurs who have built their business from scratch with a mix of savings and loans. The subsidy the project receives will allow it to undercut local prices. The risk is that, by the time it collapses, its competitors will already have done so – with a net loss of jobs and economic activity in a given local economy: an inadvertent economic scorched-earth policy.

So, is there no role for direct and subsidised enterprise establishment, as part of local economic development strategy? By this logic, neither the business units in the development centres nor Marula Natural Products should have been supported. What differentiates these from the kind of project approaches described above?

The following main features do so: firstly, the roles played and risks taken in relation to innovation; secondly, the need to overcome particular forms of market failure or constraint and thirdly, the catalytic roles played in unlocking new economic opportunities, either from an untapped local resource, in the case of marula, or by creating changed market conditions that lowered the threshold of viability for business activities in multiple sectors, as in the case of certain business units in the development centres. Do these provide sufficient rationales to support – and subsidise – such interventions? This was (and remains) contested terrain. In the end, the nature of the differences on this issue mirror wider debates on industrial policy and on innovation policy and – for better or for worse – interventions in the local economy often mirror the consequences of such policies in the national economy.

As with industrial policy, the issue is less about subsidies per se than how, when and on what terms support is provided. Are there any rules of thumb in this regard? Firstly, arguably, the lower the barriers to entry for a particular enterprise type, the more likely direct subsidies to such enterprises will crowd out other local entrepreneurs. Secondly, as far as possible, support for entrepreneurs should be provided in open-ended, demand-driven ways that rely on self-selection rather than externally driven processes of beneficiary selection.

Development centres and business development services

NUM shifted away from an approach focused at the project level (through its co-op programme) to focus on service delivery through development centres. This allowed an important shift: instead of NUM setting up projects on terms that required the selection of a limited number of participants per co-op, the users of the centres were self-selected, with no limit placed on the number of people who could use the services offered: in fact, the more the better. In the process, greater scope for agency and initiative – or entrepreneurship – were also unlocked. Certainly, outcomes, impacts and the scale of outreach all increased significantly in this phase.

The centres created an environment for networking and learning by doing: both in terms of sectoral clusters, such as for poultry, as well as supporting a more horizontal, multi-sectoral community of local enterprise practice. They also performed a 'de-risking' function – with the equipment-hire facilities allowing entrepreneurs to engage with technologies that were new to them and to test different markets without having to incur significant upfront investment, enabling applied innovation.

The business supply stores also created access to business inputs not otherwise available in the local economy but required in sub-sectors such as poultry, construction and small-scale food processing, building economies of scale that allowed demand thresholds for these inputs to be reached, in turn creating conditions for their longer-term sustainable supply. With sufficient demand created, market failures hindering the development of local production activity were overcome. The centres also provided intermediation services that limited the risks and costs in bridging the gap in value chains in selected sectors.

One of the problems confronted, however, was that, in a context of high inequality, the gains from the economies of scale and threshold effects achieved by the centres were often quickly captured by established players. Perhaps the entry of these players would have happened anyway, without MDA's development centres. It did however seem that as soon as these started to reach break-even thresholds, creating conditions for sustainability, big players from within the core economy started to enter the market in areas that had previously been underserviced. While one could claim this as a market-development effect that overcame a prior market failure, it was certainly not on the terms anticipated. Were the aim simply to extend the reach of the big players into these areas, there were probably more-cost-effective ways of facilitating such an outcome. This was not, however, the intention. Was it really overreaching on our part to imagine we might localise the ownership and economic benefits of such processes – rather than just paving the way for existing players to expand?

In practice, for those with equity to invest, the threshold at which levels of demand were sufficient to sustain a viable supplier enterprise were significantly lower than for new entrants, dependent on loan finance in a lending environment in which lending rates were well in excess of 20 per cent at the time. In other words, an investment based on equity needs lower margins to break even. This is one of the trajectories through which inequality reproduces itself: the cost of capital is cheaper for those who already have it than for those who have to borrow it. As a result, the threshold at which it became viable for the big players to enter such markets was lower than for new entrants. Overcoming this requires mechanisms to create access to capital and/or to equity, not to loans. The difficulty, however, is how to structure such access without recreating the problems described as a local development scorched-earth strategy above – so that the process actually supports emergent entrepreneurs rather than crowding them out.

MDA's role in direct service delivery through development centres came up for no small measure of scrutiny and critique as a result of the business development services (BDS) approach; we in turn returned the favour. As argued in Chapter 11, the central weaknesses of the BDS approach included a tendency to overlook the links between markets, power and poverty or the role of inequality in markets, coupled with a predilection for a rather uncritical market fundamentalism. These were reflected in the core assumptions in the Donor Guidelines: in particular that both operational and strategic business services could and would be provided by the private sector 'even for the lowest income segment of the entrepreneurial SE [small enterprise] sector' and that this segment would be willing and able to pay for such services, if only distortionary subsidies were removed (Committee of Donor Agencies 2001, p. 1).

These assumptions proved flawed. They ignored the role of threshold effects for operational or economic services and the catalytic role of strategic services – such as product development and market facilitation

– in unlocking new forms of value and opening access to new markets. The BDS approach did, however, hold certain important lessons, which carried through into the paradigm called 'making markets work for the poor' (M4P) and from which we learned important lessons.

Firstly, the BDS and M4P approaches placed discussion of markets and their impacts centre-stage in the small enterprise development discourse, where, surprising as it may now seem, they had not been. Secondly, they focused on the market effects of different forms of development intervention. This was new and it was necessary. While the debate about what that means for the types of development interventions that are 'permissible' or effective continues, the need to be aware of the market impacts of development intervention remains important. It is true that markets in marginal areas are fragile and that with the best will in the world, intervention can do damage and the process needs to be informed by mindfulness in this regard.

Then, the critique of the notion of service delivery as development purpose challenged development agencies to raise their game to play a more catalytic role and to achieve more systemic forms of change, with the concept of sustainability shifted away from the narrow confines of organisational cost recovery to this wider level. Despite the many unanswered questions about what this means for organisational sustainability and despite different perspectives on what systemic change is, this was nevertheless a more developmental framework within which to be asking such questions, in a context in which, in South Africa, the development sector as a whole was increasingly stuck in a service-delivery rut: a situation that has largely not changed up to today.

Cost recovery and the new anti-politics machine

While the BDS market development approach focused on the market impacts of development intervention in new ways, it also inadvertently drew attention to the effects that a market-driven approach to cost recovery was having on the development agenda of MDA's development centres.

As part of a wider global discourse, the focus on cost recovery in development has been a feature of the post-apartheid period, in civil society organisations beyond the enterprise sector. Organisations that had largely been focused on systemic change in the political realm in the apartheid period attempted to convert to playing a service-delivery role to support the democratic transition. With the advocacy funding characteristic of the anti-apartheid period largely drying up, cost recovery became the new imperative.

Where cost-recovery concerns pit the organisational survival of development agencies against their purpose, where competitive pressures mitigate against playing catalytic change-agent roles and cause organisations to target away from the poor, then, drawing on Ferguson's powerful term in a different context, cost recovery in development becomes the new 'anti-politics machine'.

For Ferguson, writing in the era of the post-colonial state, it was state-lead processes of development that leached the politics out of the development process. Against the later backdrop of a neo-liberal hegemony, market-driven processes of development achieved similar effects in different ways: with a development politics able to catalyse systemic change from below still elusive and constrained.

Facilitation, organisation and systemic change

The BDS and M4P approaches emphasise facilitating systemic change that makes markets work better for the poor. The first question this begs is what is meant by systemic change? At one end of the spectrum, it means deregulated markets; at the other, socialist revolution. It also depends which level of the 'system' is under scrutiny: from the micro-economics of how smallholder farmers access fertiliser to the rules governing tariffs in the World Trade Organisation.

For the arguments here, the concept of systemic change describes processes that lead to a change in institutions (in the rules of the game) and/or a change in power relations that result in better outcomes for poor people on terms that can endure.

Next on the agenda is to what extent 'facilitation' can in fact achieve such change, the role of the kind of development politics from below, to which Ferguson alludes (1990, p. 282), and how such a politics might be organised.

Part of what makes the concept of facilitation attractive is that in some respects it resonates with what would once have been understood as an organising role in South Africa: a role that was integral to the process of achieving social and political change, but that has itself almost disappeared from the development discourse: to the detriment of change processes of any kind.

A critical difference, however, is that, while the concept (and process) of organisation was always rooted in an attempt to empower participants and to change power relations, the concept of facilitation tends to be used in ways that ignore issues of power or agency. Perhaps it is not surprising that a discourse that often does this should develop an instrument for systemic change that does so too.

Most of the elements usually described as being required to make a market work, in the classic sense, can be facilitated. Facilitation can enhance access to information, create linkages, reduce transaction costs and achieve the kinds of outcomes that make markets work more effectively and efficiently. This can mean better returns for poor producers (or consumers) although efficient markets can also co-exist quite happily with high levels of inequality and poverty. The point, however, is that facilitation can achieve a range of win-win outcomes in markets, where making markets work better also happens to make them work better for the poor. At a certain threshold, this may also lead to changes in the structure of the market in a way that embeds these effects. This is all worth achieving. It has its limits, though.

At a certain point, making markets work better for the poor is likely to reach the limits of win-win solutions and to entail changing the distribution of returns in a given market in ways that require and/or lead to shifts in power relations in that market. Shifts in power relations and in the distribution of returns are not facilitated, they are negotiated, they may have to be fought for, won and defended over time and the ability to do so is likely to depend on how protagonists are organised and – to use Khan's (2012, p. 8) concept – what 'holding power' such organisations have.

A quick scan of today's M4P websites illustrates the point. To a large extent, wherever gains have been made by the poor, these have been possible because the incentives have also worked for stakeholders further up the chain: where the focus on the 'bottom of the pyramid' is a profitable exercise for all concerned. This win-win paradigm places serious limitations on the scope to address contexts in which it might be necessary to disrupt existing patterns of allocation, power and distribution in markets, where these are patently disadvantageous for the poor.

As soon as change in the way a market works entails a zero-sum shift in the distribution of benefits, it moves beyond the scope of facilitation and onto the terrain of negotiation, where outcomes are determined to a large extent by organisation and its ability to impact on power relations. This relies on players rooted in that market.

Any serious attempt to catalyse systemic change in markets or to change the distribution of benefits within them has to take serious account of the ways in which power is organised and constituted both within and in relation to markets as well as the forms of organisation and influence through which such power is exerted and through which different sets of interests are defended.

These debates link directly to theories of economic change and the role of organisation and forms of association within societies and within markets that shape the rules of the game in society, with the issue of 'holding power' a critical concept.

The centrality of the role of organisation in effecting institutional – or systemic – change applies to political processes and the state, but there is also a terrain of influence from within markets in terms of how power is constituted, how participation is organised, how influence is brought to bear, that has effects within markets – at the same time as contributing to a political economy context in which political power can potentially be held to greater account.

As a consequence, the forms through which 'the poor' constitute themselves matter – across a diverse spectrum of interests, capacities and identities – in order to influence the way markets work: as workers, consumers, producers, retailers and more. This is the case even though the interests of different constituencies of poor people can manifest in contradictory ways and be in conflict.

In practice, it is workers in trade unions that have most consistently been able to contest the terms of inclusion of the poor in a given market, doing so in the incremental and ongoing kind of way that North describes as characterising the processes of economic change. The financial independence of trade unions gives them holding power. That their roles currently face huge setbacks and may, in some contexts, have had contradictory outcomes for other sectors within the poor is not the point.

What are the equivalent forms of organisation able to represent the interests of the poor in other capacities? This is critical to contesting the terms on which the poor are integrated into markets, their ability to shape markets and to change the interests that markets serve. The answer to this is far less clear, with fewer organisational models able to exert power or influence, or to provide the kind of holding power that trade unions have demonstrated.

The exception, in certain parts of the world, has been the role of co-ops. This is arguably, however, only where co-op movements have also been mass movements, built on the foundations of a multiplicity of forms of economic co-operation, where the critical organising principle is that the larger the membership, the stronger their economic power. What such co-ops share with trade unions is the financial independence that their membership base provides. Worker co-ops have a home in this landscape, but they are not its backbone, because the number of members they can absorb is circumscribed by the labour-absorptive capacity of the enterprise, with limits on this imposed by the competitive market context.

What other forms of social organisation might tackle the market-change challenge? How will these be resourced? Without an answer to that question, their holding power will remain circumscribed.

Implications of the structure of the economy for strategy

During the co-op programme, and also in the context of service delivery through development centres, the focus was on promoting local pro-duction for local consumption – on support to enterprise activity targeted largely at local markets in poor areas. In reviewing outcomes, the impact of the structure of the economy on the scope for such an approach came into focus, with the difficulties compounded by spatial inequality, strongly correlated in turn with continued inequality in human development outcomes based on race.

As was explained in Chapter 10, the structure of the South African economy means that it is extremely difficult for small-scale producers to compete with South Africa's established industries insofar as they are competing for a market share from poor consumers in relation to basic consumption goods. Typically, small producers cannot compete on price or brand recognition and, for larger, less recurrent purchases such as furniture, they also cannot compete on the kinds of payment terms the established sector can offer. In contexts of high concentration, price is not the only means of exclusion, however, with cartel behaviour also excluding newcomers.

The net effect, however, is that the opportunities for small-scale manufacturing targeting poor consumers in local markets are largely limited to niche opportunities: that is, to products not already mass-produced in the core economy, or where the product is sufficiently differentiated that consumers are willing to pay a higher price for it. Such opportunities are more likely to exist where communities have started to see a degree of internal social stratification, and that is certainly happening in certain contexts. Today, Soweto, for example, includes a middle-class constituency willing and able to pay more for a local craft beer – such as Soweto Gold; cappuccinos now have a market in Khayelitsha. Increased disposable income at the local level immediately expands the landscape of opportunity. Often however, in South Africa, the black middle class moves out to the leafy suburbs leaving the poor spatially concentrated in areas of exclusion, with niche opportunities remaining relatively limited: despite examples of real innovation and entrepreneurship. The point however, is that these dynamics are not static, even if the overall structure of the economy has continued effects.

Despite such shifts, it remains true that, insofar as poor consumers are the target market, small producers find it hard to compete, with greater opportunities in retail and service – which is where the action is in practice. At local level, the issue is how best to support entrepreneurs to diversify and upgrade their offerings to strengthen returns.

Enterprise development opportunities in marginal contexts are not, however, confined to local markets. In a highly unequal context such as South Africa, there is no shortage of disposable wealth in markets beyond these confines. However, access into such markets requires a step-change in business sophistication and a very different kind of support strategy. A focus on local markets lends itself to more horizontal strategies – such as those the MDAs development centres provided –

where the emphasis is on networks, skills-upgrading, economies of scale and creating threshold effects. A focus on external markets tends to require a more focused sectoral approach to creating market access or access into value chains. Such approaches certainly need not be mutually exclusive, as long as the different enterprise support needs dictated by different forms of market insertion are understood. These needs are explored further below.

From local to external markets

There is no binary choice between targeting local and external markets. Both have advantages and disadvantages and, in any given local economy, there is space for both. While a focus on local markets in poor communities can at times represent a poverty trap, success in gaining access to wider external markets is by no means an easy alternative, despite the significant potential such markets hold. From a strategic perspective, what matters is to understand the different characteristics of each so that appropriate support can strengthen outcomes.

Certainly, enterprises targeting local markets have advantages. Entrepreneurs can rely on local knowledge and networks and they understand the value propositions in their own community; the barriers to entry tend to be low; the context lends itself to informality and income-generating activity can often be done part-time and from home on a flexible basis, with volumes built incrementally over time with limited risk. There is little advantage to formalisation for enterprises of this kind and many are below the radar of regulatory frameworks: yet this location in markets tends to limit their horizons to low-value opportunities with limited growth prospects.

In recognition of these limitations, MDA started to focus beyond such local markets to seek out higher-value opportunities in the wider economy. Yet, accessing these 'external' markets entailed bridging both social and spatial distances: with a new set of constraints brought into play.

In particular, the shift in focus to external markets introduced a shift from the face-to-face transactions characteristic of local markets to the arms-length or business-to-business transactions required in the interface with retailers or as part of wider supply chains. This shift to Adam Smith's 'anonymous exchange' marks the end of informality as an option. According to Douglass North:

> [o]f all the fundamental transitions that human beings have had to make, the shift from personal to impersonal exchange has been one of the most fundamental and is one that is still at the very heart of the failure of poor societies to develop. (North 2003, p. 6)

Access to wider markets holds the promise of significantly expanded returns – but it requires new levels of formality to provide the contract certainty necessary to limit the risks of exchange, as well as to enable compliance with sector-specific standards and quality measures. This typically requires a step-change in business complexity, levels of capital investment and cash-flow risk. Often, the value proposition in distant markets is also less than clear to those hoping to enter them: particularly where rural producers are targeting people and places they have never encountered before.

As a corollary, it is the nature of insertion into markets that determines the relative benefits of formalisation; there is nothing axiomatic about its advantages. In local markets, where transactions are directly with the end consumer, there may be few benefits from formalisation. Yet if the goal is to break into wider markets, informality can be an insurmountable barrier.

While much of the focus of strategy for small enterprise development has been to limit red tape to enable formalisation, there is a risk of missing this larger point: the real rationale for formality is that legal status enhances contract certainty and enables anonymous exchange, providing the basis for recourse in the event of default. Where an exchange is informal, little or no recourse exists (or such recourse is also informal). Leaving aside large-scale illegal operations, informality tends to confine transactions to the local context, limiting their scale and scope for growth. Instead of focusing on reducing the requirements for formalisation, it may matter more to support small enterprise to up their game.

It is against this backdrop that forms of intermediation enter the picture in bridging the gap between marginal producers and wider markets. In MDA, such intermediation created an interface between the often-informal networks of rural craft producers and the formal, urban and international retail sector where ever-changing design trends and complex export standards create barriers to entry. Certainly, there were contexts in which unequal power relations were abused, but there were also many instances in which intermediaries limited the risks of exchange and lowered transaction costs for both parties, creating new forms of market access and bringing disposable urban incomes into rural local economies. The roles played included insight into the value proposition in distant markets, the provision of design input and product development support, as well as upgrading the capabilities of the entrepreneurs or enterprises in ways that enabled them to transact directly or to institutionalise forms of intermediation into the value chain on sustainable terms.

The importance of intermediary roles was evident also in the development of the marula value chain. MDA's Marula Natural Products (MNP) played the role of a market intermediary embedded within the value chain, initiating product innovation, negotiating access to the resource from traditional authorities, consolidating volumes of this indigenous fruit from four thousand women in forty-two dispersed and somewhat inaccessible villages, reducing transaction costs and risks for players further up the chain and enabling the link into established volume markets in the fruit juice sector and into a global cosmetics value chain for the oil.

In both the craft and marula examples, product development and innovation allowed for new segments of a wider chain to be built from below, avoiding direct competition with existing players and using innovation to create new forms of value. In both cases, however, MDA was able to create links into existing value chains with strong links into relevant markets or strong brands on which such new products could ride.

While in the first instance, participation in value chains requires a step-change in business sophistication, once within such chains, open market transactions are replaced with supply relationships that offer continuity and within which relationships and interdependencies develop, with trust relationships off-setting the risks and transaction costs of anonymous exchange. This includes technology transfer and risk sharing. In the process, under the right circumstances, participation in value chains can assist in bridging the gap into wider markets. Participation in value chains also allows for specialisation, which can reduce the scale and complexity of the challenge facing entrepreneurs on the margins.

Implications for employment creation and poverty reduction

In the context of the significant structural constraints confronting enterprise on the margins, it is small wonder that returns are often low. This does not remove the rationale for supporting enterprise on the margins, and there are many relevant lessons to be learned from MDA's experience. It does however mean a sober assessment of the extent to which such strategies can live up to the expectations so often placed on them, in relation to employment creation and poverty reduction at scale for the poorest.

Contrary to widespread expectations, strategies for enterprise development in marginal contexts are not mass employment strategies. They can contribute to employment creation and to strengthening livelihoods, but the notion that the solution to poverty lies in poor people self-employing their way out of poverty is misplaced: all the more so if it is assumed that the process can be self-financed with a micro-loan or from funds diverted from social grants intended to feed a child or support a pensioner. After fourteen years in MDA, the limitations of small enterprise development in addressing employment creation and poverty at the speed and scale South African society currently requires was clear: as was their limited scope to directly target the people most in need of such employment.

At an overall level, there is no escape from the big-picture issues of inequality, the structure of the economy, strategies for inclusive growth, industrial policy and human development in South African society: all of which will contribute to the scope for small enterprise development in marginal contexts also.

However, these big-picture issues will take time to resolve and have thus far proven largely intractable. Yet, addressing the social costs of poverty and unemployment is urgent. A policy assumption that small enterprise development strategies will pick up this slack is tantamount to society washing its hands of the problems. There is a concerted need for complementary strategies. What might these be?

In the first instance, in South Africa, there is a need to address the social protection gap. Despite a seemingly generous social grants system, its direct beneficiaries are people who society does not expect to work: children, the elderly and people with disabilities. Vast numbers of unemployed people have no direct form of social support, leaving them dependent on goodwill transfers from within their communities, from people with jobs or access to social grants intended for other purposes. As unemployed people are mainly in poor communities, this burden is carried overwhelmingly within such communities, with impoverishing and also dis-equalising impacts in a society already so highly unequal. Instead of the cost of unemployment being shared by all as a social cost, it is shouldered disproportionately by those who can least afford to do so. Yet important as it is to address this social protection gap, it only partially addresses the negative social impacts of unemployment on society as a whole.

So, while Plan A is for the economy to develop in ways that create market-based jobs at the scale required, societies also need a Plan B. Employment matters too much to leave to markets alone. This is all the more important in a world in which the future of work appears to involve less and less of it, with the demand for labour potentially in decline. Now, more than ever, societies need to look at new ways in which to address the social need for economic inclusion through participation in work: a social need that goes beyond simply earning an income, important as that is.

It was in the light of these concerns that my own attention turned to the scope for innovation in the creation of public employment: moving beyond the traditional categories of public works to find new ways of creating work – and of creating social and economic value – in contexts in which markets are not doing so: re-asserting the social value of labour, even where it has no market value, and investing in communities in the process.

16 If Markets are Social Constructs, how Might we Construct them Differently?

> The need for a constantly changing market for its products chases the bourgeoisie over the whole surface of the globe. It must nestle everywhere, settle everywhere, establish connections everywhere.
>
> The bourgeoisie has through its exploitation of its world market given a cosmopolitan character to production and consumption in every country. To the great chagrin of Reactionists, it has drawn from under the feet of industry the national ground on which it stood. All established national industries have been destroyed or are daily being destroyed. They are dislodged by new industries, whose introduction becomes a life and death question for all civilised nations, by industries that no longer work up indigenous raw material, but raw material from the remotest zones; industries whose products are consumed not only at home, but in every quarter of the globe. In place of old wants, satisfied by the production of the country, we find new wants, requiring for their satisfaction the products of distant lands and climes. In place of old national and local seclusion and self-sufficiency, we have intercourse in every direction, universal independence of nations. And as in material, so also in intellectual production. The intellectual creation of individual nations become common property. National one-sidedness and narrow mindedness become more and more impossible and from the numerous national and local literatures, there arises a world literature. (Marx and Engels 1848)

This quote from the Communist Manifesto appears to be an ode to the dynamism of capitalism and to globalisation. Certainly, it highlights capitalism's immense powers to innovate and to create wealth – and in the process to destroy old forms of social organisation and to create new ones.

That power has impacted in differential and contradictory ways on human history and human lives ever since, because the flip side of this hubris is that poverty and exploitation have also been characteristic of capitalism's global expansion, with epic struggles focused on how to contain and resist its destructive power at the same time as to harness its ability to create wealth and reduce poverty. In essence, these are struggles over distribution; they are also struggles over power: over who gets to determine the rules of the game. Such struggles have taken many forms, with highly differential outcomes within and between societies and interest groups across the globe – with the process continuing unabated.

> Capitalism has not just survived; it has been rejuvenated and shows no
> prospect of imminent collapse, or even ageing. This is the totally unpredictable
> outcome of the twentieth century. It is still unbelieved in many circles.
> Many point to the injustices, inequities and costs of the new dispensation ...
> There is no rival mode of production on the horizon as a viable alternative.
> Capitalism is the only game in town. The contest is between rival versions.
> (Desai 2004, p. 303)

Desai wrote this before the last great financial crisis and the decimation
of jobs that followed. That crisis seemed to offer unanticipated
prospects for a reversal of capitalist triumphalism and a reassertion of
the role of societies in mitigating its worst excesses. Instead, not only
did capitalism triumph once more, it did so on terms that bailed out the
banks but left societies paying the price. Who could have anticipated
how quickly governments in the developed world would step in as
lenders of last resort? Nationalisation – the mere mention of which can
cause currencies in the developing world to plunge – was brushed off
and put to use like any other tool in the policy toolbox. No equivalent
scale of intervention was directed at mitigating the impacts in the lives
of people, however. The option of the state acting as employer of last
resort – as proposed by Hyman Minsky as an alternative approach to
the War on Poverty in the USA in the 1960s – was 'the path not taken'
(Wray 2007, p. 1).

Yet while the after-shocks of the crisis continue to impact across the
globe, Desai's central point still holds: at present, variants of capitalism
are the only game in town and the contest is indeed between rival
versions. No convincing alternative approach is even currently in
contention. Compelling as the visions of socialist *outcomes* might be,
clarity on the alternative forms of organisation of ownership, production
and exchange that might deliver such outcomes is simply lacking. These
are important details. If North is right about path dependency and the
incremental processes of institutional change, then it is also unlikely
that an alternative economic model will spring into being fully formed
to take us by surprise.

Bitter as this pill may be to swallow, it does mean that any hope of
advancing social and economic justice in today's world has to engage
seriously with changing *how* market economies and market systems
work – and the social and distributive outcomes they produce. This
is not, actually, cause for excessive doom and gloom. 'Rival versions'
of capitalism can encompass huge differences in the forms markets
take and the outcomes they deliver. From one society to the next, from
one sector or value chain to the next, the political economies that
determine the rules of the game that govern markets vary substantially.
Markets don't exist in any pure form; market economies don't either.
Both are embedded within social relations. As a consequence, the
social outcomes, rights and equity that can be achieved are also highly

diverse: they are steeped in their own particular histories, ideologies and expectations, with significant gains in social and economic justice already achieved in some contexts (threatened as these may be right now) but with scope for innovation to push these boundaries beyond the limits of our current assumptions and policy imaginaries. That's where the challenge lies.

In the first instance, however, a focus on such change is inhibited by a discourse on the role of markets that is based on a false dichotomy, that pits markets versus the state; and the economic versus the social: ignoring a history of market formation in which, far from constituting an 'intervention' in markets, the role of the state was formative in the development of markets as institutions – with 'the state' an institutional and organisational expression of society more widely, that has also taken highly varied forms.

In the dominant discourse, the social and the economic are presented as distinct and separate domains, with the market operating almost as a force of nature, variable and unpredictable: unlocking growth and development when treated right, unleashing havoc and destruction when its whims are ignored. Obvious as it is that economies – and markets – are part of societies and embedded within them, much in the public discourse feeds this notion that markets are instead somehow outside of society. For the free marketeers, that is their natural home – wild and free, unshackled, unpredictable, best left with a minimum of intervention of any kind (maybe just the equivalent of a game fence separating them from society). For many market critics, the same analogy applies – just viewed from the other side of that game fence: from where markets are seen as a kind of negative externality, a dangerous beast best kept at a safe distance from society.

The problem on both sides of this fence is that this conceptualisation cedes the terrain to the limits of neo-classical economics, in which the market 'is shorn of social relations, institutions, or technology and is devoid of elementary sociological concerns such as power, norms and networks' (Lie 1997, p. 342).

Instead, there is a need to recognise that markets are part of society; they are institutions that have emerged to govern exchange relations and as such, they are social constructs. As forms of exchange have become ever more impersonal and complex, the need for institutions to govern exchange has grown. However much we might be able to rebuild or reinvent less impersonal forms of exchange within a more social economy, we are also likely to remain part of global systems reliant on the complexities of impersonal exchange and of value chains, in which specialisation of knowledge continues to escalate and the global division of labour to mutate, taking new forms spatially and technologically. Smallholder farmers may well benefit from emergent producer-to-consumer movements yet, from Lusikisiki to New Jersey, such farmers are still also likely to rely on a mobile phone produced as part of a global value chain. Even if there is value in maximising such local systems, there is nevertheless no realistic prospect of returning to a world in which all our needs are produced locally.

Understood in this way, there's little point being 'against' markets – or against the need for institutions to govern exchange in societies. Producer-to-consumer networks also operate within systems of agreed, institutionalised rules that govern the exchange – often with the explicit goal of circumventing rules in other value chains they consider exploitative and unfair. They are a small, localised example of the social construction of a market in which, by design, power relations and the spread of benefits are more equitable; but this requires organisation and intentionality, with some level of mobilisation of consumer power, coupled with organisation amongst producers.

If, therefore, markets are understood as social constructs, the question is how they might be constructed differently – to achieve different social and distributional outcomes?

In their different ways, Polanyi, North and Chang all made the social construction of markets visible by elucidating the role of the state in market formation. That role certainly remains central, with a wide array of powerful levers, including the property rights regime, the courts, industrial policy, competition law, innovation and skills development – to name a random selection from the complex list of institutions and models that shape markets and their performance. The role of the state has also always encompassed a global dimension, with market formation inextricably linked to imperialism, colonialism and international trade. Global processes – and globalisation – are no less socially constructed than at the state level. There is nothing inexorable about a trade regime in which capital is mobile and people are not; this is a social construct. Untouchable and impervious to social processes though the rules of the game at this level have appeared to be, both Brexit and the surge of anti-globalisation politics in the USA in 2016 have these issues at their core. Too bad that, thus far, this momentum has largely been captured by the right, is tied to anti-immigration sentiments and, in the USA, looks set to deliver a form of pork-barrel protectionism that serves a particular segment of corporate interests while tossing a bone or two to the working class – called the middle class – to keep them at heel.

Yet despite the pivotal role of states, there are other powerful mechanisms through which the social construction of markets also takes place locally and globally – some of which elude the rules of the game set at state levels or agreed between states. This includes mechanisms within markets themselves, between stakeholders within sectors and value chains. These relationships straddle national boundaries, in terms of how such stakeholders organise themselves and through contestation between them, in ways that define important dimensions of how such markets operate and the power relations within them.

At all these levels, processes of economic and institutional change are strongly influenced by the role of organisation, with North arguing that organisations are the drivers of institutional change, because of how they articulate and assert specific sets of interests. While North uses the term to capture an array of forms through which people structure and formalise a common purpose, including everything from corporations to social movements, this broad definition includes a core truth, which is that any agenda of advancing the interests of the poor in shaping how markets work has to take seriously the forms of organisation through which such outcomes can be achieved, including (although not limited to) how the poor themselves are organised – not only within the political process, but also as players within markets: as workers, consumers, producers, retailers and more, if different distributional outcomes are to be achieved.

In this regard, the labour market still provides the clearest example of a constituency of the poor organising to change their share of returns from participation in a given market – in the process asserting some limits on their own commoditisation. Are there lessons that can be drawn from this for other markets? Are there contexts in which the players are not only capital and labour? What are the levers effecting such change? Work on pro-poor value chains has looked at how to secure better access and returns for small producers, consumer power has been used to influence the global behaviour of large brands and, in some countries, co-ops are significant economic players. Yet without derogating from the many examples of real impact, the forms of organisation and association required to exert influence and wield power in markets and even in specific value chains in significant ways still remain, to a large extent, lacking in scale and depth. Some of these efforts form part of what has been characterised as the social economy; but, important as this concept is, the limits associated with the 'projectising of poverty' often seem applicable in analogous ways within social economy approaches, similarly limiting the scope for more systemic-level impacts.

A lack of what Khan refers to as 'holding power' is part of the problem (2012, p.8). A simple but vital element of such holding power relates to the resourcing models available to support the emergence of social formations and organisations that enable them to stay the course. Simply put, the wealthy have resources on which to draw to sustain the organisations that serve their interests, including not only representative forms of organisation but also support organisations of diverse kinds, from lobby groups to legal services and media outlets. The poor cannot match this; their ability to do so is often further circumscribed by the imposition of market-based cost-recovery models on those forms of organisation attempting to support their interests.

The issue of how organisations representing or asserting the interests of the poor are funded may seem to be a minor, practical detail but it is actually rather fundamental. Finding new ways of addressing this is a strategic imperative for any process of durable systemic change.

This manifestation of inequality is, however, just one of the many ways in which inequality reproduces itself and in turn impacts on market outcomes, with the overall role of inequality so profound in this regard that it brings to mind the story of the Irishman, who, when asked for directions, is reputed to have advised, 'if that's where you want to go, you'd best not start from here'. This logic certainly applies to attempts to make markets work better for the poor, because of the extent to which the history of imperialism, colonialism, land dispossession, occupation, patriarchy and plunder are all inscribed in unequal endowments and patterns of power that market players bring to market processes – along with the accrued endowments that nations bring to the global economy.

Even in the local context of the marginal markets in which the Mineworkers Development Agency (MDA) operated, the role of the highly unequal structure of the economy in constraining opportunities and locking out new entrants was evident, as well as multiple other tangible ways in which inequality reproduced itself. This local experience was consistent with the growing consensus in the wider discourse on the role of inequality, which highlights that high levels of inequality constrain growth and that, even where growth does take place in such contexts, it tends to reinforce existing patterns of distribution in a self-reinforcing cycle (Ravallion 2004; Ostry et al. 2014).

This recognition is fundamental. It means that rather than seeing growth as an antidote to inequality, addressing inequality is a necessary condition for growth – and in particular, for inclusive growth. It also puts paid to any reliance on market processes leading to more equitable distribution; instead prior changes in distribution appear necessary to break the cycle. The social construction of markets on different terms – making them work better for the poor, if you will - is therefore an agenda with a distributional challenge at its core, with existing inequality potentially limiting the impacts of any changes in the rules of the game that might be achieved at other levels: a genuinely binding constraint.

The Irishman is right: we really cannot get where we want to go by starting from here. Instead, addressing inequality and issues of distribution have to be the starting point in changing the interests in which markets operate, to ensure that the productive powers of capitalism can be harnessed in ways that are good for societies. This requires a long hard look at the complexity of the distributional regime in any given context: at the nexus of factors and forces, past and present, that deliver a given distributional outcome, with these outcomes central to what constitutes 'society'. This is, in part at least, an institutionalised consensus on what we expect from each other, the contributions to our households and wider community we expect to make, the care we expect to receive when our ability to contribute is diminished, our notion of what constitutes 'the public good', and how as a collective we sustain it. Issues of distribution are in turn integrally connected to the rights regime, with direct distributional consequences from the forms taken inter alia by the right to education, to shelter, to food, to health care, to a basic income grant – or to an employment guarantee.

Within this, the property rights regime is often central, either repro-ducing the effects of history or shifting them, with choices at this level encompassing forms of tenure but also seemingly more prosaic issues such as inheritance laws and tax, with potentially significant impacts on asset inequality and intergenerational outcomes. Desirable as it may be to tackle this form of inequality directly, countries such as Sweden that have high asset inequality but low-income inequality illustrate that even where structures of asset inequality may seem intractable, societies still have choices in how they manage and mitigate the social outcomes.

In this regard, the role of labour markets is critical, both in relation to the rights framework underpinning employment, as well as in terms of how societies respond to unemployment: with the latter bringing us back to the central challenge with which this book has been concerned; and a final reflection on what it means that this market – like all others – is socially constructed.

An assumption is commonly made that unemployment is a form of market failure that market-based solutions must fix. While there is debate over the extent to which the state has a role in shaping such markets, the state of play is nevertheless confined within the parameters of market performance and how this is influenced.

Of course it makes sense to optimise outcomes at this level; there is no quarrel with doing so. Defining the challenge in this way nevertheless gives markets a primacy in relation to the role of work in society that they should not, in fact, be given.

To make an analogy, the notion that the failure to place value on the eco-services provided by the environment is a market failure assumes that responsibility for the environment vests with markets in the first place. Instead, this is a social failure: a societal-level failure to recognise the value of the environment for human survival (let alone for the survival of the rest of the planet) and the role of social systems in protecting it – including the need to protect it from markets.

Similarly, while unemployment is presented as a market failure, is it not as much a social failure? Markets have no inherent tendency to balance the demand and supply of labour: it's just not what drives them, it's not their purpose and on the whole, as history has shown, they do not do so. Technological change means imbalances in this regard may well worsen: with the future of work likely to exacerbate inequality and social tension. The need to balance the demand and supply of labour is instead a social imperative: because of the negative social consequences of high levels of unemployment and the centrality of economic participation as part of social inclusion.

It is in this context that the emergence of an employment guarantee in India, through the Mahatma Gandhi National Rural Employment Guarantee Act (MGNREGA), provides a contemporary example of the form such a social imperative might take, with a change in the rights regime that significantly reshapes the labour market. In this process, MGNREGA also illustrates how existing paradigms of rights can be transcended, through a combination of public imagination coupled with the levels of organisation necessary to translate such an idea into public policy and – thus far – to defend it.

Until now, the interpretation of the right to work has been as a right to work *when work is available* – giving markets primacy in this regard. Through MGNREGA, India has changed this to a right to work *when work is needed by the worker*: for up to a hundred days per year per rural household. Contested, uneven and sometimes flawed as the process of rolling out MGNREGA has been, over fifty million people now work on the scheme each year.

This is a radical and transformative shift, with profound implications for labour markets and for society more widely, with the need to work recognised as a social right, for which society must provide, not as something contingent purely on market demand. In the process, a limit is placed on the primacy of markets and on the extent of commodification of labour. At the same time, the power of labour to create social and economic value even when it has no market value is unlocked, with the creation of an increasing range of public goods and services.

This is a significant contemporary example of the social construction of the labour market through change to its underlying rights framework, illustrating how societies are able to set the parameters and logic within which a particular market functions.

South Africa has not managed to institutionalise such a right to work. However, as part of a wider focus on public employment (under the auspices of the Expanded Public Works Programme), the Community Work Programme was designed to put in place a model of public employment that could be scaled in this way, and that, although publically funded, is designed to be community driven, opening spaces for community agency in the identification of what work needs to be done to improve the quality of life in poor communities, and putting resources – not least labour – at their disposal to drive such change. In the process, communities are given a lever – circumscribed though it might be – with which to influence what falls within the ambit of 'public goods' at the community level: addressing social needs but also providing a lever with which to swing Polanyi's pendulum back against the encroachment of market logics into ever expanding spheres of life.

Examples of the work undertaken include a wide range of forms of care, environmental actions, support to creative endeavours, community safety, programmes tackling social issues such as drug abuse, domestic violence and the re-integration of ex-offenders, community-level media initiatives, and much more.

Not only does participation in work assist in limiting the negative impacts of long-term unemployment on individuals – and hence on their households too – the work undertaken can also address these effects at the community level.

The ability to achieve such effects becomes all the more important given the seemingly bleak prospects for the future of work, with the prospect of ever-larger numbers of people surplus to the requirements of the economy – with potentially devastating social consequences. This will require new instruments with which to respond. In addition to addressing heightened inequality, such instruments need to enable economic inclusion, the development of capabilities and the network effects associated with participation in work:

> Work is not just a means for distributing purchasing power. It is also among the most important sources of identity and purpose in individual's lives. If the role of work in society is to shrink, other sources of purpose and identity will need to grow. (Avent 2016)

All of this is why, after leaving MDA in 2002 and after some continued grappling with the challenges of enterprise development in marginal contexts, I became involved in the design and initial project management of the Community Work Programme (CWP), as one of the outcomes of a strategy project I was mandated to undertake for the South African Presidency – and approved by Cabinet during the Presidency of Kgalema Motlanthe. A nice twist of historical irony. Yet, while the CWP lead me straight back to many of the very same mining communities in which MDA had been engaged, it is nevertheless another story.

The rationale for the CWP was, however, driven to a large extent by lessons learned in MDA and from the conclusions drawn here: that a reliance on markets alone to create employment is an abdication to the primacy of markets in shaping social outcomes – and a capitulation to the logics of inequality. Employment matters too much to society to leave to markets alone. Furthermore, if markets are social constructs, then society cannot merely blame markets as if they are a negative externality on the other side of that imaginary game fence. Instead, the onus is on societies to develop the necessary institutions – the rules of the game – as well as the instruments, mechanisms, forms of organisation and resourcing models required to create employment or other forms of economic inclusion at the scale that people need, without relying on markets alone to do so – and certainly without expecting the poor to self-employ their way out of poverty on market terms.

Select Bibliography

All references to interviews are given in-text

Abt Associates and Brij Consulting (1998) Completion of a Feasibility Study for a Bulk Procurement Strategy. Johannesburg: Mineworkers Development Agency.

Adato, M. (1996) Democratic Process, Mediated Models and the Reconstitution of Meaning in Democratic Organizations: Trade Union Cooperatives in South Africa. Doctoral Dissertation. Cornell University.

All Are One Co-op (1989) 'Interview with the All Are One Co-op.' *Workteam: The Workers' Co-op Magazine 7.* CORDE, Botswana.

Allen, V.L.L. (2003 [1992]) *The History of Black Mineworkers in South Africa: Pt. 1: Mining in South Africa and the Genesis of Apartheid, 1871–1948.* Keighley: The Moor Press.

American Economic Journal: Applied Economics (2015) on Microfinance/Microcredit, 7(1), January.

Avent, R. (2016) 'A World Without Work is Coming – It Could be Utopia or it Could be Hell.' *The Guardian*, 19 September.

Barton, S. (2001) 'A Strategy for the Commercialisation of Marula Products from the Wild: Creating Incomes for the Rural Poor.' Paper presented at 'Bridging the Gap' Conference, February 2011. Johannesburg: MDA.

Bateman, M. (2014) 'South Africa's Post-Apartheid Microcredit-Driven Calamity'. *Law, Democracy and Development* 18, pp. 92–135.

Baumann, T. (1998) 'Mhala Development Centre: Local Economic Development – A Civil Society Perspective.' Bay Research and Consultancy Services, Muizenberg, South Africa.

Bear, M., Gibson, A. and Hitchins, R. (2003) 'From Principles to Practice – Ten Critical Challenges for BDS Market Development.' *Small Enterprise Development* 14(4), pp. 10–23.

Berold, R. (1991) 'Co-operatives: The Struggle for Survival.' *New Ground: A Journal of Development and the Environment* 3, March 1991.

Callinicos, L. (1980) *A People's History of South Africa Volume One: Gold and Workers 1886–1924.* Johannesburg: Ravan Press.

Chang, H.-J. (2001) 'Breaking the Mould: An Institutionalist Political Economy Alternative to the Neoliberal Theory of the Market and the State.' Available at: www.unrisd.org/80256B3C005BCCF9/(httpAuxPages)/44552A491D461D-0180256B5E003CAFCC/$file/chang.pdf (accessed: 11 July 2016).

—— (2002) *Kicking away the Ladder: Development Strategy in Historical Perspective.* London: Anthem Press.

—— (2006) 'Understanding the Relationship between Institutions and Eco-

nomic Development', UNU-WIDER: Working Paper. Available at: www.
wider.unu.edu/publication/understanding-relationship-between-institu-
tions-and-economic-development (accessed: 11 July 2016).

Chiloane, F. and Phala, J. (2002) 'Evaluation of the Marula Project in Bushbuckridge.' Danish Co-operation for Environment and Development (DANCED)
and the Department of Water and Forestry (DWAF) South Africa.

Committee of Donor Agencies for Small Enterprise Development (2001) 'Business Development Services For Small Enterprises: Guiding Principles
for Donor Intervention 2001.' Washington, DC: World Bank. Available at:
www.enterprise-development.org/wp-content/uploads/BDS-Guiding-Prin-
ciples-2001-English.pdf (accessed: 15 July 2016).

CORDE/CSFS (1993) 'Co-ops and Democracy: Lesotho Workshop Report.' Unpublished report to MDA.

Cornforth, C. (1983) 'Some Factors Affecting the Success or Failure of Worker
Co-operatives: A Review of Empirical Research in the United Kingdom.'
Economic and Industrial Democracy 4(2), pp. 163–90.

—— (1995) 'Patterns of Co-operative Management: Beyond the Degeneration
Thesis.' *Economic and Industrial Democracy* 16(4), 487–523.

Department of Trade and Industry (2005) Sector Development Strategy, Craft
Version 1, ExBoFile 1. Pretoria, South Africa.

Desai, M. (2004) *Marx's Revenge: The Resurgence of Capitalism and the Death
of Statist Socialism.* London: Verso Books.

Du Toit, A. (2009) 'Adverse Incorporation and Agrarian Policy in South Africa:
Or, How Not to Connect the Rural Poor to Growth.' Cape Town: Institute for
Poverty, Land and Agrarian Studies. Available at: http://repository.uwc.ac.
za/xmlui/bitstream/handle/10566/65/duToit_Adverse2009.pdf (accessed:
15 July 2016).

Du Toit, A. and Neves, D. (2007a) 'In Search of South Africa's Second Economy.'
Africanus 37(2), pp. 145–74.

Du Toit, A. and Neves, D. (2007b) 'In Search of South Africa's Second Economy:
Chronic Poverty, Economic Marginalisation and Adverse Incorporation in
Mt Frere and Khayelitsha.' Chronic Poverty Research Centre Working Paper
102. Bellville, South Africa: Programme for Land and Agrarian Studies.

Ferguson, J. (1990) *The Anti-Politics Machine: 'Development', Depoliticization,
and Bureaucratic Power in Lesotho.* Cambridge, UK: Cambridge University
Press.

Field, M., Hitchins, R. and Bear, M. (2000) 'Designing BDS Interventions as if
Markets Matter.' Bethesda, MD: Development Alternatives Inc.

Gay, J. and Hall, D. (2000) 'Poverty and Livelihoods in Lesotho: More than a
Mapping Excercise.' Maseru, Lesotho: Sechaba Consultants.

Gereffi, G., Humphrey, J. and Sturgeon, T. (2005) 'The Governance of Global Value Chains'. *Review of International Political Economy* 12(1), pp. 78–104.

Gibson, A. (1999) 'The Development of Markets for Business Development Services: Where We Are and How to Go Further.' ILO and USAID for Committee of Donor Agencies for Small Enterprise Development.

Hassan, Fareed M.A. (2002). 'Lesotho: Development in a Challenging Environment.' World Bank, Washington, DC. https://openknowledge.worldbank.
org/handle/10986/14252 (accessed 13 January 2018).

Heras-Saizarbitoria, I. and Basterretxea, I. (2016) 'Do Co-ops Speak the Managerial Lingua Franca? An Analysis of the Managerial Discourse of Mondragon Cooperatives.' *Journal of Co-operative Organization and Management* 4, pp. 13–21.

Hitchins, R., Elliott, D. and Gibson, A. (2004) 'Making Business Service Markets Work for the Poor in Rural Areas: A Review of Experience.' Available at: www.springfieldcentre.com/ making-business-service-markets-work-for-the-poor-in-rural-areas-a-review-of-experience (accessed: 16 July 2016).

Humphrey, J. and Schmitz, H. (2001) 'Governance in Global Value Chains'. *IDS Bulletin* 32(3), pp. 19–29.

ICA – International Co-operative Alliance (1995) 'Co-operative Identity, Values & Principles.' Available at: http://ica.coop/en/whats-co-op/co-operative-identity-values-principles (accessed: 15 July 2016).

ICA – International Co-operative Alliance (2017) The Capital Conundrum for Co-ops. Report of the ICA Blue Ribbon Commission. Available at: http://ica.coop/en/media/library/the-capital-conundrum-for-co-operatives (accessed: 13 August 2017).

Jensen, A., Patmore, G. and Tortia, E. (2015) *Cooperative Enterprises in Australia and Italy*. Italy, Firenze University Press. Available at: www.fupress.com/catalogo/cooperative-enterprises-in-australia-and-italy/2960 (accessed: 15 July 2016).

Johnson, A. (2005) 'Making Market Systems Work Better for the Poor (M4P): An Introduction to the Concept.' Manila: DFID. Available at: www.eldis.org/vfile/upload/1/document/0708/DOC21034.pdf (accessed: 15 July 2016).

Kasmir, S. (2016) 'The Mondragon Cooperatives and Global Capitalism: A Critical Analysis.' *New Labor Forum* 25(1) 52–9.

Khan, M. (2012) 'The Political Economy of Inclusive Growth.' OECD Publishing. Available at: http://eprints.soas.ac.uk/17301/1/Political%20Economy%20of%20Inclusive%20Growth%20an%20Application%20to%20Thailand.pdf (accessed: 9 November 2016).

Langmead, K. (2016) 'Challenging the Degeneration Thesis: The Role of Democracy in Worker Cooperatives?' *Journal of Entrepreneurial and Organizational Diversity* 5(1), pp. 79–98. Available at: www.euricse.eu/wp-content/uploads/2017/02/5.-Langmead.pdf (accessed: 5 August 2017).

Ledger, T. (2016) *An Empty Plate*. Johannesburg: Jacana.

Lie, J. (1997) 'Sociology of Markets.' *Annual Review of Sociology* 23, pp. 341–60.

Mahlati, V. (2011) 'Establishing Viable and Sustainable Rural Economic Development Programmes in a Competitive Global Economy: Analysis of Marula Commercialisation in South Africa.' PhD Dissertation, University of Stellenbosch. Available at: https://scholar.sun.ac.za/bitstream/handle/10019.1/18068/mahlati_establishing_2011.pdf (accessed: 15 July 2016).

Major, G. (1996) 'Solving the Underinvestment and Degeneration Problems of Workers' Cooperatives.' *Annals of Public and Cooperative Economics* 67(4), pp. 545–601.

Malan, R. (2015 [1990]) *My Traitor's Heart*. London: Vintage Books.

Mander, M., Cribbins, J., Shackleton, S.E. and Lewis, F. (2002) 'The Commercial Marula Industry in South Africa: A Sub-Sector Analysis.' DFID Country Report. London: Department for International Development.

Markham, C. and Mothibeli, M. (1987) 'The 1987 Mineworkers Strike.' *South African Labour Bulletin* 13(1), pp. 102–20.

Marshall, E., Newton, A.C. and Schreckenberg, K. (2003) 'Commercialisation of Non-Timber Forest Products: First Steps in Analysing the Factors Influencing Success.' *International Forestry Review* 5(2), pp. 128–37.

Marx, K. and Engels, F. (1848) *Manifesto of the Communist Party*. Available at: www.marxists.org/archive/marx/works/download/pdf/Manifesto.pdf (accessed: 16 July 2016).

Mbeki, T. (2003) 'Address to the National Council of Provinces', 11 November. The South African Presidency. Available at: www.polity.org.za/article/mbeki-address-to-ncop-11112003-2003-11-11 (accessed: 21 August 2017).

MDA – Mineworkers Development Agency (2000) 'Annual Report.' Johannesburg: MDA.

—— (2002) 'Annual Report.' Johannesburg: MDA.

Meyer-Stamer, J. (2006) 'Making Market Systems Work? For the Poor?' *Small Enterprise Development* 17(4), pp. 21–32.

Meyer-Stamer, J. and Wältring, F. (2007) 'Linking Value Chain Analysis and the "Making Markets Work Better for the Poor" Concept.' Duisburg and Dortmund: gtz. Available at www.mesopartner.com/fileadmin/user_files/other_publications/Meyer-Stamer%2BWaeltring_-_VC%2BM4P.pdf (accessed: 15 July 2016).

Miehlbradt, A. (2002) 'Assessing Markets for Business Development Services: What Have We Learned So Far?' SEED Working Paper 28. Geneva: ILO. Available at www.ilo.org/wcmsp5/groups/public/---ed_emp/---emp_ent/---ifp_seed/documents/publication/wcms_117708.pdf (accessed: 15 July 2016).

Miehlbradt, A.O. and McVay, M. (2002) Developing Commercial Markets for Business Development Services: 'Are "How-To-Do-It" Recipes Possible?' Seminar reader for the Third Annual Seminar, Turin, Italy. Small Enterprise Development Programme, International Labour Organization.

—— (2004) *Developing Markets for Business Development Services: Pioneering Systemic Approaches*, seminar proceedings of the Fifth Annual BDS Seminar held in Chiang Mai, Thailand. Small Enterprise Development Programme, International Labour Organization.

Moodie, T.D., Ndatshe, V. and Moodie, D.T. (1994) *Going for Gold: Men, Mines and Migration*. Oakland, CA: University of California Press.

Neves, D. and Du Toit, A. 2013. 'Rural Livelihoods in South Africa: Complexity, Vulnerability and Differentiation.' *Journal of Agrarian Change* 13(1), pp. 93–115.

Nippard, D., Hitchins, R. and Elliott, D. (2014) *Adopt-Adapt-Expand-Respond: A Framework for Managing and Measuring Systemic Change Processes*. Briefing Paper, the Springfield Centre. Available at: www.springfieldcentre.com/wp-content/uploads/2014/06/2014-03-Adopt-Adapt-Expand-Respond-Briefing-Paper1.pdf (accessed: 30 December 2016).

North, D.C. (1990a) *Institutions, Institutional Change and Economic Performance*. Cambridge, UK: Cambridge University Press.

—— (1990b) 'Institutions and their Consequences for Economic Performance', in K.S. Cook and M. Levi (eds), *The Limits of Rationality*. Chicago, IL: University of Chicago Press, pp. 383–401.

—— (1991) 'Institutions.' *Journal of Economic Perspectives* 5(1), pp. 97–112.

—— (1994) 'Economic Performance through Time.' *American Economic Re-*

view 84(3), pp. 359–68.

—— (2003) 'The Role of Institutions in Economic Development.' Discussion Paper Series 2003.2. Geneva: United Nations Economic Commission for Europe. Available at: www.unece.org/fileadmin/DAM/oes/disc_papers/ECE_DP_2003-2.pdf (accessed: 15 July 2016).

NUM Co-op Unit (n.d.) 'Let's Fight Bad Habits in the Co-op.' Democratic Management Workshop Training Materials, unpublished.

Oakeshott, R. (1990) 'Workers as Entrepreneurs, Two Striking Success Stories from Italy.' Unpublished Report prepared by Partnership Research Ltd, London.

Ostry, J., Berg, A. and Tsangarides, C. (2014) 'Redistribution, Inequality and Growth.' IMF Staff Discussion Note 14/02. Washington, DC: International Monetary Fund.

Pepstores (2007) 'Can Retailers Maintain Price War on School Uniforms?' Available at: www.pepstores.com/news/article/can-retailers-maintain-price-war-on-school-uniforms (accessed: 23 July 2016).

Philip, K. (1988) 'Producer Co-ops in South Africa: Their Economic Limits and Potential.' Labour Studies Research Report 4, Sociology of Work Programme. Johannesburg: University of the Witwatersrand.

—— (1989) 'The Private Sector and the Security Establishment', in J. Cock and L. Nathan (eds), *War and Society: The Militarisation of South Africa.* Cape Town: David Philip, pp. 202–16.

—— (1991) 'Union Co-ops on the Road to Success.' *Workteam: The Workers' Co-op Magazine* 11. CORDE, Botswana.

—— (2001) 'Bridging the Gap', Bridging the Gap Between Craft Producers and Markets Conference, Sunnyside Park Hotel, Johannesburg, 29 March. Johannesburg: Mineworkers' Development Agency.

—— (2002) 'The Quest for Rural Enterprise Support Strategies that Work: The Case of Mineworkers' Development Agency.' *Small Enterprise Development* 13(1), pp. 13–25.

—— (2003) 'Putting Development Back at the Centre of BDS.' *Small Enterprise Development* 14(4), pp. 24–30.

Pinder, C. (1999) 'Gender Appraisal of Mineworkers Development Agency.' Unpublished report. London: Department for International Development (Southern Africa).

Pinder, C. (2000) 'Impact Assessment of MDA's Training and Related Enterprise Development Services in South Africa.' Unpublished report. London: Department for International Development (Southern Africa).

Polanyi, K. (2001 [1944]) *The Great Transformation: The Political and Economic Origins of our Time.* Boston, MA: Beacon Press.

Ravallion, M. (2004). 'Pro-Poor Growth: A Primer.' World Bank Policy Research Working Paper 3242. Washington, DC: Development Research Group, World Bank.

Roelants, B., Hyungsik, E. and Terrasi, E. (2014) *Co-operatives and Employment: A Global Report.* CICOPA and Desjardins Group. Available at: www.cicopa.coop/IMG/pdf/cooperatives_and_employment_a_global_report_en__web_21-10_1pag.pdf (accessed 18 August 2017).

Rumney, R. (2005) 'Who Owns South Africa: An Analysis of State and Private Ownership Patterns', in J. Daniel, R. Southall and J. Lutchman (eds), *State of the Nation: South Africa 2004–2005*. Pretoria: HSRC Press.

Satgar, V. (2007) The State of the South African Cooperative Sector. Johannesburg: The Co-operative and Policy Alternative Center (COPAC).

Schreckenberg, K. (2003) 'Appropriate Ownership Models for Natural Product-based Small and Medium Enterprises in Namibia.' Ministry of Trade and Industry (MTI) Trade and Investment Development Programme (TIDP). Available at: www.odi.org/sites/odi.org.uk/files/odi-assets/publications-opinion-files/3904.pdf (accessed: 18 July 2016).

Schreckenberg, K., Marshall, E., Newton, A., Te Velde, D.W. et al. (2006) 'Commercialisation of Non-timber Forest Products: What Determines Success?' ODI Forestry Briefing 10. London: Overseas Development Institute.

Shackleton, C. and Shackleton, S. (2003) 'Communal Rangelands in Savannas of South Africa: What do they Contribute to Rural Livelihoods', in N. Allsopp, A. Palmer, S. Milton, K. Kirkman et al. (eds), *Rangelands in the New Millennium, Proceedings of the VIIth International Rangelands Congress.* DTT, Durban. pp. 1695–7.

Shackleton, C.M., Botha, J., Emanuel, P.L. and Ndlovu, S. (2002) 'Inventory of Marula (*Sclerocarya birrea*, subsp. *caffra*) Stocks and Fruit Yields in Communal and Protected Areas of the Bushbuckridge Lowveld, Limpopo Province, South Africa.' Unpublished research report, Rhodes University.

Shackleton, S. and Shackleton, C. (2005) 'The Contribution of Marula (*Sclerocarya birrea*) Fruit and Fruit Products to Rural Livelihoods in the Bushbuckridge District, South Africa: Balancing Domestic Needs and Commercialisation.' *Forests, Trees and Livelihoods* 15(1), pp. 3–24.

Sievers, M., Haftendorn, K. and Bessler, A. (2003) 'Business Centres for Small Enterprise Development: Experiences and Lessons from Eastern Europe.' Seed Working Paper 57. Geneva: International Labour Office. Available at: http://oit.org/wcmsp5/groups/public/---ed_emp/---emp_ent/---ifp_seed/documents/publication/wcms_117676.pdf (accessed: 15 July 2016).

Staff Reporter (2011) 'It's the Big Guys: Allen.' *Mail & Guardian*, 18 March. Available at: http://mg.co.za/article/2011-03-18-its-the-big-guys-allen (accessed: 14 February 2017).

Storey, J., Basterretxea, I. and Salaman, G. (2014). 'Managing and Resisting "Degeneration" in Employee-Owned Businesses: A Comparative Study of Two Large Retailers in Spain and the UK.' *Organization* 21(5), pp. 626–44.

Tendler, J. (2002) 'Small Firms, the Informal Sector, and the Devil's Deal.' *IDS Bulletin* 33(3), pp. 1–15.

—— (2004) 'Why Social Policy is Condemned to a Residual Category of Safety Nets and What to Do About It', in T. Mkandawire (ed.), *Social Policy in a Development Context*. Basingstoke: Palgrave Macmillan, pp. 119–42.

Vilakazi, S. (2002) 'Bulk Supply Stores: Status Report on Stores and Proposals.' Unpublished report: Mineworkers Development Agency.

Webb, B. and Webb, S. (1914) 'Special Supplement on Co-operative Production and Profit Sharing.' *The New Statesman* 2(45).

Wolpe, H. (1972) 'Capitalism and Cheap Labour-Power in South Africa: From Segregation to Apartheid.' *Economy and Society* 1(4), pp. 425–56.

Workteam (1988) 'Bad Habits in the Co-op.' *Workteam: The Workers' Co-op Magazine* 5. CORDE, Botswana.

World Bank (2001) 'World Development Report 2002: Building Institutions for

Markets.' New York: Oxford University Press, for The World Bank, Washington, DC.

Wray, L.R. (2007) 'Minsky's Approach to Employment Policy and Poverty: Employer of Last Resort and the War on Poverty.' Working Paper 515. Annandale-on-Hudson, NY: The Levy Economics Institute of Bard College. Available at: www.levyinstitute.org/pubs/wp_515.pdf (accessed: 17 January 2017).

Wynberg, R.P., Laird, S.A., Shackleton, S., Mander, M. et al. (2003) 'Marula Commercialisation for Sustainable and Equitable Livelihoods.' *Forests, Trees and Livelihoods* 13(3), pp. 203–15.

Zamagni, V. (2012) 'Interpreting the Roles and Economic Importance of Cooperative Enterprises in a Historical Perspective.' *Journal of Entrepreneurial and Organisational Diversity (JEOD)* 1 (1), pp. 21–36. Available at: www.euricse.eu/wp-content/uploads/2016/06/jeodzamagniinterpretingtheroles-sandeconomicimportanceofcooperativeenterprisesinahistoricalperspective.pdf (accessed: 13 August 2017).

Index

Adato, M. 63, 71
agriculture 21, 35, 36, 60, 73, 114,
    183, 184, *see also* co-ops
    subsistence 4, 17, 113, 114, 115
agro-processing 112, 145, 113-14,
    190
Amarula Cream 164, 166, 179
Amcoal 76, 94, 96, 97
African National Congress 5, 6, 34,
    36, 37, 42, 43-4, 50, 51, 79, 93, 109,
    162
Andersson, Gavin 72
Anglo American Corporation 18, 20
anonymous exchange 13, 14, 101,
    150-1, 155, 156, 197, 198, 199
anti-politics machine 35-6, 79, 134-9,
    140, 144, 192-3
apartheid 1, 3-6, 7, 15, 17, 18, 22, 31,
    36, 38, 143, 183, 192
    post-apartheid 2, 8, 51, 84, 92, 93,
    112, 114, 120
Arnot Colliery 94, 95, 96, 133
Association of Mineworkers and Con-
    struction Union (AMCU) 2, 3,

Barton, Susan 137, 154, 168, 173,
    174, 176
Basotho Congress Party (BCP) 35, 36,
    37, 41-2, 44
Basotho Mineworkers Labour Co-op
    (BMLC) 40, 41, 42-4, 72, 78, 79,
    82, 157
Basotho National Party (BNP) 35, 37
Bateman, Milford 120
Baumann, Ted 100, 101, 102, 131
Bhala, Elliot Nomazele 23, 24, 25, 26,
    29-32, 54
Body Shop 164, 175, 178, 183, 176
Brecker, Carl 72
Bridging the Gap Conference 148,
    149, 151, 152, 153, 157, 160
Bronpro 177-9, 181, 183

business centres, *see also* develop-
    ment centres 138-9
Business Development Services
    market development approach *see
    also* business services, develop-
    ment agencies, facilitation, subsi-
    dies, systemic change
    overview 117-22
    critique 123-8, 139-41, 191-2, 192-
    4
    Donor Guidelines 119, 122, 123,
    124, 191
    implications for MDA 129-44
business services
    economic or operational services
    98, 99, 103, 118, 125, 131-4, 135,
    139, 187, 190-2
    equipment hire 99, 100, 101, 103,
    125, 131, 162, 190
    poultry supply centres 81, 96, 99,
    103, 131, 132, 133, 139, 140
Business supply stores 100, 103, 132,
    133, 135, 139, 190
    strategic services 99, 118, 124-6,
    131, 135, 162, 190, 191-2
    subsidies to 45, 95, 99, 113, 118,
    121-4, 126
Butha Buthe Agricultural Co-op 52,
    58, 65, 78, 82
Butha Buthe Sewing Co-op 52, 76,
    148

Cape Craft and Design Institute 154,
    157
capital *see* finance
capitalism, market economy
    history of in South Africa
    7, 10, 11, 12, 15, 17, 47, 47, 48, 49,
    84, 112, 122, 150, 201-2, 204, 205,
    206
Ceres 112, 178, 182
Chamber of Mines 3, 18, 21, 26, 28